STRONG GOVERNMENTS, PRECARIOUS WORKERS

STRONG GOVERNMENTS, PRECARIOUS WORKERS

Labor Market Policy
in the Era of Liberalization

Philip Rathgeb

ILR Press

AN IMPRINT OF CORNELL UNIVERSITY PRESS   ITHACA AND LONDON

First published 2018 by Cornell University Press

Printed in the United States of America

Library of Congress Cataloging-in-Publication Data

Names: Rathgeb, Philip, 1987– author.
Title: Strong governments, precarious workers : labor market policy in the era of liberalization / Philip Rathgeb.
Description: Ithaca : ILR Press, an imprint of Cornell University Press, 2018. | Includes bibliographical references and index.
Identifiers: LCCN 2018012025 (print) | LCCN 2018015603 (ebook) | ISBN 9781501730597 (pdf) | ISBN 9781501730603 (epub/mobi) | ISBN 9781501730580 | ISBN 9781501730580 (cloth ; alk. paper)
Subjects: LCSH: Precarious employment—Austria. | Precarious Employment—Denmark. | Precarious employment—Sweden. | Manpower Policy—Austria. | Manpower policy—Denmark. | Manpower policy—Sweden. | Labor unions—Austria. | Labor unions—Denmark. | Labor unions—Sweden.
Classification: LCC HD5858.A9 (ebook) | LCC HD5858.A9 .R38 2018 (print) | DDC 331.25/727—dc23
LC record available at https://lccn.loc.gov/2018012025

To Anja

Contents

Preface

"Economic history reveals that the emergence of national markets was in no way the result of the gradual and spontaneous emancipation of the economic sphere from governmental control. On the contrary, the market has been the outcome of a conscious and often violent intervention on the part of government which imposed the market organization on society for non-economic ends."

Karl Polanyi (1944 [1957]), 250

"What makes most Western economies still viable is that the organization of interests is yet only partial and incomplete. If it were complete, we would have a deadlock between these organized interests, producing a wholly rigid economic structure which no agreement between the established interests and only the force of some dictatorial power could break."

Friedrich August von Hayek (1979), 93

Why do some European welfare states protect precarious workers from economic uncertainty better than others? This study of labor market policy in three small states—Austria, Denmark, and Sweden—explores this fundamental question. It does so by examining the power-distributional interaction between trade unions and governments. Inclusive trade unions have high political stakes in the protection of precarious workers because they incorporate the margins of the workforce into their representational outlook. Yet in the era of liberalization, the impact of union *preferences* has declined over time, with a shift in the balance of class *power* from labor to capital across the advanced capitalist countries. National governments, even those of a Social Democratic character, have accordingly prioritized flexibility for employers over the protection of precarious workers. As a result, organized labor can only be successful when governments are reliant on union consent for consensus mobilization. When governments have a united majority of seats, however, they are strong enough to exclude trade unions, to the detriment of precarious workers. Variations in government strength best explain why Danish and Swedish trade unions faced remarkable defeats at the cost of social solidarity, whereas their Austrian counterparts remained much more influential and could thus enhance the protection of precarious workers.

This argument is buttressed with evidence from shadow case studies of Italy and Spain.

Perhaps strong government is not what most observers would spontaneously associate with precarious workers. In fact, it is often said that the strengthening of the market requires the weakening of government. In this way, so the logic goes, the state's redistributive function can be cut back in favor of free enterprise. But the historical record of modern capitalism shows that the *politics* behind the expansion of market forces requires a strong government. Economic liberalization cannot proceed without a government that is able to remove constraints on capital and fend off political demands for material compensation at the same time. Scholars from fundamentally different ideological outlooks and political persuasions came to similar conclusions a long time ago, as illustrated by the quotations shown at the start of this Preface. In fact, these passages indicate that liberal forces have been normatively committed to the notion of a strong government—one that can enforce free markets against the resistance of organized interests in general and trade unions in particular—for quite some time, even if their political rhetoric might suggest otherwise.

However, their insight about the instrumental role of government strength was somewhat lost over time, although this was quite understandable. In the postwar period of high economic growth, national governments of the advanced capitalist countries faced little incentive to create precarious employment in return for successful economic performance. In fact, at that time, such a strategy was not even a serious option, given the influence of powerful labor movements and Keynesian economics. Yet the economic crisis of the late 1970s set in motion a new material and social context, one in which union demands seemed no longer conducive to capitalist prosperity while employer associations started a counteroffensive against the Keynesian class compromise. Governments of the right as well as the left responded accordingly by initiating the contemporary era of liberalization. But the distributive outcomes of this historical change were not uniform for precarious workers. The present book explains this variation by recovering a plain truth of capitalist democracies: only when governments are strong can they liberalize labor markets without compensating the losers this creates. Otherwise, trade unions oblige them to make concessions. In the end, this finding calls into question the electoral responsiveness of national governments—and thus political parties—to the social needs of an increasingly numerous group of precarious workers.

Acknowledgments

This book relied on the support of many people to whom I want to express my deepest gratitude. At the European University Institute, Hanspeter Kriesi provided me with invaluable feedback, guidance, and advice all along the way. Without him, this book would not have been possible. Pepper Culpepper contributed to this book with his sharp reflections throughout. His work on business power was an important source of inspiration in the process of researching and writing this book. I want to express my thankfulness to Lucio Baccaro and Wolfgang Streeck for their encouraging comments to push this project forward. At the University of Konstanz, Marius Busemeyer and his working group provided me with an excellent academic environment to turn this into a book and gave me great comments on the first chapter. I am grateful to them for all the numerous discussions we had about this book. I thank Julian Garritzmann for his excellent feedback on the concluding chapter.

A number of scholars provided me with invaluable advice at various stages of this project. I thank Johannes Lindvall, Carlo Knotz, Thomas Brambor, Per Andersson, and Johan Bo Davidsson for their useful feedback and for giving me the opportunity to be a visiting researcher at Lund University at a crucial stage of this project. I am also grateful to Hans-Peter Blossfeld, László Bruszt, Johan Christensen, Dominik Geering, Patrick Emmenegger, Christian Lyhne Ibsen, Mara Yerkes, Christine Musselin, and Alex Reisenbichler for valuable feedback on earlier parts of this book. This project also benefited from numerous stimulating conversations I had with Fabio Wolkenstein over the past roughly six years. I feel unable to list here the many other names of scholars who supported my research with their ideas at conferences, workshops, and elsewhere. Nevertheless, they should all know that I am very grateful to them.

Portions of chapter 3 were previously published as "Relying on Weak Governments: Austrian Trade Unions and the Politics of Smoothed Dualization" in *Austrian Journal of Political Science* 45, no. 3 (2017): 45–55. Parts of chapter 4 were previously published as "No Flexicurity without Trade Unions: The Danish Experience" in *Comparative European Politics* (preview; 2017): 1–21. Parts of chapters 3 and 5 previously appeared as "When Weak Governments Confront Inclusive Trade Unions: The Politics of Protecting Labour Market Outsiders in the Age of Dualization" in *European Journal of Industrial Relations* 24, no. 1 (2018): 5–22.

I thank Emmerich Tálos very much. He taught me welfare state research during my diploma studies at the University of Vienna and has been my mentor ever since. Without his invaluable support, I would not have made it to the European University Institute, which has turned out to be the greatest privilege I can imagine. Moreover, I would like to thank all of my forty-six interviewees, without whom I would not have been able to pursue this research. I want to thank Fran Benson and her colleagues at Cornell University Press for believing in this project and their brilliant support in turning my manuscript into a book. I also thank Mary Ribesky and the Westchester editorial staff for excellent copyediting.

I warmly thank my parents, Andrea and Günter, my brother, Mathias, and my grandmothers, Hildegard and Helga, for their love and their support in providing me with the opportunity to pursue third-level education. I also thank Helga and Karl Sahora for their personal support at every stage of this process. Finally, I would like to thank my wife, Anja, for being the greatest source of support all along the way and for the wonderful moments we had when this book was in its making. It is to her I dedicate this book.

Abbreviations

ALMP	active labor market policy
ATS	Österreichischer Schilling (Austrian Schilling)
BAK	Kammer für Arbeiter und Angestellte (Austrian Chamber of Labour)
BAWAG	Bank für Arbeit und Wirtschaft (Bank for Labour and Business)
BMASK	Bundesministerium für Arbeit, Soziales, Gesundheit und Konsumentenschutz (Federal Ministry of Labour, Social Affairs, Health and Consumer Protection)
BMS	Bedarfsorientierte Mindestsicherung (needs-oriented minimum income scheme)
BZÖ	Bündnis Zukunft Österreich (Alliance for the Future of Austria)
CGIL	Confederazione Generale Italiana del Lavoro (Italian General Confederation of Labour)
CISL	Confederazione Italiana Sindacati Lavoratori (Italian Confederation of Workers' Trade Unions)
CiU	Convergència i Unió (Convergence and Union)
DA	Dansk Arbejdsgiverforening (Confederation of Danish Employers)
DGB	Deutscher Gewerkschaftsbund (German Trade Union Confederation)
DI	Dansk Industri (Confederation of Danish Industries)
DPP	Dansk Folkeparti (Danish People's Party)
ECB	European Central Bank
EIRO	European Industrial Relations Observatory
EMCC	European Monitoring Centre on Change
EMU	European Economic and Monetary Union
EPL	employment protection legislation
EU	European Union
EU-21	All EU countries prior to the accession of the ten candidate countries on 1 May 2004, plus the four eastern European member countries of the OECD, namely Czech Republic, Hungary, Poland, Slovak Republic (OECD definition)
EU-28	all twenty-eight EU countries (from July 2013)

FDI	foreign direct investment
FPÖ	Freiheitliche Partei Österreichs (Freedom Party of Austria)
FSG	Fraktion Sozialdemokratischer Gewerkschafter (Group of Social Democratic Unionists)
GDP	gross domestic product
GPA-djp	Gewerkschaft der Privatangestellten, Druck, Journalismus, Papier (Union of Private Sector Employees, Printing, Journalism, and Paper)
IAF	Inspektionen för arbetslöshetsförsäkringen (Swedish Unemployment Insurance Board)
IV	Industriellenvereinigung (Federation of Austrian Industries)
LAS	Lagen om Anställningsskydd (Employment Protection Act)
LO (Denmark)	Landsorganisationen i Danmark (The Danish Confederation of Trade Unions)
LO (Sweden)	Landsorganisationen i Sverige (Swedish Trade Union Confederation)
OECD	Organisation for Economic Co-operation and Development
ÖGB	Österreichischer Gewerkschaftsbund (Austrian Trade Union Federation)
ÖKSA	Österreichisches Komitee für Soziale Arbeit (Austrian Committee for Social Work)
ÖVP	Österreichische Volkspartei (Austrian People's Party)
PD	Partido Democrático (Democratic Party)
PES	public employment system
PP	Partido Popular (Spanish People's Party)
PRO-GE	Produktionsgewerkschaft (Union of Production Workers)
PSOE	Partido Socialista Obrero Españo (Spanish Socialist Workers' Party)
RC	Partito della Rifondazione Comunista (Communist Refoundation Party)
RV	Radikale Venstre (Danish Social Liberal Party)
SACO	Sveriges Akademikers Centralorganisation (Swedish Confederation of Professional Associations)
SAF	Svenska Arbetsgivareföreningen (Swedish Employers Association)
SAP	Sveriges socialdemokratiska arbetareparti (Swedish Social Democratic Party)
SEK	Svensk krona (Swedish krona)
SPÖ	Sozialdemokratische Partei Österreichs (Social Democratic Party of Austria)

TCO	Tjänstemännens Centralorganisation (Swedish Confederation of Professional Employees)
UA	unemployment assistance
UGT	Unión General de Trabajadores (General Union of Workers)
UI	unemployment insurance
UIL	Unione Italiana del Lavoro (Italian Labour Union)
UK	United Kingdom of Great Britain and Northern Ireland
VF	Verkstadsföreningen (Swedish Engineering Employers' Association)
VoC	Varieties of Capitalism
WIFO	Österreichisches Institut für Wirtschaftsforschung (Austrian Institute of Economic Research)
WKÖ	Wirtschaftskammer Österreich (Austrian Federal Economic Chamber)

STRONG GOVERNMENTS, PRECARIOUS WORKERS

THE PROTECTION OF OUTSIDERS IN THE ERA OF LIBERALIZATION

Introduction

This book is about the losers of the liberalization era. Social scientists often call them "outsiders," because their precarious labor market situation excludes them from the employment and social rights enjoyed by "insiders" on regular jobs. The resulting lack of security is associated with several trends that are adverse in their implications for democracy and society: declining voter turnout and political resignation (Schäfer 2013), diverging life chances and growing poverty (Tomlinson and Walker 2012) as well as poor health, and even an increased relative risk of suicide (Nordt et al. 2015). The willingness of the state to protect workers from the risks of being unemployed or "atypically employed" is thus of great political and social significance.

"Outsiderness" as a particular expression of economic inequality can be traced to the retreat of the state from its political commitment to ensure full employment, which occurred in response to the inflation crisis of the late 1970s (Harvey 2010; Streeck 2011). Faced with rising unemployment rates, during the 1980s, the welfare states of Western Europe expanded exit routes out of the labor market such as early retirement schemes and incapacity benefits, especially for people who found themselves excluded from the rapidly growing service sector due to low or obsolete skills, chronic health problems, or weak labor demand (Ebbinghaus 2006). In this context, labor supply management by means of preretirement options took the place of Keynesian aggregate demand management.

With the tightening constraints of fiscal austerity, however, the European welfare states of the 1990s no longer had the public resources available to ease the situation of mass unemployment through "labor-shedding" strategies. As a result, the main option left for adjusting national models of capitalism in the interest of successful employment performance was the one of *liberalization*; including the differentiation of wage levels and the deregulation of employment contracts, as well as cuts in social security. Part of this transformation in welfare statehood is the turn toward "activation," whereby the provision of social security for the unemployed has become conditional on active job-search, which may include the willingness to take up any job deemed "suitable" or participation in training (Clasen and Clegg 2006, 2011; Bonoli 2010). Given the growing emergence of precarious employment and welfare standards, the active reconfiguration of labor market institutions to the social needs of outsiders has become crucial to the redistributive capacity of the welfare state. Figure 1.1 sheds some light on the growing number of outsiders in the European Union.

Despite the common reform trajectory just described, political actors could still shape the liberalization of work and welfare in different ways. That is to say, even though the neoliberal transformation of global capitalism pointed to a general expansion of market mechanisms and economic inequality over time (Streeck 2009; Baccaro and Howell 2011), the political practice of liberalization

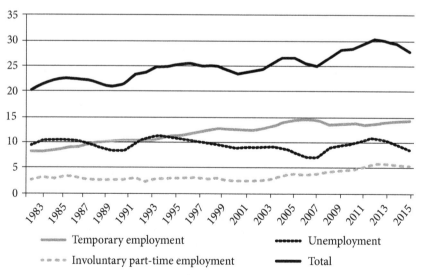

FIGURE 1.1. Share of unemployment, temporary employment, and involuntary part-time employment in total employment in the EU-28, 1983–2015.

Source: OECD statistics.

at the national level has resulted in divergent distributive outcomes for outsiders (Emmenegger et al. 2012; Thelen 2014). Therefore, the common liberalization of Keynesian postwar capitalism did not rule out variation in the reform trajectories of national welfare states, nor did it imply convergence in the redistributive capacities of European public policy regimes.

One example of this lack of convergence can be seen in the case of Austria, which deviated from the Continental European adjustment path of "pronounced dualization" between workers with stable employment ("insiders") versus unemployed and atypically employed workers ("outsiders") (Obinger et al. 2012). In fact, the Austrian policy output ran directly counter to the reinforcement of status divisions in such diverse areas as job security arrangements, social insurance coverage, and active labor market policy spending. Outsider-oriented patterns of liberalization appear puzzling in a prototype of the Conservative welfare regime, which has a segmented and male-dominated institutional legacy. Existing theory would expect otherwise. It is interesting, by contrast, that the reform trajectory in the Social Democratic prototype of Sweden differed profoundly from that of Austria: Sweden substantially curtailed both the coverage and generosity of benefit entitlements, while deregulating the job security of temporary workers at the same time. As I will show, labor market policy has therefore become more egalitarian in Austria than in Sweden. Denmark, by contrast, stands in between Austria and Sweden as it reveals substantial variation over time. It attracted widespread attention for undermining social divides with a policy combination of inclusive social security, human capital formation, and flexible job security arrangements. During the 2000s, however, the security-related components of this "Flexicurity" model came under strain, while legislative interventions additionally curtailed the long-term power base of the union movement.

Despite the many similarities between their political economies—small size, trade openness, corporatist legacy, relative macroeconomic success, periods of center-right coalitions, and mature welfare states—the reform trajectories of Austria, Denmark, and Sweden, not only differed markedly but also evolved in very counterintuitive directions. Conventional theories of partisanship (Rueda 2007; Huo 2009; Häusermann 2010) and producer group coalitions (Palier and Thelen 2010; Martin and Swank 2012; Thelen 2014) generally suggest continued regime variation between the Social Democratic–Nordic and Conservative-Continental welfare states in the distributive outcomes of economic adjustment. These two dominant lines of research in comparative political economy, however, do not hold with respect to the puzzling policy outputs observed in three small states of Western Europe. Austria and Sweden, for example, crossed levels of outsider protection in opposite directions, while the recent Danish reform trajectory underlying the erosion of Flexicurity has also been less "solidaristic" than the Austrian case.

Research Question and Argument in Brief

The brief presentation of three nationally distinct political responses to the distributional tensions of the neoliberal era poses a general question of interest to academia and society alike: *Why do some European welfare states protect outsiders better than others?* I examine this broad question through a comparative investigation of reform trajectories in the area of labor market policy. The rationale for this choice is that labor market policy represents a crucial area that may either mitigate, reproduce, or reinforce the socially corrosive effects of economic liberalization on the weakest segments of society (e.g., Emmenegger et al. 2012; Rovny 2014; Rueda 2015).

I analyze reform trajectories in three dimensions of labor market policy: employment protection legislation (EPL), unemployment insurance (UI), and active labor market policy (ALMP). The main reason for investigating change in all three dimensions is that they closely interact with each other in shaping the material situation and employment prospects of outsiders. UI and ALMP are distributive policy areas in that they provide income support and reintegration programs for the unemployed. Conventional welfare state research examines these two policy dimensions to find out how policy-makers react to the emergence of postindustrial labor markets (Clasen and Clegg 2011). Yet, as Crouch and Keune (2012) rightly point out, welfare states not only react to changing risk patterns emanating from postindustrial work and family patterns, but also co-shape them by regulating the "hiring and firing" conditions for different employment contracts. Employment protection legislation may also exist as a functional equivalent to unemployment benefits in the provision of economic security (Locke and Thelen 1995; Bonoli 2003). For example, the maintenance of strict employment protection for regular workers in combination with residual unemployment support contributes to a dualization between well-protected insiders and precarious outsiders in the Mediterranean and Continental European political economies (Palier 2006). The direction of institutional change in these three areas thus has a profound impact on the distributive character of economic liberalization in any capitalist regime (OECD 2008, 2011, 2015; Thelen 2014).

To explain why political actors in some European welfare regimes protect outsiders better than others, I compare the reform trajectories of Austria, Denmark, and Sweden over the past three decades, complemented with shadow case studies of Italy and Spain. The reason for concentrating on these three countries in particular is that they represent similar corporatist legacies of economic governance and three different reform trajectories. Following a most-similar systems design, the three cases are thus picked from among the small states of Northwestern Europe that are particularly challenged by the vagaries of global capitalism and have small populations with tightly knit policy-making elites (Katzenstein 1985). The shadow case studies of Italy and Spain serve to illustrate the generalizability of the book's argument beyond the small corporatist states of Northwestern Europe.

Challenging conventional explanations, I argue that the variation observed between Austria, Denmark, and Sweden does not result from differences in partisanship or producer group coalitions, but rather from differences in the *power-distributional interaction* between trade unions and governments. High levels of inclusiveness continue to provide trade unions with an acute interest in the protection of outsiders. But the causal significance of union preferences has declined in the course of the past three decades, with a shift in the balance of class power from labor to capital across the advanced capitalist countries of the Western world. National governments have accordingly prioritized the flexibility demands of employers over the social protection of outsiders. When they had a united majority of seats in parliament, they were therefore strong enough to pursue a unilateral reform strategy that excludes unions to the detriment of outsiders. When they were weakened by intracoalitional divides or a hung parliament, on the other hand, they negotiated political deals with trade unions to mobilize an extraparliamentary channel of consensus mobilization. This kind of weakness was instrumental in forcing governments to compensate outsiders for labor market liberalization.

The core argument of this book can therefore be summarized in one sentence: the weaker the government, the stronger becomes the capacity of inclusive trade unions to enhance the protection of outsiders through an extension of job security regulations, unemployment benefit entitlements, and active labor market policy spending.

Varieties of Liberalization and the Protection of Outsiders

Liberalization refers to the expansion of market mechanisms in the allocation of material resources and life chances as the political response to the crisis of postwar democratic capitalism (Streeck 2009; Harvey 2010). Faced with rising inflation in the late 1970s, Anglo-American governments put an end to the Keynesian class compromise and initiated the evolutionary stages of liberalization in capital, product, and labor markets (Hacker and Pierson 2010). The neoliberal era took off with the rise of monetarism (late 1970s), followed by a gradual departure from the commitment of the state to provide full employment (1980s), and it continued with fiscal consolidation in tandem with the deregulation of capital markets (1990s) and the subsequent (post-2008) global financial crisis (Streeck 2011). National trajectories of liberalization had in common a conversion of the function of labor market institutions from market-constraining social rights toward market-conforming economic competitiveness (Baccaro and Howell 2011). Central to this process was the removal of legally binding constraints on employers' strategies of capital accumulation. In terms of concrete institutional changes, this political practice implied a (partial) deregulation of job security regulations and the recommodification of labor through activation strategies targeted at people who were out of work.

The socially corrosive effects of liberalization have become visible in the growing emergence of workers in precarious employment and welfare standards—that is, the so-called outsiders. Following Rueda's definition, I use the term "outsiders" to describe workers that "are either unemployed or hold jobs that are characterized by low levels of protection and employment rights, lower salaries, and precarious levels of benefits and social security regulations" (2006, 387). The literature on "new social risks" pointed to the social groups that face the highest probability of being unemployed or atypically employed on postindustrial labor markets. First, *low-skilled* workers in both the manufacturing and service sectors are exposed to greater (long-term) unemployment risks and flexibility demands. Second, *female* workers, largely irrespective of skill levels, are often pushed into atypical employment contracts with reduced working hours in their attempt to reconcile the demands of work and family life. Finally, *young* workers face difficulties in entering the primary labor market due to weak labor demand and the deregulation of fixed-term employment (Taylor-Gooby 2004; Bonoli 2007; Häusermann and Schwander 2015).

Liberalization, however, took divergent forms and distributive outcomes in different national contexts due to the mediating impact of the interplay between historically evolved institutions and domestic politics. Kathleen Thelen famously animated this empirical identification of different regimes of social solidarity by arguing that the common trend of liberalization did not rule out institutional variation in the redistributive capacities of national public policy regimes (Thelen 2014). All the same, her understanding of social solidarity is markedly different from traditional notions of decommodification or social citizenship, and this perhaps best explains why she observes pronounced cross-country variation. Drawing on a vast body of welfare state scholarship, Thelen claims that the institutional heritage of the industrial postwar era ceased to produce "solidaristic" effects in a postindustrial environment. In this perspective, ongoing high levels of social solidarity require an institutional reconfiguration of European welfare states toward more emphasis on market-conforming human capital formation and universal minimum benefit entitlements. This argument relates to the perceived mismatch between postindustrial labor market change and industrial welfare arrangements, which can be said to have caused a declining scope in, and generosity of, risk protection (Hacker 2004). The erosion of manufacturing employment implied greater demands for wage differentiation and (re-)training, given the lower productivity growth potential and higher qualification requirements of the service sector. At the same time, the erosion of the male breadwinner model and demographic aging called for state support in care services, while the concomitant rise of atypical employment contracts reinforced problems of in-work poverty and insufficient benefit entitlements.

In terms of empirical outcomes, Thelen finds three different varieties of liberalization in the areas of industrial relations, vocational training and labor market policy. From a distributive point of view, her typology resonates in characterizing Esping-Andersen's three worlds of welfare capitalism: social solidarity in Scandinavia, status protection for a (shrinking) manufacturing sector in Continental Europe, and deregulation across the board in Anglo-American countries. Table 1.1 summarizes her typology with a focus on labor market policy.

First, liberalization through embedded flexibilization describes a combination of policy choices that may be subsumed under the (admittedly vague) concept of "Flexicurity" (Clasen and Viebrock 2009; Burroni and Keune 2011; Rathgeb 2017). It combines inclusive social security and reintegration programs ("security") with liberal job security arrangements ("flexibility"). In this strategy of supply-side solidarity, risk collectivization rests on welfare state support to enable outsiders in finding poverty-free jobs and receiving security in the event of joblessness (Baccaro and Locke 1998). Second, liberalization through dualization

TABLE 1.1.   Varieties of liberalization in labor market policy.

	EMBEDDED FLEXIBILIZATION	DUALIZATION	DEREGULATION
Country regimes	Scandinavian coordinated market economies (CMEs)	Continental CMEs	Anglo-American liberal market economies (LMEs)
Employment protection	Low for all	High for insiders, low for outsiders	Low for all
Generosity of unemployment insurance	High and homogenous	Earnings-related	Residual and homogenous
Inclusiveness of unemployment insurance	High	Medium	Low
Spending on active labor market policy	High	Medium	Low

Source: This typology draws on Thelen (2012, 2014).

describes increased differentiation between insiders and outsiders in the three dimensions of the dependent variable. The maintenance of job security and social security for insiders goes hand-in-hand with institutional deregulation for outsiders. Finally, liberalization through deregulation describes the full dismantling of job security and welfare arrangements, with no compensation for outsiders through an expansion of active labor market policies at the same time. It thus implies an individualization of risks at the expense of labor as a whole.

Following Thelen's definition of "embedded flexibilization," I conceptualize an expansion in the protection of outsiders as a set of institutional changes consisting of three elements: (1) the extension of benefit entitlements to workers with employment contracts who previously lacked coverage, (2) the expansion of spending on active labor market policy, and (3) the homogenization of job security regulations between permanent and temporary workers. Conceived in this way, "embedded flexibilization" enhances the social security of outsiders in the event of unemployment, while smoothing the chance of reemployment into the primary labor market and impeding the growth of precarious employment contracts at the fringes of the labor market.

Conventional Explanations

Why should national models of capitalism diverge in their scope of risk protection, despite powerful structural pressures for cross-national convergence? International competition, European integration, deindustrialization, demographic aging, "financialization" and declining growth of the real economy, inter alia, pose undeniable constraints on the domestic capacity of national sovereign democratic states to reconcile the distributional tension between social solidarity and capital accumulation (Garrett 1995; Rhodes 1996; Kaufmann 1997; Pierson 1998; Scharpf 2000; Alber 2002; Stockhammer 2004). To simplify somewhat, the principal empirical studies of comparative political economy offer two different theoretical approaches to the question of cross-national variation in risk protection, which can be summarized under the rubric of (1) producer group theory versus (2) partisanship theory.

The first theoretical approach—producer group theory—highlights the role of employers and unions in shaping interest group coalitions to achieve their preferred policy output. Leaving aside important details for the moment, the primary focus of this research agenda is to explain how different strategies of interest group action emerge in the face of a given set of domestic institutions and power relationships. Recent contributions have placed strong emphasis on the inclusiveness of producer groups as the dominant cause of variation in the protection of outsiders (Martin and Swank 2012; Thelen 2014), whereas contemporary classics were more attuned to differences in class power (Korpi 1978; Esping-Andersen 1985).

The second theoretical explanation—partisanship theory—emphasizes the vote-seeking action of political parties. Putting voters and elections front and center, this research agenda looks at how parties respond to electoral demands against the backdrop of fiscal constraints and institutional legacies. Central to electoral theory is the assumption that differences in the electoral alliance behind party coalitions reflect the dominant cause of variation in the protection of outsiders (Rueda 2007; Pontusson 2011; Beramendi et al. 2015). In sum, conventional theories look at either interest groups or political parties. Neither approach, however, allows for an interaction between these two types of agencies. Perhaps even more important, however, is that both lines of research tend to underestimate the shift in the capitalist context in which the politics of labor market reform plays out. I will now review these existing explanations to show that my empirical puzzle empirically contradicts their theoretically derived predictions. Then, I will delineate my alternative argument from these two lines of research.

Producer Group Theory

The classic interpretation among producer group theory is that redistributive state action hinges on labor's power resources, that is, the relative strength of the alliance between Social Democratic parties and union movements (Korpi 1978, 1983). According to this power resource approach, differences in labor power explain variations in the size of the welfare state. A central assumption is that industrial welfare states are not only a product of working class mobilization, but, once in place, also turn into a power resource per se, because social security arrangements have a decommodifying impact on labor (Esping-Andersen 1985; 1990). It follows that the power resource approach assigns employers the role of profit-seeking antagonists against the welfare state, given the strict relationship between labor power and politically achieved social rights (Korpi 2006; see also Streeck 1997).

The general claim that employers are hostile to welfare states evoked a revisionist counterattack in the institutionalist study of national capitalisms. At its most basic, the literature along the lines of the varieties of capitalism (VoC) framework linked institutional variation to differences in national production strategies of firms, and not to the historically specific strength of labor vis-à-vis capital (Hall and Soskice 2001). Accordingly, centralized business associations help recalibrate domestic welfare arrangements with a view to fostering skill development and competitive advantages, thereby creating opportunities for states to draw on cross-class cooperation and pursue social investment policies (Swenson 2002; Mares 2003). All-encompassing neocorporatist policy forums—composed of centralized peak-level associations and the state—are thus posited to be the necessary condition for protecting the most vulnerable social segments of society (Martin and Swank 2012; Martin and Thelen 2007).

Yet the firm-centered argument of the VoC framework does not hold with respect to the forceful demands of employers' associations for market-clearing adjustment strategies in the neoliberal era in general (Hassel 2009) and the forceful escape of Swedish employers from corporatist bargaining arrangements in particular (Lindvall and Sebring 2005). If anything, in fact, a growing amount of contemporary literature powerfully contests the central role assigned to organized employers by VoC approaches, arguing that business consented to welfare state expansion only in the face of political constraints in order to preempt further market correction (Hacker and Pierson 2002; Korpi 2006; Baccaro and Howell 2011; Paster 2012; Emmenegger 2014).

Unlike the revisionist literature, Thelen (2012, 2014) claims that the protection of outsiders—or "embedded flexibilization" as she termed it—rests on the capacity of unions to incorporate the growing number of service-sector workers into their traditionally manufacturing-dominated membership base. Here, encompassing unions are seen as the only type of organization that can mobilize social support for redistributive state action on behalf of outsiders and new social risk groups. By contrast, shrinking trade unions in economies with large industrial outputs in countries such as France and Germany prioritize the interests of manufacturing core workers (Palier and Thelen 2010). Accordingly, the second necessary condition of "embedded flexibilization" is the capacity of the state to coerce peak-level associations into an agreement when tripartite negotiations appear deadlocked or employers are simply unwilling to participate in corporatist bargaining. This kind of state capacity resonates with the "shadow of hierarchy" argument, providing governments with legislative and executive tools of economic governance (Scharpf 1997).

Central to Kathleen Thelen's coalitional theory is the claim that the inclusiveness of national peak-level associations is the key factor in explaining institutional variation: the more encompassing the inclusiveness, the more egalitarian is the policy output. While the presence of centralized business associations remains important in her account, Thelen places stronger emphasis on high levels of labor organization than revisionist contributions inspired by the VoC-framework. Therefore, accordingly, we should expect more "solidaristic" reform trajectories in Scandinavia than in Austria. Yet this is not the case: today, outsider protection through labor market policy is stronger in Austria than in Sweden, while Denmark has started to move from egalitarian levels into a (modest) dualist direction in the past decade.

Thelen's work was pioneering in highlighting the relationship between the distributive outcomes of liberalization and the mobilization of producer group coalitions. Her approach appears persuasive in explaining continued regime variation in wage inequality, given the relative membership strength of Scandinavian peak-level associations vis-à-vis their Continental European counterparts. Yet my empirical focus is on public policy, and not industrial relations. Thus, the membership strength emphasized by Thelen (2014) or the administrative power position derived from the Ghent system highlighted by Clegg (2012) does not necessarily translate into strong union influence on the design of public policy changes. Union-based explanations ignore the fundamental fact that governments may turn against negotiated reform to exclude organized labor from the policy-making process, irrespective of membership strength and corporatist legacies. Scholarship on social pacts and corporatism demonstrates that ideological and programmatic unity facilitate the capacity of majority governments to impose unilateral reform ambitions on organized labor (Baccaro and Simoni 2008; Afonso 2013). The omitted factor in producer group theory is thus the political choice of whether to share policy-making authority with organized labor. This is a serious shortcoming for a theory of institutional change because it assumes that there is no possibility of having a strong government with an autonomous reform agenda.

The general claim emerging from my emphasis on unilateral government action is that change in labor market policies does not necessarily originate in industrial relations. Producer group approaches argue that the political roots of institutional dualisms are to be found in the shrinking coverage of collective bargaining (Palier and Thelen 2010). The logic behind this argument stems from the notion of "institutional complementarities" (Hall and Soskice 2001), whereby the gradual erosion of industrial relations systems unravels the economic viability of labor market and welfare policy arrangements. In essence, this mechanism attributes dualistic labor market and welfare reforms to functional pressures generated by industrial relations, leaving little room for government agency. Certainly these policy domains are tightly interrelated in the functioning of economic models, but the mechanism underlying dualization may also work precisely the other way around. That is to say, unilateral government action may set in motion dualistic tendencies in state policy without any preceding impetus from industrial relations. The Swedish case is illustrative in this regard. Thanks to encompassing unionization and collective bargaining coverage, Thelen herself finds that Sweden displayed the second lowest percentage of employees in low-wage work in 2010 (Thelen 2014, 130). Yet the picture looks very different in the area of labor market policy: dualistic job security arrangements go hand-in-hand with sharply declining unemployment insurance coverage and spending on active labor market policy. Related to this policy output, Sweden experienced the fastest growing relative poverty rate in the OECD, slipping from the most poverty-free country in 1995 to fourteenth place, behind Germany and Ireland, in 2010 (OECD 2013). In a similar vein, the Danish center-right government (2001–2011) passed various institutional reforms that threatened the viability of encompassing unionization, which might well impact collective bargaining coverage in the future (Ibsen et al. 2013). Theories of producer group action fail to capture these trends. I will now turn to previous research of partisanship theory to detail existing explanations based on the policy-making action of political parties.

Partisanship Theory

Contemporary partisanship theory scholarship highlights the impact of socio-structural change on the interaction patterns between parties and voters (Oesch 2006; Kriesi et al. 2008; Häusermann 2010; Beramendi et al. 2015). Deindustrialization, immigration, demographic aging, and rising female labor market participation reshaped the traditional class- and family- basis on which parties had competed for votes in the postwar era. This new postindustrial context drove a wedge between the policy preferences of low-skilled and low-educated constituencies, on the one hand, and the highly educated "sociocultural professionals," who were mostly employed by the public sector, on the other. While the former classic working class prefers income transfers and high job security to cope with current social needs, the latter group prefers social investment policies that have favorable long-term effects on their capacity to reconcile work and family life and on lifelong learning. Part of the explanation for the growing intralabor divides comes from the emergence of conflicts over postmaterial values and immigration (Kriesi et al. 2008). In political-economic terms, the explanation comes from the heterogeneity of postindustrial risk profiles, which assumes there are divergent policy demands from different labor constituencies (Rueda 2007). In this perspective, the protection of outsiders hinges on the capacity of parties to forge an electoral alliance between the traditional working class and sociocultural professionals (Beramendi et al. 2015, 27–29).

The recognition of intralabor divides in the electoral arena is an essential contribution to the study of electoral politics and economic adjustment. Yet among partisan theorists, there is disagreement over the effects of labor heterogeneity on the policy-making action of parties, especially those with a Social Democratic character. This disagreement plays out between the labor dualism theory of David Rueda (2007) and the classic partisanship theory reinvigorated by Jonas Pontusson (2011). Rueda's powerful contention is that Social Democratic parties have strong incentives to prioritize the interests of insiders over outsiders. He argues that, when faced with fiscal constraints, social democracy lost the capacity to pursue maximalist solutions on behalf of insiders and outsiders, thereby facing a new electoral trade-off. Pontusson (2011), however, points to evidence showing that some (e.g., Nordic) political economies with strong Social Democratic parties remain more inclusive and egalitarian than other (e.g., Continental European) countries with strong Christian Democratic parties. More fundamentally, Schwander (2012) questions the very potential for a full politicization of the insider-outsider divide. Accordingly, the heterogeneity of workers in class, age, gender, and skills interact in shaping welfare state preferences, thereby pointing to other cleavages than simply employment risk.

This contested debate about the role of social democracy appears indicative of the fact that even center-left governments are prone to pursuing dualization. In the most extensive volume on dualization to the present day, the authors concluded that "the chapters in this book do not report strong differences between left- and right-wing governments with regard to dualization" (Emmenegger et al. 2012, 311). In theory, however, the protection of outsiders—in terms of job security, unemployment benefits, and training opportunities—would be an essential vote-seeking device that reflects the egalitarian preference structure of the Nordic electorate (Larsen 2008; Svallfors 2011). Universalist welfare state legacies, low tax burdens for business, and broad public sector employment have traditionally appealed to labor as a whole, thus holding together an encompassing pro-welfare coalition between "old" and "new" electoral constituencies (Beramendi et al. 2015, 29–32). Hence, an electoral logic of labor market reform should translate into strong incentives for Nordic governments, especially those from the center-left, to combat growing insider-outsider divides. However, the Danish and Swedish center-right coalitions managed to deuniversalize unemployment protection and cut active labor market policy spending (Goul Andersen 2012b), while in Austria they homogenized job security arrangements and expanded training. Austrian grand coalitions improved the social protection of outsiders, while the opposite is the case for Swedish Social Democratic single-party governments (Obinger et al. 2012) and, to a lesser extent, Danish center-left governments (Goul Andersen 2012b; Rathgeb 2017). It seems that the partisanship narrative about the left-right cleavage is too simplistic to capture these developments.

An obvious problem with theories of vote-seeking agency is that they tend to ignore shifts in class power and their implications for organized interests. Labor-inclusive negotiations over the design and implementation of institutional changes condition the strategic calculations of partisan reform ambitions and provide trade unions with access to public policy-making. Trade unions have important stakes in this policy domain because labor market reforms interact with, and impinge on, the institutional landscape of collective bargaining and effective labor power. By contrast, electoral mobilization on the grounds of unemployment support has traditionally been constrained by low political solidarity for the unemployed (Alber 1982). As Pierson (1994, 103) argued, voters pay less attention to labor market policy than to social security for pensioners and the sick or disabled, thereby underscoring the explanatory significance of class power. Therefore, the historical context of declining union strength does not naturally "give more prominence to electoral partisan competition" (Beramendi et al. 2015, 26), but may rather help explain the common liberalizing trend in labor market reform. Moreover, the neocorporatist literature points to the diverse mechanisms through which governments continue to fall back on negotiated reform in the neoliberal era (Visser and Hemerijck 1997; Ebbinghaus and Hassel 2000; Culpepper 2002; Traxler 2010; Afonso 2013).

Second, the partisanship literature tends to conflate trade unions with insiders that resist any attempt to enhance the material situation of outsiders in order to defend their own status quo (Rueda 2007; Häusermann 2010). Yet a number of studies show that high levels of labor organization and unity create an acute interest in the representation of outsiders (Becher and Pontusson 2011; Thelen 2014; Gordon 2015), which can be underpinned by institutional incentives attached to the administrative setup of the unemployment protection system (Clegg 2012). An inclusive representational outlook, however, is not necessarily confined to strong unions with encompassing membership bases. Naczyk and Seeleib-Kaiser (2009), for example, demonstrated how preinstitutional settings led labor movements in such diverse cases as Belgium, Britain, France, and Germany to push for an extension in the coverage of supplementary pension schemes to less privileged segments of labor. Moreover, as Benassi and Vlandas (2016) point out, the ideological working-class orientation of unions in the Mediterranean countries may trump an insider-oriented, occupational egoism in the preference-formation process. This claim resonates with findings from the union revitalization literature, which documents the fact that weaker unions opened up their bargaining and recruiting strategies to the non-unionized margins of the workforce (Baccaro et al. 2003; Heery and Adler 2004; Jódar et al. 2011).

That shrinking trade unions did accept policy deals to the detriment of outsiders often reveals their long-term power considerations in the face of declining union power, and certainly does not reflect their policy preference (Emmenegger 2014). Previous studies showed that even the rapidly declining union movement of Austria was the most forceful advocate of outsider efforts in labor and employment law (Tálos 1999; Obinger et al. 2012). Unions in the Nordic countries have traditionally been the central actors with stakes of an organizational

(Ghent system) and representational (encompassing membership) nature on behalf of the weakest segments of the labor market. If anything, in fact, universal access to benefits and training had been the core demands of union confederations in Denmark and Sweden long before the idea of Flexicurity had gained prominence in scholarly debates and policy circles.

The capacity of organized labor, however, to assert favorable concessions for outsiders rests on the political choice of parties to share policy-making authority; that is, the calculus of governments to ensure successful economic performance, and thus their electoral fortunes, by means of political exchange and labor acquiescence (Baccaro and Lim 2007; Baccaro and Simoni 2008; Afonso 2013). Even if permanent austerity and globalization challenge the policy-making autonomy of governments, they may still opt for different actor configurations at the bargaining table: they can work with unions or pursue reforms unilaterally. This political choice has important implications for the power relationships at the bargaining table. Union exclusion eases the adoption of welfare cuts and employment deregulations that stimulate an internal devaluation of the economy, while union inclusion requires political exchanges between the state, capital, and labor. Conventional approaches focusing on either partisanship or producer group coalitions miss this power-distributional interaction between political parties and organized labor.

The Argument: Unions and Governments in the Era of Liberalization

Partisanship and producer group approaches share two features. First, both argue that the viability of social solidarity rests on encompassing pro-welfare coalitions. The causal mechanism behind these claims is that only a united intra-labor coalition has the capacity to push for inclusive policy choices that satisfy divergent social demands. Partisan scholars such as Beramendi et al. (2015) have highlighted the partisan task of reconciling the policy demands of divided electoral constituencies, while producer group scholars like Thelen (2014) have emphasized the unionist task of incorporating service-sector workers into the traditionally manufacturing-dominated union movement. Although one of these theories looks at parties and the other one at unions, they have in common the same underlying logic. Moreover, they focus on either parties or unions to understand the national dynamics of change in OECD capitalism. Both lines of research have been very instructive insofar, as their arguments have helped us to understand the electoral calculations of political parties and material interests of producer groups in the politics of economic adjustment. However, neither approach focuses on the interaction between parties and producer groups under the influence of shifts in class power.

In challenging conventional explanations, I argue that the variation observed between Austria, Denmark, and Sweden does not result from differences in partisanship or producer group coalitions, but rather from differences in the power-distributional interaction between governments and unions. In the Keynesian postwar era, governments in all three countries routinely involved organized labor to cope with the vulnerability of small nation-states in the international capitalist economy (Katzenstein 1985). During the era of liberalization, however, the distribution of policy-making influence between governing parties and unions evolved in very different directions. Austrian governments, largely irrespective of partisanship, continued to work with unions in labor market policy through the process of policy concertation, thereby securing for organized labor the opportunity to strike important concessions for outsiders. After turbulent years of party system change, Danish center-right governments returned to consensual modes of adjustment with organized labor, enabling unions to demand strong state support for training in exchange for welfare-to-work activation. The pattern of union involvement in Denmark, however, turned out to be more fragile than in Austria, thus paving the way for unilateral welfare cuts at the cost of encompassing social security. By contrast, over time, the Swedish unions were gradually marginalized from the policy-making process. Union influence has traditionally been reliant on Social Democratic government partisanship, but party-union ties came under strain and the center-right bloc gained strength as well as unity over time. While the policy preferences of the Austrian, Danish, and Swedish unions were very similar, their political capacity to influence the reform process differed markedly.

My theoretical framework attempts to account for this variation in the capacity of organized labor to protect outsiders. I argue that the capacity of trade unions to achieve concessions for outsiders is conditional on the interaction with a politically weak government. Weakness, in this context, refers to a low level of capacity for autonomous reform, which makes governments unable to formulate or pass a unilateral reform strategy that excludes unions. As I will show, weakness often results from intracoalitional divisions between ideologically divided governing parties or a lack of parliamentary support behind minority governments. Trade unions are influential under these conditions because their support provides weak governments with an extraparliamentary channel of consensus mobilization. This creates powerful incentives for governments to delegate policy-making authority to trilateral negotiations between the state, capital, and labor. Unions can credibly demand substantial concessions from a weak government because their assent to new policies can make the difference between a reform's success and failure.

The presence of a weak government became necessary for union influence, because unions themselves lost the structural power to impose tight constraints on the unilateral reform ambitions of partisan actors. Overall, unions lost members, unity, and thus electoral significance, while the global turn to monetarism and austerity under the conditions of exogenous competitive pressures disciplined their political bargaining power vis-à-vis business as well as governments. I therefore expect the preferred policy output of parties to prevail under the conditions of a strong government because a united majority allows them to pursue their preferred policy output against weakened unions. In the era of liberalization, when parties of all complexions face a structural incentive to reduce the reservation wage and increase labor market flexibility, the policy output of strong governments precludes concessions to unions to the detriment of outsiders.

The argument I will present next in more detail draws on a variety of earlier contributions, especially the power resource approach of Walter Korpi (1978, 1983) and Gøsta Esping-Andersen (1985) as well as the liberalization theory advanced by Wolfgang Streeck (2009), and Lucio Baccaro with Chris Howell (2017). It builds on the assumption that differences in the balance of class power are central to the causal dynamics of national liberalization paths. But it also deviates from the focus of the power resource approach on Social Democratic partisanship by highlighting instead the role of organized labor in capitalist development. Neoliberal economic ideas, fiscal austerity, globalized market competition, and changes in the electorate, among others, cut across the left-right divide in important ways (Blyth 2001; Rueda 2007; Mair 2013), which means that even Social Democratic parties have proved willing to dualize labor markets and welfare. By contrast, inclusive union confederations continue to mobilize political support for outsiders because their organizations incorporate workers who are hit hardest by inequality in employment and social rights (Thelen 2014, Gordon 2015).

Yet the preferences of unions are not causally omnipotent, given their loss of structural power vis-à-vis capital in the neoliberal era. My argument therefore emphasizes the political opportunities unions face when governments are weak. Under conditions of weakness, governments are more responsive to the demands of unions because they need support from extraparliamentary actors in the pursuit of consensus mobilization. This claim about weak governments draws on the social-pact literature and extends to governments of the partisan right as well as the left (Baccaro and Lim 2007; Baccaro and Simoni 2008; Afonso 2013).

The presentation of my argument proceeds as follows. First, I will consider how the gradual stages of liberalization shifted the balance of class power from labor to capital. An appreciation of this shift is necessary to understand why governments had a structural incentive to prioritize the preference of employers in pursuing dualistic policy choices to the detriment of outsiders. Second, I will shift the analysis to the role of organized labor and explain why inclusive union movements—which are characterized by high density or organizational unity— resist partisan attempts aimed at increased inequality through dualization. Third, and finally, after having outlined the contrasting preferences between governments and unions, I will discuss the opportunities unions face to influence the distributive outcomes of national paths of liberalization when governments are weak.

Why Governments Followed the Preference of Capital for Dualization

Governments operating in capitalist democracies have to reconcile the distributive tension between capital accumulation and social stability (Polanyi 1944 [1957]). But they found themselves increasingly unable to perform this dual task when egalitarian redistribution seemed no longer conducive to capitalist growth. This historical change in the capitalist context not only implied a fundamental constraint on the policy-making autonomy of governments. It also caused a shift in the balance of class power by creating opportunities for employers to push governments in relatively egalitarian countries toward dualization. Governments, in other words, have come under enhanced pressure to facilitate capital accumulation by responding to the policy demands of employers. This is not the place for a comprehensive review of the reasons for this shift in the capitalist context. For the purpose of this book, it suffices to discuss the class power implications of the transition from the Keynesian public policy regime to the gradual stages of liberalization over roughly the past four decades (Silver 2003; Glyn 2007; Streeck 2011; Emmenegger 2014; Baccaro and Howell 2017).

The era of liberalization started with the *collapse of Keynesian macroeconomic management* in response to the two oil price shocks of the 1970s. One of the main problems posed by the economic turmoil of the time was that flexible monetary policy adjustment in combination with full employment policies no longer seemed capable of controlling inflation. The Keynesian class compromise therefore began to be seen as the cause of the capital accumulation crisis rather than as its solution. This rethinking ultimately led the Federal Reserve Bank of the United States, under chairman Paul Volcker, to switch to a restrictive monetary policy in an attempt to put the wage demands of unions under severe pressure and thereby undermine inflationary wage-price spirals, in a move that was retrospectively called the "Volcker shock." National governments in Western Europe were quick to follow the U.S. lead in sharply raising interest rates and containing government spending.

The global shift to *monetarism* called into question the functional effectiveness of Keynesian policy instruments for national governments. This had two profound consequences for the political assertiveness of national trade unions vis-à-vis capital. On the one hand, it implied that unions had to discipline their wage demands in order to avoid increasing unemployment. As monetary policy was used to combat inflation, it could no longer serve the unions in stabilizing employment performance. This led to the return of mass unemployment in the advanced capitalist countries (Lindvall 2010), which enhances the bargaining position of employers vis-à-vis unions. On the other hand, the shift to a restrictive monetary policy undermined the incentive for governments to trade wage restraint in return for policy concessions from the unions (Scharpf 1987). However, this capacity to hold back wage demands in the interest of inflation control was the main asset that the unions, which were characterized by an encompassing, centralized, and hierarchical structure, could offer governments to promote their inclusion in the policy-making process (Lehmbruch and Schmitter 1982). A nonaccommodating monetary policy thus called into question the viability of the corporatist "political exchange" between governments and unions (Goldthorpe 1984) because governments were no longer reliant on the capacity (and willingness) of the unions to internalize wage restraint in return for successful economic performance.

In addition to monetarism, nationally anchored unions and governments were confronted with the accelerated expansion of market relations beyond national frontiers, which is also known as *globalization* (Garrett 1995). As employers became less dependent on their home countries for the pursuit of profits, they could threaten unions and governments alike to exit the domestic arena by shifting production sites to more favorable political jurisdictions with lower tax obligations and lower nonwage labor costs (Rhodes 1996; Scharpf 2000). This change in power relations brought about by global trade and capital account liberalization went hand-in-hand with a massive increase in the supply of low-paid workers in the global South, which began to compete with high-paid workers of the global North in the manufacturing sector (Milanovic 2016). Globalization was thus linked to the subsequent deindustrialization of Europe, because it allowed for cheaper production opportunities outside European borders. In other words, increased capital mobility and foreign direct investment (FDI) under the conditions of freer trade pushed national economies into a situation of strong pressures for international competitiveness. Capital could therefore threaten to punish unions and governments by refraining from domestic investment and thereby cause growing unemployment. The credibility of this threat was buttressed by a concerted counteroffensive on the part of employers' associations and their affiliated think tanks to advance neoliberal economic ideas and reverse the tide of squeezed profits against ever more demanding union movements (for Europe, see, e.g., Pontusson 1992; Glyn 2007; for the United States, see, e.g., Lafer 2017; MacLean 2017).

While monetarism and globalization empowered capital vis-à-vis labor, the *emerging fiscal crisis* of the 1990s enhanced the political assertiveness of employers in their demands for cuts in the reservation wage and pension entitlements (Pierson 1998; Bonoli 2007). The creation of the European Economic and Monetary Union (EMU) contributed to this shift in class power by delegating authority over monetary policy to the European Central Bank (which is designed to be even more independent than the German *Bundesbank*) and requiring the achievement of economic convergence criteria as well as the removal of all barriers to capital mobility (Baccaro and Howell 2017, 187–191). The subsequent Stability Pact, which obliged governments to rein in public spending and inflation rates, therefore underpinned the fiscal consolidation agenda of this period (Scharpf 2002). In the absence of strong economic growth and Keynesian aggregate demand management, national governments had to impose social spending cuts on organized labor to consolidate the public budget without lifting taxes on business to prevent capital flight. Declining productivity growth due to deindustrialization as well as demographic aging aggravated the need to reduce public debt, with the result that a strategy of "labor shedding" or "public deficit spending" was no longer a viable option (Ebbinghaus 2006).

To reconcile the popular demands from voters and unions with the structural demands of capital accumulation, governments liberalized their finance markets instead. As Crouch (2009) argues, this liberalization was used to stimulate access to cheap credit when governments could no longer embed market relations with public spending, thereby essentially "privatizing" Keynesian deficit spending. The socialization of bad loans in response to the collapse of the U.S. financial system reinforced the problem of fiscal austerity because it led to suspicions about the sustainability of record high public debt levels. Global financial investors and institutions therefore required sovereign nation states to consolidate public finances in exchange for access to sound money (Streeck 2013).

Finally, deindustrialization, growing white-collar and female employment, and ethnic heterogeneity, in tandem with an increasingly individualist lifestyle, led to a *heterogenization of the working class* (Oesch 2006). Even though a number of unions remained externally encompassing (e.g., in Denmark and Sweden) and internally centralized (e.g., in Austria), these social changes nevertheless weakened the mobilizing capacity of organized labor. To be sure, governments continued to pursue negotiated reforms with organized interests as unions possessed an institutionalized veto-position on social security boards while partisan actors pursued a political cover for unpopular spending cuts, especially in the area of pension policy (Pierson 1996). But the strength of unions to achieve substantial concessions in return for their consent to controversial policy packages was in decline, as labor became more fragmented in terms of skills, earnings, and ideological orientation. The impact of liberalization on class power relationships was thus complemented by a fragmentation and decline of the unionized workforce.

To summarize, the stages of liberalization—the monetarist turn and liberalization of trade and capital accounts (late 1970s), the political acceptance of unemployment (1980s), the fiscal consolidation agenda and creation of the EMU (1990s), and the socialization of bad loans (post-2008), complemented with an ongoing decline and fragmentation of organized labor—gradually altered the distribution of class power and thus facilitated shifts in labor market policy toward the preferred direction of employers. Increased wage differentiation and labor market flexibility have thus become the dominant policy instruments available to stimulate job creation (Culpepper and Regan 2014, Baccaro and Howell 2017). In countries that were previously committed to high levels of social solidarity, the resulting pressures for liberalization started at the fringes of the labor market and thus affected outsiders in particular (Palier and Thelen 2010).

Although the labor market policy preferences of political parties have shifted towards the right in light of these structural constraints, partisan differences have certainly not disappeared. Political parties still cater to diverse electoral constituencies and thus fight over policy choices. Social-democratic parties, for example, are increasingly composed of (high-skilled) outsiders and should thus be more moderate than the political right with respect to dualization (Gingrich and Häusermann 2015; Häusermann et al. 2015). Such an electoral assumption would be in line with the declared goal of the Social Democratic "Third Way" to promote labor market flexibility only to the extent that it reconciles social solidarity with the competitiveness demands of globalization (Blair and Schröder 1998). The Social Democratic motive behind (moderate) dualization contrasts with the more general objective of center-right parties to individualize the risks of becoming unemployed or atypically employed (Jensen 2014, chap. 6). We should thus expect center-right parties to be more radical than their center-left counterparts in pursuing insider-outsider divides. My argument about the impact of class power on the policy preference of governments is thus compatible with a common *direction* of partisan reform ambitions, but also with remaining partisan differences in the *degree* of dualization.

While the shift in the balance of class power from labor to capital was a common trend in the Western world, its effect on union preferences was not equally pronounced or influential across different national models of capitalism. What we have yet to discuss are therefore the conditions under which unions retain the strategic capacity to incorporate outsiders into their representational outlook and resist dualizing reform plans by governments. In the next section of this chapter, I will elaborate on this question.

Why Inclusive Union Movements Resist Dualization

A core finding in the dualization literature is the recognition that encompassing and centralized unions are better able to mobilize political support for outsiders than small and decentralized unions (Palier and Thelen, 2010; Thelen 2014; Gordon 2015). First, encompassing unions organize a higher share of outsiders, thereby directly incorporating their demands into the interest formation process. Second, centralized unions prevent the formation of particularistic policy priorities because the confederal elite incorporates the policy demands from union affiliates that are exposed to a growing number of outsiders. In other words, centralized unions give voice to the sectors that are hit hardest by atypical employment and unemployment. Moreover, administrative roles in the provision of unemployment insurance give trade unions strategic stakes in the protection of the unemployed (Clegg 2012). Drawing on Gordon (2015), my three cases are among the five most inclusive unions in eighteen countries of the OECD (see table 1.2). Gordon's index of inclusive unionism comprises measures of average union density rates, centralization rates, and involvement in unemployment benefit administration for the period from 1985 to 2005.

Sweden and Denmark rank first and second in inclusive unionism, scoring 78.7 and 73.6, respectively, and both featuring very high density and a central union role in the unemployment benefit system. Austria ranks fifth, at 59.2, which puts it well above the remaining countries. We should expect the relatively high levels of inclusiveness in labor movements in Austria, Denmark, and Sweden to produce a stake in the protection of outsiders. Danish and Swedish unions display the highest density rates, while Austrian unions boast the highest levels of concentration and centralization in the OECD. High union density rates in Denmark

TABLE 1.2.   Index of the five most inclusive unions in eighteen countries of the Organization for Economic Co-operation and Development, 1985–2005.

COUNTRY	AVERAGE UNION DENSITY	AVERAGE UNION CENTRALIZATION	INVOLVEMENT IN UNION BENEFIT ADMINISTRATION	INCLUSIVE UNIONISM
Sweden	80.8	55.3	100.0	78.7
Denmark	75.2	45.6	100.0	73.6
Finland	75.2	39.1	100.0	71.4
Belgium	53.0	48.5	100.0	67.2
Austria	41.7	85.9	50.0	59.2

Source: Gordon (2015), 91.

and Sweden are, in large part, a product of unions' responsibility over the administration of voluntary and state-regulated unemployment insurance; that is, the so-called Ghent system (Rothstein 1992). The cost-benefit attractiveness of joining unemployment insurance traditionally acts as a recruitment device for trade unions in the Ghent countries of Denmark, Sweden, Finland, and Belgium (see Clasen and Viebrock 2008 on this mechanism in detail). By contrast, Austrian unions cannot rely on a "Ghent effect," given that membership in unemployment insurance is mandatory and the social partners in the corporatist institutional setting share responsibility for its administration. The Austrian labor movement has experienced a significant membership loss over time, with unionization declining from almost 68 percent in 1960 to a mere 28 percent in the early 2010s. Yet unlike the Ghent countries, the Austrian union confederation, the Österreichischer Gewerkschaftsbund (ÖGB) can draw on its unquestioned leadership and political mandate on behalf of its union affiliates to provide levels of concentration and centralization that are unmatched from an international comparative perspective (Traxler and Pernicka 2007).

The implication is that organizational unity through centralization and concentration can be an effective functional equivalent to high density rates in the political representation of outsiders. As in the case of Austria, it allows the weaker unions to push the confederal elite to resist dualization by offsetting an unequal distribution of sectoral intraunion power in the interest formation process (Thelen 2014; see also Western 1997, chap. 3). Union mergers further enhanced organizational unity in the interest of outsiders because they created a growing share of member unions affected by the usage of "atypical" employment contracts, which were often characterized by a lack of social rights. Notably, the number of member unions gradually declined from 16 in 1978 to 7 in 2009, with the result that even the traditionally male-dominated metalworkers union—the Produktionsgewerkschaft (PRO-GE, established in 2008)—came to include sectors with female part-time workers, albeit to a moderate degree relative to the service sector.

While organizational unity implicates Austrian unions in the fate of outsiders despite a significant membership loss, precisely the opposite relationship seems to underpin labor solidarity in Denmark and Sweden. High density rates incorporate a high number of workers who are at risk of unemployment directly into their membership base (Becher and Pontusson 2011), but union fragmentation between the three separate confederations for manual, white-collar, and professional employees poses a challenge to the effective representation of outsiders. This problem is particularly acute in Sweden, where the main voice for outsiders—blue-collar peak union confederation (LO)—lost its hegemonic position due to a transfer in membership to white-collar unions, which was mainly the result of deindustrialization. As a result, the two nonmanual confederations have come to exceed the membership levels of the LO. In Denmark, LO faced a similar membership shift but was more successful in maintaining its dominant position as it has traditionally included lower-level white-collar grades as well. That said, generous and inclusive unemployment support has been central, not only to the interest representation of the Danish and Swedish LOs in particular, but to the membership recruitment strategy of the labor movements as a whole (Clasen and Viebrock 2008).

In addition to high rates of organizational unity and density, recent studies have identified two alternative mechanisms underlying the political support of unions for outsiders. First, as Vlandas (2013) concludes, French unions pushed for regulation of temporary work contracts to undermine the "replaceability" of permanent workers. He attributes this political choice to the presence of general skills, low wage coordination, and similar educational attainments, which, all together, increased the competition posed by temporary workers vis-à-vis permanent workers. This claim, as he himself points out, does not hold in cases involving a more specific skill set and high levels of wage coordination. Second, as Benassi and Vlandas (2016) argue, a strong ideological working-class orientation broadened the representational outlook of unions in Southern Europe toward temporary agency and marginal worker groups. But such an argument also cannot underlie the choices of unions in the corporatist economies of Northwestern Europe because their postwar identity evolved on the basis of class cooperation and state involvement, not class conflict. Still, these findings are in line with my claim that unions are not necessarily dualizing forces in the era of liberalization.

The formation of inclusive union preferences, however, is not sufficient for the successful protection of outsiders because the gradual decline in union power has weakened the assertiveness of labor in the policy-making process. My argument is that the decline in union power enhances the relevance of national governments in conditioning the level of union influence on policy outputs. They can still grant concessions to unions, but a unilateral reform strategy that excludes unions has become less risky for successful reelection and economic performance than in the Keynesian postwar era. Yet despite a decline in union power, governments are not always the driver behind the reform process. They are often unable to shape public-policy outputs, in particular when they are internally divided or lack a parliamentary majority. In this situation, governments face powerful incentives to share policy-making authority with the unions because they are too weak to formulate and pass a common reform agenda independent of an extraparliamentary channel of consensus mobilization. The presence of a weak government is therefore the main condition under which unions can gain influence despite a decline in power resources.

Government Strength and Union Influence

Weakness often results from intracoalitional divisions between ideologically divided governing parties or a lack of parliamentary support behind minority governments. Both conditions increase the reliance of a government on the support of others for consensus mobilization, which creates opportunities for unions to influence state policies. To assess the strength of a government, I look at its vote share and partisan composition. Put simply, when governing parties come from the same partisan left-right bloc and enjoy a majority in parliament, they have a high capacity to pursue a unilateral reform path that excludes union influence, and vice versa. The following section proceeds to illustrate the logic of this operationalization by discussing different formations of government according to their autonomous reform capacity, which I call government strength. I will thereby draw on the literature of government formation (Crombez 1996; Laver and Shepsle 1996), social pacts (Baccaro and Lim 2007; Hamann and Kelly 2007; Baccaro and Simoni 2008), and recent contributions to the politics of consensus building (Afonso 2013; Alexiadou 2013; Knotz and Lindvall 2015).

First, a *single-party majority government* obviously reflects the strongest possible formation in democratic political systems. It may legislate its preferred policy output without any need to rely on the support of other parties or interest groups. Such governments are common in Anglo-liberal countries with first-past-the-post electoral systems that usually produce stable majorities for single parties. Second, a *single-party minority government* implies the presence of a hegemonic party that dominates the parliamentary majority-building process. Otherwise, it would aim to build a coalition government with other parties. Such a powerful position facilitates the governing party's capacity to find support for its preferred policy output. The Swedish Social Democratic Party (SAP) government (1994–2006) is a case in point, especially from 1994 to 1998. Thanks to a vote share of 45.25 percent it was able to rely on the support of only one party among a diverse set of six opposition parties. Judging from my argument, we should expect even the SAP to use its high level of government strength to downgrade union influence for dualistic policy choices in the interest of job creation. By contrast, the formation of a Liberal single-party minority government in Denmark (2015–2016) resulted from failed coalition talks with the other three parties from the center-right bloc. With a vote share of 26.70 percent, it had a very weak support base, which increased the likelihood of a labor-inclusive reform strategy (Rathgeb 2017).

Third, *ideologically united majority coalitions* are composed of parties from either the left bloc or the right bloc of the parliament. A cohesive ideological outlook enhances their capacity to formulate a common reform agenda, which they are able to pass in parliament due to a majority of seats. The Austrian center-right coalition of the Christian-democratic/Conservative Austrian People's Party (ÖVP) and the right-wing populist Freedom Party of Austria (FPÖ) in 2000–2006, on the one hand, and the first tenure of the Swedish four-party center-right "Alliance," in 2006–2010, on the other, reflect this type of government formation. Notably, the latter did not rely on support from the far-right Sweden Democrats, which should enhance its internal unity relative to the ÖVP-FPÖ coalition. This is because right-wing populist parties—like the FPÖ and the Sweden Democrats— might face an electoral incentive to mitigate the welfare retrenchment typically pursued by center-right parties, as they have attracted an increasing share of working-class voters in, roughly, the past two decades (Afonso 2015; Röth et al. 2017).

Fourth, the government strength of *ideologically united minority coalitions* is contingent on the willingness of the opposition to cooperate with the government holding office. In a polarized party system, such a government would face difficulties trying to achieve a majority in parliament. The resulting hung parliament provides opportunities for unions to achieve policy influence because the government requires an extraparliamentary channel of consensus mobilization (Baccaro and Lim 2007). By contrast, in a consensual party system, such a government has more autonomy in relation to organized labor (Alexiadou 2013). The Danish case demonstrates both propositions, as the frequent formation of minority coalitions led party leaders to establish norms of cross-bloc agreements and inter-party cooperation, thereby augmenting government strength over time (Green-Pedersen 2001). Finally, *ideologically divided majority coalitions* refer to grand coalitions that are composed of heterogeneous policy preferences across the left-right divide. They should thus be less able to find an intra-coalitional compromise relative to pure left- or right-wing governments because they have to reconcile a broad range of partisan interests, especially when they have an equally strong share of parliamentary seats. To overcome internal divisions, grand coalitions often delegate contested issues to trilateral policy forums and thereby draw on a less politicized channel of consensus mobilization (Hamann and Kelly 2007; Afonso 2013).

In sum, we should expect minority coalitions in polarized party systems and grand coalitions between similarly strong parties to be more prone to fall back on a labor-inclusive reform strategy than the other types of government, because the former has a low capacity to *pass* its preferred policy output in parliament, whereas the latter has a low capacity to *formulate* a common reform agenda. The presence of either of these two weaknesses creates opportunities for unions to enhance the protections of outsiders.

Case Selection

To explain why some countries protect outsiders better than others, this book compares the reform trajectories of Austria, Denmark, and Sweden, complemented with shadow case studies on Italy and Spain. The rationale for comparing these three countries in particular is that they represent cases that are similar in important theoretical respects but differ on the empirical outcome of interest. Following a most-similar systems design, the principal objective behind this strategy is to evaluate my argument for divergent reform trajectories while controlling for alternative explanations at the same time. The three cases I have selected are similar in three conditions that are proposed to cause outsider-oriented policy choices: small size and corporatist legacies (Martin and Swank 2012), inclusive union movements (Thelen 2014), and strong Social Democratic parties (Rueda 2007; but cf. Pontusson 2011).

First, the three cases represent *small states* of Western Europe that are characterized by economic openness, relatively simple political-institutional environments, and corporatist legacies. In his seminal study, Katzenstein (1985) showed how the common perception of economic and political vulnerability in small West European states translated into an ideology of social partnership that paved the way for tripartite power sharing. Small size allowed for the cooperation between centralized elite networks that could coordinate policy adjustments more flexibly than larger states with complex and pluralist intermediation patterns. Yet among the small states of Western Europe, the distributive outcome of democratic corporatism varied markedly. In consequence, Katzenstein distinguished between "liberal" and "social" types of corporatism. Austria, Denmark, and Sweden shared the core trait of social corporatism in that they had strong union movements. Unlike Austria and Denmark, however, Sweden represented a mixed type due to the presence of a strong union movement (social) as well as a strong business association (liberal). However, as of the 1990s, the three cases diverged in their patterns of interest mediation, moving Sweden, and to a lesser extent Denmark, to a pluralist direction while Austria revived the corporatist decision-making patterns of the Keynesian postwar era (Öberg et al. 2011; Afonso 2013). To take these different pathways into account, we should speak of common corporatist legacies, and not static structures. However, it is clear that small size and the presence of centralized peak-level associations reflect methodologically important similarities, since these two factors are often portrayed as important conditions for the improved protection of outsiders (Martin and Swank 2012; Wilensky 2012). That is to say, the variation in reform trajectories that we observe in the three cases must be attributed to other factors than country size or corporatist legacies.

Second, and related to the first point, all three countries have *inclusive union movements* from an international comparative perspective. As we saw above, this inclusiveness has different sources: Austria has the highest level of union centralization, while Denmark and Sweden have the highest levels of union density in the OECD. Union centralization enhances bargaining power, reduces coordination costs, and gives greater voice to the less organized union affiliates, thereby boosting the strategic capacity of union confederations to support outsider policies. Union density, on the other hand, provides for financial, political, and organizational means to further labor's interests. Despite their undeniable retreat in the past decades, the three union movements thus remain relatively inclusive from an international comparative perspective. This is another important methodological similarity, given that Thelen (2014) points to the necessity of encompassing unionization for the protection of outsiders. If anything, in fact, the higher levels of inclusiveness would suggest a more "solidaristic" direction of reform in Sweden relative to the case of Austria. From this theoretical perspective, therefore, it would be impossible to attribute cross-national variation between the three cases to differences in the level of unionization.

Third, all three cases share an electorally strong and organizationally united political left in the form of *Social Democratic* parties. In Austria, the alliance between the Catholic Church and liberal elites during the historical struggles for nation building (against Protestant Prussia and affiliated Hapsburg peoples) preempted the possibility of a split between different factions of the working-class movement (Lipset and Rokkan 1990, 132; Bartolini 2000, 552). By contrast, the structural origin of working-class unity in Denmark and Sweden lay largely in Protestant state religiosity and cultural homogeneity (Castles 1978). As Bartolini (2000, 304–305) showed for the period between 1918 and 1985, the three cases represented the most organized and electorally successful socialist parties in Western Europe. Partisan state penetration, tight linkages to centralized union confederations, and the historical absence of intralabor divides were the common core factors underlying this exceptional strength. Unsurprisingly, the Social Democratic parties of Austria, Denmark, and Sweden played an influential role in the neoliberal era as well. Between 1970 and 2015, the Austrian Sozialdemokratische Partei Österreichs (SPÖ), or Social Democratic Party of Austria, and the Swedish Sveriges socialdemokratiska arbetareparti (SAP), or Swedish Democratic Party, led the government for 39 and 28 years, respectively. The Danish Social Demo-

crats (Socialdemokraterne) were less successful in terms of government participation (Esping-Andersen 1985), even though they provided the prime minister
for twenty-two years during the same period. Leaving aside important differences
for the moment, the relative strength and unity of center-left parties forms another similarity that adds to the puzzle of divergent reform trajectories in Austria, Denmark, and Sweden. While the causal predictions derived from Social
Democratic partisanship remain contested (Rueda 2007; but cf. Pontusson 2009),
it seems fair to say that additional factors need to be taken into account to resolve this puzzle of cross-national variation.

Taken together, the reform trajectories of Austria, Denmark, and Sweden
evolved in markedly different directions, although all three cases are similar in
important theoretical respects: small size and corporatist legacies, relatively strong
union movements, and Social Democratic parties. Against the backdrop of these
similarities, the outcome of interest would have been *possible* in all three countries (Mahoney and Goertz 2004). Yet only Austria expanded the protection of
outsiders, whereas Sweden and, to a smaller extent, Denmark did the opposite.
This variation is definitely counterintuitive within contemporary political economy and welfare state research. Conventional producer group and partisan
explanations generally suggest continued regime variation between the Social
Democratic–Nordic regime (Denmark and Sweden) and the Conservative-
Continental regime (Austria).

While Austria represents the positive case of outsider protection, the cases of
Denmark and Sweden highlight how temporal variations in government strength
explain differences even within the same welfare regime. In both countries, trade
unions are very inclusive and build on a Social Democratic institutional legacy.
Yet in crucial moments of time, they faced diverse opportunities to compensate
outsiders for liberalizing pressures. In Denmark, they benefited from the presence of weak center-right governments, which were reliant on union support for
consensus mobilization. In Sweden, by contrast, they faced a hegemonic Social
Democratic government that was becoming more receptive to neoclassical economists than union demands. As a result, during the 1990s, the national reform
trajectories came to diverge: Unions secured Flexicurity in Denmark, while being sidelined in Sweden. However, the Danish case also highlights the importance
of time and within-case variation in my argument. An increase in government
strength during the 2000s led to a decline in union influence and thus social
solidarity in labor market policy—similar to what happened a decade earlier in
Sweden.

The obvious problem of selecting these three cases is the one of generalizability. It could be argued that the three countries are too similar to reveal findings
that could be applicable to other cases. I therefore complement my selection with

shadow case studies of two countries that are neither small in size or corporatist nor characterized by the presence of strong Social Democratic parties and inclusive union movements: Italy and Spain. Although these two countries are very different from the small, corporatist states of Northwestern Europe, they reveal similar observations about the impact of variations in government strength on union influence. Only when governments were weak did these unions have the capacity to influence labor market reforms (Italy), whereas under conditions of strong government, the outcome precluded concessions to unions and, as a result, any protections for the workforce (Spain). Yet union influence tended to prioritize the defense of achievements for insiders, while consenting to deregulation for outsiders. This suggests that union movements in such cases are less effective in fighting for outsiders, even though they also use their influence, as long as it exists, to prevent growing divisions within the workforce. But they not only face institutional legacies and liberalizing pressures that are hostile to the protection of outsiders; without high levels of union membership and centralization, they are also less able to represent them. The shadow cases of Italy and Spain therefore buttress the relevance of high levels of union inclusiveness and suggest that variations in government strength have explanatory merit for a larger universe of cases.

Methodology

The methodological approach used here is primarily one of qualitative case study research over time and space. This research strategy—often called "process-tracing"—focuses on historical trajectories within a particular case rather than correlations of data across many cases at one point in time (George and Bennett 2005). In this way, the mechanism of policy change can be more specifically observed, since the values of the explanatory variables as well as the historical contexts in which they operate fluctuate over time. Previous theories focusing on producer group coalitions (Martin and Swank 2012; Thelen 2014) or partisanship (Rueda 2007; Pontusson 2011) have outlined expectations about the political process we should observe if their mechanisms are the most adequate explanations of policy change. I will compare their expectations with those derived from my *power-distributional interaction framework* and confront them with the empirical observations in each case. More specifically, in Hall's terms, "the point is to see if the multiple actions and statements of the actors at each stage of the causal process are consistent with the image of the world implied by each theory" (Hall 2008, 312). Much information would get lost if I aggregated such complex political dynamics into country-year observations on a limited number of explanatory and dependent variables.

Counterfactual analysis in the concluding sections of each empirical chapter attempts to back up the causal inference drawn from my methodological approach. In counterfactual analysis, the objective is to lend additional plausibility to the causal significance of an argument by making an explicit statement about what would have happened to the dependent variable, Y, if the factor X had not been present. For example, my claim is that Austrian unions had the political capacity to protect outsiders because intracoalitional divisions made governments unable to pursue a unilateral reform strategy that excludes them. So what would have happened *without* the presence of weak governments? The 2003 pension reform provides a sound factual scenario in which the government was not weak; that is, it could draw on an autonomous reform capacity generated by intracoalitional cohesiveness. The 2003 pension reform thus reflects a useful and instructive piece of evidence on which I can build a counterfactual claim from a different point in time. To back up my claim, then, we need to find evidence showing that under the conditions of a strong government the policy output that emerges does not cater to outsiders.

To assess the explanatory merits of different theories I mainly use primary and secondary sources as well as semistructured interviews with policy-making elites (party spokespeople, interest group representatives, bureaucrats, and academic country experts). Following the operationalization described earlier, I measure government strength in terms of the size and unity of the government's parliamentary support base. In the case of minority governments, I also look at the number of options available to build up a majority for their preferred policy in parliament. More specifically, a small number of parliamentary seats composed of parties from different party families suggest a weak government, and vice versa.

The collection of data from semistructured interviews was necessary to understand the political processes leading to institutional change in labor market policy. I conducted twenty-one interviews in December 2013 and August 2014 in Copenhagen, fifteen interviews in December 2014 and spring 2015 (various months) in Vienna, and nine interviews in May and September 2015 in Stockholm (one interview via Skype). For each key event in the causal chain, I gathered interview evidence from at least one representative of the strongest governing party, the national peak-level employers' association, the national peak union confederation, and the Ministry of Labor Market Affairs. The spokespeople of the respective actors were contacted for an interview once I had sufficient information documenting that they were directly involved in the reform process. Most of my interviewees were therefore spokespeople for labor market and social policy. When the responses of different actors were consistent with each other as well as with primary and secondary sources, I ceased to collect additional interview evidence.

My interview questions attempted to grasp the policy-making influence of different actors and the extent to which the final policy output corresponded to the initial policy demands of these actors. For instance, I asked party representatives and bureaucrats about the calculations behind the inclusion (or exclusion) of organized labor in the reform process. Moreover, I asked party and interest group representatives about the initial policy preferences prior to the reform negotiations and the strategic preferences developed in the face of political constraints; that is, second-best choices. Importantly, I adapted my questionnaire to the period in which my interviewees were official representatives of the organization of interest. Following this strategy, I attempted to enhance the reliability of the interview evidence for the historical reconstruction of the reform trajectories. I recorded almost all interviews and evaluated them through reports immediately written down afterwards. On average, the interviews lasted between 45 and 60 minutes.

The usage of interview evidence required a careful interpretive consideration of various empirical sources, given that political actors may tend to give stylized justifications of their action. Therefore, the quotes used from my interviews are the result of extensive triangulation with written documents and other interviews. I used direct interview quotes when they seemed to illustrate the core mechanism at work. I sent all direct quotes to the interviewees for approval in order to check the accuracy of their statements and rule out any misunderstanding. A few quotes had to be modified slightly, but none of these changes altered the meaning of the statements substantially. The list of interviewees can be found in the Appendix. Moreover, I sought advice from experts of the countries I studied to avoid any misunderstanding and draw on existing findings (Emmerich Tálos for Austria, Jørgen Goul Andersen and Henning Jørgensen for Denmark, and Johannes Lindvall and Johan Bo Davidsson for Sweden).

Outline of the Book

Chapter 2 provides a quantitative overview of institutional change in labor market policy for Austria, Denmark, and Sweden from a comparative West European perspective. To assess the direction of reform in labor market policy, it relies on aggregate data on change (and stability) in employment protection legislation, unemployment protection, and active labor market policy spending. As noted previously, and in contrast to the conventional wisdom, it shows that labor market policy has become more "solidaristic" in Austria than in Sweden, with the Flexicurity model of Denmark coming under strain in the 2000s and early 2010s.

The following three chapters constitute the empirical core of the book and address the puzzle of variation described above. Chapter 3 is an inquiry into the reasons why Austrian political actors enhanced the social protection of outsiders despite tightened fiscal constraints (1990s), neoliberal assaults from the political right (2000–2006), and the onset of the Great Recession (post-2008). Challenging the partisan explanatory perspective, it shows that governing parties were not important players in this process. Across partisan differences, they faced difficulties in coming to issue-specific agreements and thus found it more expedient to fall back on a labor-inclusive reform strategy, which enabled unions to strike concessions for outsiders. A business-oriented explanatory perspective is also not borne out by the evidence. Employers reacted strongly against concessions for outsiders, but were unable to overcome the resistance posed by organized labor in the face of weak governments. The chapter instead highlights the strategic capacity of concentrated and centralized unions in supporting the social demands of outsiders. Despite a substantial decline in membership, the Austrian union confederation (ÖGB) not only fought hard for an extension of prevailing labor market protections to "atypical" workers who previously lacked coverage; it also managed to remain influential due to the intracoalitional divisions of the Austrian governments, which ruled out a unilateral reform strategy.

Chapter 4 explores why Danish political actors enhanced the protection of outsiders in the 1990s but did the opposite in the 2000s and early 2010s. Against its ideological preferences, the center-right government of the late 1980s and early 1990s resorted to labor-inclusive negotiations in order to overcome a hung parliament between two opposing party blocs. This way the unions secured a Flexicurity-deal with the political right, which was immediately implemented by the subsequent center-left government. Unlike in Austria, the weakness of Danish governments was not intracoalitional divisions. What caused a reform deadlock was a lack of parliamentary support in a divided party system. However, subsequent minority governments gained less by involving unions, because enhanced flexibility in the parliamentary majority-building process allowed them to seek their preferred policy output independent from union consent. The onset of the Great Recession therefore allowed governments of the right as well as the left to dismiss the one single actor that mobilized political support for outsiders. *Pace* partisanship theory, partisan differences were of minor importance, because center-right as well as center-left governments were in power during the rise of Flexicurity as well as its erosion. *Pace* producer group theory, policy deals between unions and employers lost causal influence with the dominance of parliamentary decision-making processes. Organized interests were actively involved only so long as minority governments were unable to find a parliamentary majority (late 1980s and early 1990s). When that changed, union influence declined, followed by the security-related components of Flexicurity. Unlike unions, employers did not resist unilateral reform changes; governments moved state policy in their preferred direction anyway.

Chapter 5 addresses the puzzle of why Sweden departed from universalism toward a German-like path of pronounced dualization, even though it displays the strongest Social Democratic Party and union movement in the world. Sweden shared with Austria and Denmark a labor movement that advocated outsider-oriented policy demands. As in Denmark, the core institutional recruitment mechanism of unions in Sweden is the Ghent system, which contributed to the member-based strength of Swedish unions and thus shaped their policy preference for universal labor market protections. However, the Swedish governments were neither ideologically divided (as in Austria), nor in the position of having a hung parliament (as in Denmark during the late 1980s and early 1990s). They were thus the clear driver of reform at a time when the SAP came to consider moderate dualisms necessary for job creation (1990–2006), while the center-right bloc gained the unity and strength to reinforce these dualisms (2006–2014). The apparent loser of this process was the labor movement, especially the Swedish Trade Union Confederation (LO), with its demands for outsider protection. This was in the interest of employers, which not only supported the government's direction of reform, but also forcefully withdrew from corporatist policy-forums as a way of undermining union influence.

Chapter 6, the final chapter of the book, revisits the theoretical argument, discusses its limitations and extensions through shadow case studies of Italy and Spain, and considers the general lessons drawn from the book's findings. It concludes with a reflection on opportunities to recenter class power in the study of politics and the relationship between unions and governments in contemporary capitalism.

LABOR MARKET POLICY IN AUSTRIA, DENMARK, AND SWEDEN

Introduction

This chapter presents the puzzle of cross-national variation by describing the development of labor market policies in Austria, Denmark, and Sweden. By doing so, the chapter is concerned with the *distributional profile* of different reform trajectories. That is, it analyzes not only institutional change in terms of job security regulations, unemployment replacement rates, and spending patterns as such, but also the extent to which labor market policies cover and protect the growing share of atypical and unemployed workers: the outsiders.

I attempt to demonstrate, first, that institutional change in labor market policy made the level of dualism between (well-protected) insiders and (precarious) outsiders higher in Sweden than in Austria. In other words, Austria extended state support for outsiders, while Sweden restricted it to insiders and, to some extent, dismantled public unemployment protection for the whole workforce. Second, it calls into question the common assessment that Denmark represents a stable variety of egalitarian capitalism. Instead, it shows that the universal cohesiveness of Danish Flexicurity came under strain during the 2000s and early 2010s, while Austria continued to improve the social situation of outsiders in the same period.

My dependent variable—labor market policy—may be disaggregated into three distinct policy dimensions: (i) employment protection, (ii) unemployment protection, and (iii) active labor market policy (ALMP). Employment protection legislation distinguishes between the discretion of employers in "firing" *permanent* workers on the one hand, and "hiring" *temporary* workers on the other. The former, for example, refers to statutory notice periods before the termination of a permanent employment relationship or constraints on arbitrary dismissals for noneconomic reasons (e.g., political views). Such constraints on the ability of employers to fire at will are intended to enhance the job security of permanent workers. The latter, by contrast, implies regulations on the use of temporary forms of employment, such as fixed-term contracts or temporary agency work. Such constraints on the ability of employers to hire at will are meant to constrain the ability of employers to reduce labor costs by replacing permanent workers with temporary forms of employment that lack access to employment and welfare rights; that is, to replace well-protected "insider" jobs with precarious "outsider" jobs. Taken together, it follows that the maintenance of strict dismissal protection clauses for permanent contracts in combination with the deregulation of temporary contracts creates dualization, whereas a homogenous distribution of regulations on hiring and firing practices undermines it.

Unemployment protection and ALMP deal with the social protection and labor market reintegration of the unemployed. The common trend from decommodification toward the "activation" of the unemployed has made these two policy areas strongly interlinked. *Activation* refers to the tightened connection of benefit payments with obligations to actively demonstrate job-search activities and attend reintegration measures such as subsidized employment, training, or job-search activities (Clasen and Clegg 2006; Bonoli 2010). For analytical reasons, the present chapter separates these two areas from each other to identify the distinct reform trajectories of cash benefits and reintegration measures.

From a welfare point of view, unemployment protection is concerned with the degree of coverage, the duration of benefit receipt, and the level of replacement rates for people who are out of work. Coverage refers to the proportion of the workforce that is insured or entitled to income protection against the risk of unemployment. The degree of coverage depends on the specific qualifying conditions associated with social insurance and assistance programs, typically including the requirement of having been in employment for a certain amount of months or years. In addition, the maximum duration of benefit receipts conditions the inclusiveness of the benefit system by setting time limits on the availability of cash benefits. Finally, the replacement rate defines the proportion of the previous wage paid out by the state in the event of unemployment.

ALMP aims to combat structural unemployment by improving the match between the supply of and demand for labor. It thus forms a supply-side-oriented instrument for adjusting labor markets in the interest of employment growth. An important distinction in discussions of ALMP is between "demanding" versus "enabling" labor market programs (see, e.g., Barbier 2005; Dingeldey 2007; Eichhorst and Konle-Seidl 2008). Demanding ALMP refers to the pressure exerted by legal regulations to actively seek employment and accept jobs that are deemed suitable. It typically involves the use of sanctions and a tightened definition of jobs that the unemployed must be prepared to accept. Enabling ALMP targets the employability of job seekers by tackling the perceived lack of skills and service provision needed to facilitate the transition into employment. It typically involves the provision of training and education, but also counseling or mobility grants. Both types of interventions, demanding and enabling labor market programs, largely target outsiders who find themselves excluded from the labor market due to low skills, chronic health problems, or weak labor demand. Existing evaluations suggest that the expansion of training is a central outsider-oriented policy device through which ALMP may contribute to the social inclusion and labor market reintegration of the most disadvantaged and low-skilled groups of labor (Konle-Seidl 2008, 80; Eichhorst and Konle-Seidl 2008, 23). It is important to note that job seekers are always confronted with both demanding and enabling measures at the same time (Bonoli 2010).

Employment Protection Legislation

To illustrate changes in job security regulations, I rely on data from the employment protection legislation (EPL) dataset provided by the OECD. It measures the procedures and costs involved in dismissing individuals or groups of workers and the procedures involved in hiring workers on fixed-term or temporary work agency contracts. The dataset includes two versions, which differ according to: (i) the time span they cover and (ii) the number of data items they incorporate. The first version available ("Version 1") covers the period from 1985 onward and does not incorporate all the data items covered by the second version. By contrast, the second version ("Version 3") covers the period from 2008 onward and incorporates additional indicators of job security arrangements provided by collective agreements and case law. Version 3 reflects an updated database that led to a significant revision of Version 1. Therefore, I use Version 1 only for the time span not covered by Version 3.

This section, first, compares the strictness of employment protection of permanent workers against dismissals ("firing") and regulations on the use of temporary forms of employment ("hiring") in 1985 by using indicators of Version 1. Second, I look at data from Version 3 for the latest year available (2013) to compare the status quo with the legal regulations found in 1985. The rationale behind this research strategy is to capture institutional change over time and the updated dataset at the same time. When the data are handled in this way, they provide an indication of the *direction* of the reform trajectory and identify the *level* of dualism in job security regulations between permanent and temporary contracts.

Figure 2.1 provides data from the OECD index on the strictness of employment protection for permanent workers and regulations on temporary forms of employment in Austria, Denmark, and Sweden in 1985. It shows that Austria had a dualistic distribution of job security that disadvantaged workers on temporary contracts, as protections for permanent workers were much stronger than regulations on the use of temporary employment. The situation in Austria contrasts with the conditions in the two Scandinavian countries, Sweden and Denmark. Sweden in particular put strong legal constraints on fixed-term contracts and thereby facilitated the employment of permanent workers. Austrian dualism was thus very different from the kind of dualism observed in the cases of Denmark and Sweden. Austrian job security arrangements promoted the emergence of temporary forms of employment, while Denmark and Sweden clearly did not promote such arrangements

The global turn to monetarism and deindustrialization massively changed the environment in which postwar job security arrangements had been put in place and put political actors under growing pressure to adopt a supply-side

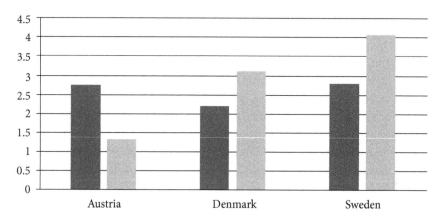

■ Protection of permanent workers against (individual) dismissal

▨ Regulation on temporary forms of employment

FIGURE 2.1.   Employment protection legislation for permanent and temporary forms of employment in 1985.

Source: OECD statistics, EPL database (Version 1).

policy logic of job creation. An important part of this logic was the liberalization of employment protection (Regini 2000; Scharpf 2002). However, the scope and direction of liberalization diverged in this policy area, and the cases of Austria, Denmark, and Sweden reveal the potential for cross-national variation very well.

Figure 2.2 provides data from the OECD index on the strictness of employment protection in 2013. It shows that the distribution of job security between permanent and temporary contracts changed in very different directions. Austria relaxed restrictions on permanent contracts and tightened regulations on temporary contracts, while Denmark deregulated temporary contracts somewhat. In fact, Austria now puts slightly tighter regulations on temporary forms of employment than those by which it protects permanent workers from dismissals, while the opposite is the case in Denmark. The dualism in Sweden strongly deviates from the other two cases. Sweden deregulated temporary contracts and maintained strict dismissal clauses for permanent contracts at the same time. In sum, it strongly reinforced a dualization in EPL, while Austria did the complete opposite. As Eichhorst and Marx (2012) show, this homogenous distribution of job security facilitates the upward mobility of outsiders on the Austrian labor market. Accordingly, the use of temporary contracts in Austria remained limited in size and has not translated into rising levels of involuntary part-time contracts.

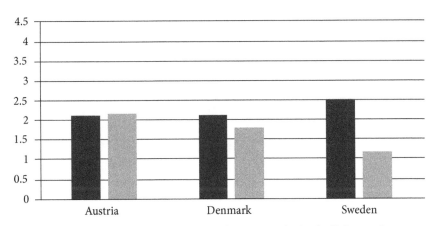

■ Protection of permanent workers against (individual) dismissal
▨ Regulation on temporary forms of employment

FIGURE 2.2. Employment protection legislation for permanent and temporary forms of employment in 2013.

Source: OECD statistics, EPL database (Version 3).

In 2013, the youth unemployment rate in Austria remained slightly below 10 percent, while involuntary part-time employment accounted for 11.4 percent of total part-time employment.[1] By contrast, Sweden experienced steep increases in youth unemployment (23.5 percent) and involuntary part-time employment (36.4 percent), whereas permanent workers continue to enjoy strong employment protection at the same time. Denmark, on the other hand, stands somewhat in the middle between these two cases, with both youth unemployment rates (13.1 percent) and involuntary part-time employment (17.6 percent) slightly above those in Austria and sharply below those in Sweden.

Time series data on temporary employment may shed some additional light on the distributive implications of diverse liberalization paths in EPL. Figure 2.3 illustrates the levels of temporary employment in Austria, Denmark, Sweden, and the average of the EU-21 from 1997 to 2014.[2]

The incidence of temporary employment remained below 10 percent in the former two countries, whereas it increased to 18 percent in Sweden, thereby significantly exceeding the average of the EU-21 countries. In Sweden, fixed-term contracts are particularly widespread among young people, and according to the European Monitoring Centre on Change, they constituted 56 percent in 2011 (EMCC 2013).

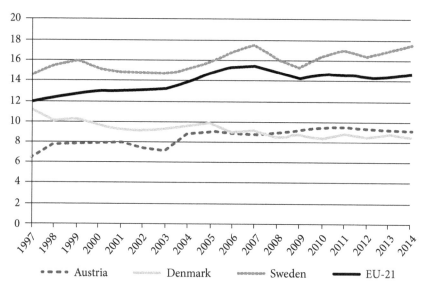

FIGURE 2.3. Incidence of temporary employment in percentage of total workforce in Austria, Denmark, Sweden, and EU-27, 1997–2014.

Source: OECD statistics.

Unemployment Insurance

This section examines the development of the: (i) inclusiveness, and (ii) generosity of the unemployment insurance systems of Austria, Denmark, and Sweden. The reason for analyzing these two dimensions in particular is that they determine the degree of insider-outsider divides in welfare, as inclusive and redistributive benefit schemes protect outsiders better than segmented and exclusive alternatives. First, the *inclusiveness* of unemployment insurance refers to specific qualifying conditions associated with social insurance and assistance programs. In addition, the maximum duration of benefit receipt influences the inclusiveness of the benefit system by setting time limits on the availability of cash benefits. Second, the *generosity* of unemployment insurance refers to the income-replacing level of unemployment benefits ("replacement rates"). To examine the redistributive degree of the generosity dimension, I will first present the development of replacement rates for medium-income earners over time and then present the development of replacement rates for different earnings levels for the latest date available.

The three cases feature two different types of unemployment insurance: the Conservative and contribution-financed type offered in Austria and the Social Democratic and voluntary and state-subsidized type of Denmark and Sweden (Esping-Andersen 1990). The Austrian case represents a typical Conservative-Continental model insofar as the benefit generosity and the maximum duration of receipts are tied to the individual's contribution record. It traditionally reproduces inequalities in the labor market within the welfare system by linking the individual employment biography to the level of benefit entitlements. By contrast, Denmark and Sweden have voluntary and state-subsidized unemployment insurance, which enables the trade unions to administer the conditions for benefit payments (the so-called Ghent system). Generous benefit levels, especially for low-wage earners, and low direct membership fees traditionally have enhanced the cost-benefit attractiveness to join unemployment insurance for workers and trade unions alike (see Rothstein 1992; Scruggs 2002; Clasen and Viebrock 2008). The egalitarian quality of the Ghent system rests on inclusive access to unemployment benefits and redistributive benefit entitlements, largely irrespective of an individual's employment record and the length of unemployment tenure.

Inclusiveness of Unemployment Insurance

My empirical analysis of the inclusiveness of unemployment insurance systems presents, first, comparative information on the qualifying conditions, the maximum duration of benefit receipt, and the requalification period. Second, it reviews coverage and recipient rates to measure inclusiveness in terms of social outcome, and not policy output. Coverage rates describe the proportion of the whole workforce that is insured with unemployment benefits in the event of unemployment. Recipient rates describe the share of all unemployed that receive unemployment benefits. High coverage and recipient rates indicate a high level of inclusiveness, and vice versa. These data sources thus reveal the actual effectiveness of unemployment insurance systems in providing inclusive access to welfare (see also Scruggs 2007). On the other hand, purely institutional analyses of eligibility conditions would fail to capture changes in outcome that result from changes in the economic context (Hacker 2004; Streeck and Thelen 2005).

Table 2.1 describes the different benefit tiers and eligibility conditions for receiving benefits. The first important difference between the three unemployment insurance systems lies in the number of benefit tiers. While Denmark has a single-tier system for all benefit claimants, Austria and Sweden have two tiers: unemployment insurance (UI), on the one hand, and unemployment assistance (UA),

TABLE 2.1. Unemployment insurance systems compared: Benefit tiers, qualifying conditions, maximum benefit duration, and requalification period in Austria, Denmark, and Sweden in 2013.

	AUSTRIA	DENMARK	SWEDEN
Benefit tiers	Unemployment insurance Unemployment assistance (follow-up insurance benefit)	Unemployment insurance	Unemployment insurance Unemployment assistance (flat-rate basic allowance)
Qualifying conditions (i)	Employment condition: 52 weeks within 2 years	Employment condition: 52 weeks within 3 years. Membership condition: 1 year.	Employment condition: 6 months within 1 year Membership condition: 1 year
Maximum benefit duration (ii)	Unemployment insurance: from min. 4 months to max. 2 years (dependent on age and contribution record) Unemployment assistance: unlimited	Unemployment insurance: 2 years	Unemployment insurance: 300 days Unemployment assistance: 300 days
Requalification period	28 weeks	52 weeks	No separate requalification period

Notes: (i) For Austria: 26 weeks within 1 year for young unemployed in Austria; for Sweden: 80 hours/month for at least 6 months within 1 year or 480 hours during six consecutive months and at least 50 hours/month. (ii) For Sweden: 450 days for unemployed people with children under 18.

on the other. In Austria and Sweden, UA provides access to benefit payments for the unemployed who fail to qualify for UI benefits. In Austria, unemployed workers who have exhausted the maximum benefit duration of UI have access to UA for an unlimited period. Means testing in this second tier of UI derives from the condition that the unemployed, whose married partners receive a certain wage level, are not eligible for UA. The generosity of the Austrian UA is only slightly less generous than is the case for UI (95–92 percent of the previous UI benefit level). Unlike social assistance, both UI and UA are financed by mandatory contributions from employees and employers on a parity basis. In Sweden, unemployed workers who are not members of an unemployment benefit fund may have access to UA under the condition that they have been in employment for at least six months within a one-year reference period. The benefit level of the Swedish UA is equivalent to a basic flat rate.

Another crucial difference lies in the type of qualifying conditions. In Austria, access to unemployment benefits rests on the employment condition, which requires benefit claimants to have been in employment for at least fifty-two weeks within a two-year reference period. This employment condition has remained unchanged over the last three decades. By contrast, in Denmark and Sweden, access rests on both employment and membership conditions. Both countries require membership in one of the unemployment benefit funds for at least one year.

In Austria, the maximum benefit duration rests on age and employment record, but participation in training measures automatically extends the length of time for receiving benefits. During the last three decades, the only restrictive change with respect to inclusiveness was the extension of the requalification period from 20 to 28 weeks. Still, access via requalification is more inclusive in Austria than in Denmark and Sweden. In Denmark, the center-left government (1994–2001) gradually reduced the benefit duration from eight and a half years to four years, on the one hand, and doubled the employment condition from 26 weeks to 52 weeks, on the other. In 2010, the center-right government (2001–2011) with support of the Danish People's Party halved the benefit duration, from four years to two years, and doubled the requalification period, from 26 weeks to 52 weeks. Unlike in Austria and Sweden, the Danish system does not allow for an extension of the maximum duration of benefit receipt via participation in training measures. In Sweden, the center-left government (1994–2006) extended the qualification period to six months and abandoned the possibility of requalification through training. In 2006, the Swedish center-right coalition (2006–2014) additionally removed access to benefit receipt via education or periods of study. At the same time, the reform reduced the benefit duration to 300 days, while a so-called job and development guarantee may extend the duration for another 300 days at the lower level of UA.

Unlike the mandatory system of Austria, membership data reflect the degree of coverage in the Ghent systems. Table 2.2 shows the proportion of the labor force covered by an unemployment benefit fund in Denmark and Sweden. It shows that membership rates significantly declined in both countries, while the relative drop was stronger in Sweden than in Denmark. Danish benefit funds registered a gradual and slow membership loss from almost 80 percent in 1995 to 71.5 percent in 2012. In contrast, Swedish benefit funds experienced a sudden and dramatic drop within a few years, resulting in a decline from 84.4 percent in 2005 to 71 percent in 2009. Today, approximately seven in ten employees are members of an unemployment benefit fund in Denmark and Sweden.

What explains the declining coverage of the Ghent systems? What is sure is that the 2006 reform by the Swedish center-right government drastically reduced the cost-benefit attractiveness of the Ghent system. Most notably, it differentiated the level of membership fees along sector-specific unemployment risks, thereby dramatically shifting the total funding of benefit payments away from public taxation. The share of general outlays covered by membership fees increased from 9.4 percent in 2004 to a full 46 percent in 2007 (Clasen and Viebrock 2008, 444). As a result, membership in UI funds dropped from 82.8 to 72.0 percent in 2007 (Kjellberg 2015). Unlike in Sweden, an important part of the explanation for declining coverage in Denmark seems to be the remarkably favorable labor market development there between the mid-1990s and 2008. As Lind argues (2009), there is a negative relationship between the unemployment rate and the membership rate of Ghent systems, albeit with some time lag. Accordingly, the gradual decline of Danish unemployment rates to levels below 4 percent "had a clear impact" (Lind 2009, 515) on the coverage ratio because a growing share of employees trusted in the viability of employment security during good economic times (see also Goul Andersen 2011b, 193). From 2000 to 2008, the unemployment benefit funds lost 120,000 members, or 6 percent of the entire membership. However, the fact that membership rates did not increase in response to the onset of the Great Recession suggests a lasting membership loss, irrespective of the level of unemployment rates (Due et al. 2012).

TABLE 2.2.   Membership of unemployment benefit funds (as a percentage of the labor force), selected years.

	1995	2001	2005	2009	2010	2011	2012
Denmark	79.6	76.7	74.8	70.2	71.5	71.1	71.5
Sweden	87.0	85.0	84.4	71.0	70.6	70.3	70.4

Source: Due et al. (2012, 4) for Denmark; Comparative Welfare Entitlements Dataset of Scruggs et al. (2014) and Kjellberg (2015, 57f.) for Sweden.

The membership condition, however, is not the only Achilles heel of the Ghent systems. In addition, restrictions in the employment condition also curtailed the inclusiveness of unemployment protection, contributing to growing shares of unemployed workers who fail to meet the requirements for receiving benefits (see Klos 2014 for Denmark and Swedish Unemployment Insurance Board [IAF] 2009 for Sweden). Table 2.3 shows the proportion of unemployed workers receiving unemployment benefits from 2008 to 2013 ("recipient rates"). It shows that recipient rates are substantially higher in Austria than in Denmark and Sweden. The main reason why UI in Austria provides income support to a higher ratio of unemployed workers lies in the relatively open access to UA. On average, 38 percent of the unemployed received UA benefits from 2008 to 2013. Without UA, the mean recipient rate would decline to 51 percent. In addition, the Austrian governments have extended the coverage of benefit eligibility to some atypical forms of employment (Obinger et al. 2012). By contrast, recipient rates in Denmark do not in the least reflect the commonly assumed universal quality of the so-called Flexicurity model. On average, more than one third of registered unemployed workers received no income support from UI during the Great Recession. Moreover, a study showed that the 2010 reform, which took effect as of January 2013, in combination with rising unemployment, prevented 33,900 unemployed workers from receiving unemployment benefits (Klos 2014). Shorter benefit duration and more demanding requalification criteria, on the one hand, and declining membership rates of the voluntary benefit funds, on the other, have amounted to a significant deuniversalization of Danish unemployment protection (see also Goul Andersen 2012b).

Sweden stands out in unequal access to unemployment benefits. Drawing on a study of the umbrella organization of Swedish unemployment benefit funds, the share of unemployed workers without social rights to receive benefits increased from 30 percent in 2005 to almost 50 percent in 2008 (IAF 2009). In particular, younger adults and immigrants lost access to benefit entitlements in this period

TABLE 2.3. Recipient rates in Austria, Denmark, and Sweden, 2008–2013.

	2008	2009	2010	2011	2012	2013
Austria	90	91	91	90	91	91
Denmark	54	64	59	56	60	57
Sweden	57	54	52	43	41	44

Notes: Share of all unemployed receiving unemployment benefits, including unemployment assistance (UA) for the cases of Austria and Sweden.

Source: AMS (Arbeitsmarktservice) for Austria, own calculation; Statistics Denmark (AUL 01 dataset) for Denmark; Arbetsförmedlingen (Swedish Public Employment Service) (2014, 20) for Sweden.

(Sjöberg 2011, 217). In 2013, only 44 percent of unemployed workers received benefit payments from UI. According to IAF (2009), high unemployment rates among groups with weak labor market attachment and restrictive changes in eligibility conditions may explain this development. First, a growing share of the unemployed workers who had exhausted their entitlements were transferred to active labor market policy (ALMP) programs, which pay out benefits from a different public authority (Försäkring-skassan). Second, the proportion of new entrants with low attachment to the labor market (e.g., young people and immigrants) increased over time. Third, tightened work conditions and the abolition of the possibility to qualify for benefits via tertiary education or periods of study additional served to deprive young unemployed people of benefits.

In sum, from an outcome perspective, the analysis illustrates that the inclusiveness of UI is higher in Austria than in the Ghent countries. Declining membership rates and tightened restrictions in eligibility conditions contributed to the shrinking effectiveness of voluntary UI in providing encompassing access to social security. In Austria, by contrast, the mandatory character of social insurance, almost no decisions with respect to the eligibility conditions, and the inclusion of atypical forms of employment (e.g., quasi-freelancers) contributed to relatively high levels of inclusiveness. Somewhat surprisingly, Swedish UA could not absorb declining membership rates in the voluntary benefit funds. Arguably, the strong dualization in job security arrangements had a detrimental impact on the inclusiveness of UI, which permitted the rise of temporary contracts with weak attachments to the primary labor market.

Generosity of UI

My empirical analysis of the generosity of unemployment benefits relies on the development of net replacement rates over the period from 1971 to 2009. The dataset used here represents an updated, extended, and modified version of Lyle Scruggs's Welfare Entitlements Dataset (Van Vliet and Caminada 2012). It separates replacement rates of the "average production worker" into two different family types: single people and one-earner couples with two children. My comparison, which follows, reflects the mean of these two family types.

Figure 2.4 shows that the gradually declining generosity of the Ghent systems led to a downward convergence between the three countries toward an average net replacement rate of around 60 percent. Average replacement rates in Austria remained almost unchanged across time, albeit starting at a substantially lower level than in Denmark and Sweden. Slight cutbacks led to a reduction of the net replacement rate from 57.9 percent to 55.0 percent for single people, whereas de-

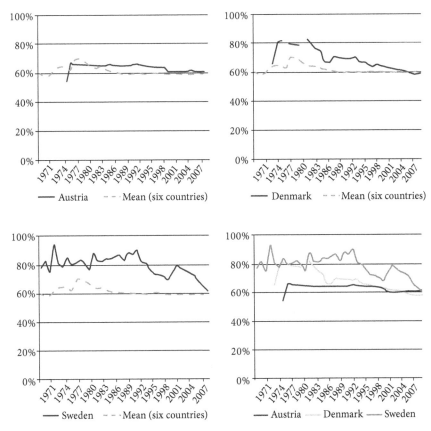

FIGURE 2.4. Net replacement rates for an average production worker (mean of two family types: single people and one-earner couple with two children) in Austria, Denmark, and Sweden, 1971–2009.

Source: Unemployment replacement rates dataset (Van Vliet and Caminada 2012).

Notes: The dotted line represents the mean replacement rate of six mature West European welfare states that were selected on the basis of Esping-Andersen's welfare regime typology: Ireland and the UK (Liberal/Anglo-Saxon regime), France and Germany (Conservative/Continental regime), Norway (Social Democratic/Nordic regime) and the Netherlands (mixed Conservative-Nordic regime). Data do not include the years from 1971 to 1976 for Austria and the years of 1978 and 1982 for Denmark.

pendents continue to receive relatively high family surcharges on top of the basic replacement rate (Lindvall 2010, 161).

Since the early 1980s, average replacement rates in Denmark have continuously decreased, although the formal benefit level remains at 90 percent. A temporary benefit freeze for three years, during which the inflation rate rose to almost 10 percent annually, implied a de facto cutback, whereas the subsequent indexation mechanism did not link the benefit ceiling to the development of average wage increases at the full level (Green-Pedersen et al. 2012, 135). In 2012, the Social Democratic–led government reduced the generosity of the indexation mechanism in order to finance tax cuts for people in employment, thereby reinforcing the trend of declining average net replacement rates in the future (Goul Andersen 2012a). Unlike in Denmark, average replacement rates in Sweden remained relatively constant until the early 1990s. In response to the economic crisis, however, Swedish governments of all partisan complexions agreed to decouple the benefit ceiling from average wage increases. In addition, the center-right coalition unilaterally cut the maximum replacement rate from 90 percent to 80 percent in 1993. In 2001–2002, the Social Democrats interrupted this trend of falling average net replacement rates by twice raising the benefit ceiling. However, these single interventions did not reverse the overall trend toward declining benefit generosity, given the abolition of annual benefit indexation. In 2006, the center-right government accelerated this development by lowering the benefit ceiling and introducing regressive replacement rates of 80 percent of the previous income during the first 100 days, 70 percent for the following 200 days and then 65 percent after 300 days of joblessness.

The Austrian governments thus largely maintained the generosity of benefit levels, while the income replacing character of the Ghent systems declined over time, leading to a gradual process of convergence between the two types of UI. The fact that average net replacement rates converged toward the Austrian level, however, does not tell us anything about the redistributive profile of the benefit system. The OECD Benefits and Wages Database gives us insight into this question by providing data on net replacement rates for low-income, middle-income, and high-income earners. It deviates from Van Vliet and Caminada (2012) in three important ways (see table 2.4). First, it calculates the level of replacement rates based on the "average worker wage," and not the "average production worker," thereby including occupations within the service sector. Second, it shows the mean ratio of six family types, rather than just two. Third, it shows data from 2012, and not only up to 2009.

TABLE 2.4. Net replacement rates by earnings levels (67 percent, 100 percent and 150 percent of average wage) and mean ratio of six family types in 2012.

	67 PERCENT OF AW	100 PERCENT OF AW	150 PERCENT OF AW
Austria	70.0	67.3	55.6
Denmark	88.3	66.5	52.0
Sweden	72.3	54.8	43.8
EU median	74.3	66.8	54.7

Source: OECD benefits and wages database; author's calculation.

Table 2.4 confirms the earnings-related character of the Austrian system, albeit providing slightly higher benefit levels for unemployed workers with previously low-income earnings. Denmark, by contrast, stands out as the most redistributive system, with net replacement rates of 88 percent for low-income earners. However, it also shows that the middle-income groups in Austria and Denmark receive similarly high net replacement rates in the event of unemployment. It is interesting that the Swedish system seems to be significantly less generous as portrayed in the OECD dataset than in Van Vliet and Caminada (2012). This divergence appears to be related to differences in the calculation method and the delayed effects of the 2006 reform. The Swedish system is the least generous one in the sample while providing only slightly higher replacement rates for low-income groups than the Austrian system.

Active Labor Market Policy

Figure 2.5 uses data from the OECD social expenditure database to show the development of public spending on active labor market policy (ALMP) as a percentage of gross domestic product (GDP) over the period from 1985 to 2012. It divides these spending data by the level of harmonized unemployment rates to control for the economic context of ALMP in a given country. Austria started with a relatively low level of ALMP spending compared to Denmark and Sweden. In the late 1990s, spending rates increased but remained at a modest level until the mid-2000s, and they started to rise again thereafter. In response to the Great Recession in 2009, the grand coalition increased the budget of ALMP by 44 percent (400 million Euro) (Atzmüller et al. 2012, 27). In 2010 and 2011, Austria recorded the third and, respectively, fourth highest ALMP expenditure rates in proportion to the unemployment rate in the OECD (BMASK 2012, 2013). In sum, Austrian governments have steadily expanded ALMP, currently reaching a relatively high level of spending from an international comparative perspective.

Starting with a medium level of spending, Denmark expanded ALMP spending to unprecedented high levels during the 1990s, clearly outperforming the rest of the OECD. The subsequent center-right government (2001–2011) gradually reduced spending and tightened the work-first approach of activation demands (Jørgensen 2009). Declining spending went hand in hand with the full transfer of the administrative responsibility over ALMP from corporatist bodies to the municipalities, thereby breaking the institutional capacity of the Danish unions to influence the regional design and local implementation of labor market programs. Although high levels of spending persisted from a comparative between-case perspective, the within-case direction reveals a decline in spending during the 2000s.

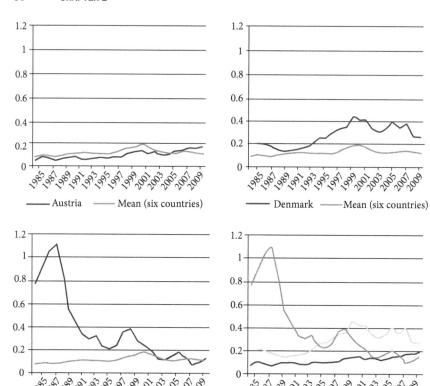

FIGURE 2.5.   Spending on ALMP as a percentage of GDP and divided by
the unemployment rate in Austria, Denmark, and Sweden, 1985–2010.

Source: OECD Social Expenditure Database.

Notes: The dotted line represents the mean ALMP spending rates of six mature West European welfare states
that were selected on the basis of Esping-Andersen's welfare regime typology: Ireland and the UK (Liberal/
Anglo-Saxon regime), France and Germany (Conservative/Continental regime), Norway (Social Democratic/
Nordic regime), and the Netherlands (mixed Conservative-Nordic regime).

By contrast, figures from Sweden reveal that the importance of ALMP has declined considerably throughout the last two decades. Remarkably high levels of
ALMP spending dramatically decreased in the wake of the economic crisis of the
early 1990s. After a three-year period of increased spending (1996–1999), Social
Democratic—and Conservative-led governments cut expenditures again. As a result, by the late 2000s this Social Democratic prototype and ALMP pioneer country spent less on this policy area than Austria. Taken together, the comparative
pattern of change in ALMP resonates with what we observed in the areas of employment and unemployment protection. Austria smoothed insider-outsider divides by expanding active state support for the unemployed, while Sweden did the

complete opposite. Denmark outperforms Austria and Sweden, but there are signs of erosion through union exclusion and declining spending during the 2000s.

Varieties of Liberalization in Labor Market Policy

Political actors in all three small states liberalized their institutions of labor market policy by advancing market mechanisms according to a supply-side logic of economic adjustment. In this process, governments departed from their commitment to full employment and expanded the discretion of employers instead. Two central changes reveal this paradigm shift in labor market policy. First, the (partial) removal of legal restrictions in statutory employment protection promoted the volatility of national labor markets. A process of so-called activation, the second element of liberalization in labor market policy, implied cutbacks in the level and duration of unemployment benefits on the one hand, and mandatory participation in active labor market programmers on the other. Taken together, the institutions of labor market policy changed their function from market-constraining social entitlements toward market-conforming economic competitiveness (Streeck 2009, Baccaro and Howell 2011).

The common trend of liberalization, however, did not rule out cross-national variation in the distributive profile of reform trajectories, nor did it imply convergence in the governance of labor market policy over time and space. Instead, the comparative review of institutional change in the three small states points to nationally distinct varieties of liberalization that markedly diverged in their impact on inequality in labor markets and welfare (Thelen 2012, 2014). Table 2.5 summarizes the reform trajectories of the empirical cases.

TABLE 2.5. Summary of labor market policy change in Austria, Denmark, and Sweden.

		AUSTRIA	DENMARK	SWEDEN
Employment protection (level of strictness)	Permanent contracts	↓	–	–
	Temporary contracts	↑	↓	↓
Unemployment Protection	Inclusion	↑	↓	↓
	Redistribution	–	–	↓
Active labor market policy (spending rates)		↑	↑	↓

Notes: (↑) = expansion; (−) = no significant change; (↓) = contraction.

Austria made its job security regulations uniform by decreasing the protection of permanent workers against dismissals and tightening regulations on the use of temporary forms of employment, while additionally including some atypical employment contracts in the social insurance system. Although the generosity of benefit levels did not decrease significantly, earnings-related social insurance continues to reproduce status-oriented divisions within the labor market in the welfare system. Finally, expanded spending on ALMP provided an increase in state support for the unemployed in a context of tightened activation demands. Compared to Sweden, Austria: (i) has a homogenous job security framework; (ii) grants income support to a substantially higher share of unemployed, and (iii) spends more public resources on ALMP. The outsider-oriented character of the Austrian variety of liberalization is thus undeniable, but in essence, this process of adjustment remains rooted in the institutional framework of the Continental-Conservative welfare regime and was connected to tightened activation demands for people out of work (Atzmüller, Krenn, and Papouschek 2012).

Denmark also made its statutory employment protections homogenous, but unlike Austria, it did so by deregulating temporary forms of employment. Low employment protection for permanent workers and redistributive unemployment protection are part of the Danish welfare state legacy, and are thus far from new. By contrast, the expansion of ALMP spending was a novel response to the economic crisis of the early 1990s and completed the "golden triangle" of Flexicurity (Madsen 1999). Largely unnoticed by conventional wisdom, however, the Social Democratic components of encompassing social security and ALMP have come under strain in the last two decades. Declining inclusiveness reflects dualism in welfare, while the erosion of benefit generosity for middle-income earners threatens to undermine the political support coalition behind the Ghent system in the future. In addition, the center-right government converted the training-based character of Danish activation policies into a work-first regime by placing more emphasis on work incentives than on education (Jørgensen 2009). The case of Denmark still appears egalitarian from a comparative between-case perspective, but a diachronic within-case perspective reveals an eroding institutional capacity to narrow insider-outsider divides.

Sweden dualized statutory employment protection by deregulating the strictness of regulations on temporary forms of employment while maintaining strong dismissal clauses for permanent contracts. In the area of UI, the 2006 reform strongly shifted the funding of benefit payments from general taxes to insured wage earners, leading to rapidly falling membership and recipient rates. Therefore, low-income earners with high unemployment often lack legally binding social rights. By contrast, high-income earners tend to top up their UI by joining private providers because their statutory benefit levels became too low. In 2012,

35 percent of the workforce paid additional membership fees to their benefit funds to gain private top-ups in the event of unemployment (Rasmussen 2014). Therefore, Sweden underwent an encompassing privatization of risk through the rise of (union-administered) private insurance providers and the declining coverage of the Ghent system. Another development that contributed to rising inequality was the dramatic decline of ALMP spending, albeit starting from a very high level. As a result, a growing share of wage earners lack significant employment protection, access to UI, or training in the event of unemployment. Taken together, it seems fair to say that Swedish labor market policy no longer represents a case of Social Democratic universalism, as instead it is moving toward a type of liberal welfare regime with dualized job security regulations.

RELYING ON THE WEAK

Austrian Unions and Smoothed Dualization

Introduction

Austria is well known for its conservative and male-oriented welfare state legacy. Declining coverage rates to the detriment of outsiders would be the most likely distributive outcome produced by this Conservative-Continental regime prototype in a postindustrial context. Perhaps not surprisingly, contemporary debates indeed view the Austrian political economy against the backdrop of a German-like dualization that shifted the burden of economic adjustment to workers of the service sector (Palier and Thelen 2010; Thelen 2014). However, the reality of the Austrian liberalization path was quite distinct from that of Germany. Despite similar historical, cultural, and institutional legacies (Katzenstein 1976), Austrian political actors did not emulate the German adjustment path of *pronounced* dualization like other cases among the Conservative-Continental welfare regime type. Instead, the liberalization of Austrian capitalism entailed elements that ran directly counter to the reinforcement of institutional status divides.

The findings I present in this chapter follow the empirical assessment developed by Obinger et al. (2012), that Austria may be considered a case of *smoothed* dualization. In the area of labor market policy, this claim refers to a set of institutional changes that (i) made consistent the protection of permanent workers against dismissals and regulations on temporary employment, (ii) extended the coverage of the social insurance, and (iii) expanded active labor market policy (ALMP) spending; that is, policies enhancing the protection of outsiders. Existing comparative studies lend additional credibility to the claim that the Austrian reform trajectory has been more "solidaristic" relative to similar Conservative-Continental welfare states such as Belgium, Germany, France, and the Netherlands (Eichhorst and Marx 2012). Even though the Austrian politics of labor market adjustment have been by no means free of the broad neoliberal trend toward the recommodification of labor (Atzmüller et al. 2012; Fink and Krenn 2014), the reform of labor market policy has also been used to cushion the socially corrosive effects of capital liberalization on the weakest labor market segments.

A relatively limited share of temporary and involuntary part-time contracts on the one hand, and an expanded coverage of the social insurance on the other, perhaps best illustrate the distributive outcome of "smoothed dualization" within the historically evolved institutional constraints of a Conservative-Continental welfare regime (Bock-Schappelwein and Mühlberger 2008; Eichhorst and Marx 2012; Fervers and Schwander 2015). This chapter is an inquiry into the reasons why Austrian political actors enhanced the social protection of outsiders despite tightened fiscal constraints and neoliberal assaults from the political right.

So how, then, can we explain the policy outcome of smoothed dualization in a prototypical Bismarckian regime? One potential explanation may link this distributive outcome to relatively favorable labor market performance with low unemployment rates. The successful macroeconomic adjustment of corporatist small states such as Austria might well have prevented the pattern of pronounced dualization found in Germany and France (Obinger et al. 2012, 185). This claim, however, conflates socioeconomic *outcome* with policy *output*. Low unemployment rates do not necessarily induce political actors to legislate "solidaristic" policy changes, nor do they rule out across-the-board deregulation. If anything, in fact, the gradual growth of public debt to more than 80 percent of GDP could have induced governments to legitimize increased status divides as a matter of "economic responsibility." Instead, however, the crisis response to the Great Recession did not entail any significant retrenchment of benefit entitlements as in other countries, but rather an expansion of training-based ALMP and short-term work arrangements.

A partisanship explanation highlights the dominant role of the Social Democratic Party (SPÖ) in Austrian politics (Huo 2009; Häusermann 2010; Pontusson 2011). Between 1970 and 2000, the SPÖ has remained the largest party and thereby provided the chancellor of the federal government. The subsequent center-right coalition between the Conservative/Christian Democratic People's Party (ÖVP) and the populist right-wing Freedom Party (FPÖ) interrupted this dominance for six years. However, in 2006, the SPÖ once again took office by leading a grand coalition with the ÖVP. While the party's emphasis on "social fairness" (Kalina 2007) in response to the controversial policy performance of the previous center-right coalition was important for attempts to expand the coverage of welfare arrangements (Obinger 2009), a straightforward argument on partisan differences appears unconvincing for at least two reasons. First, the policy demands of the SPÖ are linked to the priorities of its powerful trade union wing, and not only vote-seeking calculations per se. In that sense, a view that puts elections front and center misses the essence of Austrian politics, which rests on strong personal and institutional linkages between the SPÖ and organized labor on the one hand, and the ÖVP and organized business on the other (Tálos 2008b). Second, although the SPÖ certainly blocked many of the ÖVP's reform plans that were aimed at the individualization of unemployment risks, it would be difficult to contend that its party leaders remained markedly more egalitarian-minded than their counterparts in Social Democratic welfare states such as Denmark and Sweden. It is clear that the party leadership gradually developed market-conforming problem definitions in response to the challenges posed by the neoliberal era (Müller 1988, 322; Tálos and Wörister 1998, 283; Seeleib-Kaiser et al. 2008, 103–121).

A producer group approach attributes the enhanced protection of outsiders to the influential role of macro-corporatist institutions involving national peak-level associations and the state (Martin and Thelen 2007; Martin and Swank 2012; Thelen 2014). The resilience of national tripartite policy forums may help safeguard the interests of working people through negotiated reform between employers, unions, and the state. In this "varieties of capitalism" perspective (Hall and Soskice 2001), centralized and encompassing peak-level associations mediate the policy preferences of business, thereby enabling governments to draw on cross-class cooperation and pursue social investment policies. However, the producer group claim is not consistent with the fact that the Austrian employers' association, the Federal Economic Chamber (WKÖ), continuously demanded welfare cuts for the unemployed and blocked any attempt to establish minimum benefit entitlements. Even more important is that the producer group argument ignores the fundamental fact that union involvement in public policy is not an institutionalized constant in corporatist economies. Instead, union involvement rests on the *political* choice of governments to share policy-making authority with organized interests. When confronted with shrinking unions, governments may well refrain from acquiescence to labor to pursue their preferred policy output.

I contend that neither the favorable labor market performance nor the influence of the SPÖ or neocorporatist institutions explain the Austrian adjustment path of smoothed dualization. Rather, I argue that the crucial reason why Austria deviated from the "Bismarckian" mainstream was the persistent reliance of governments on trade union support in designing, implementing, and legitimizing reforms of the labor market and welfare state. Perhaps not surprisingly, Austrian governments at various points actively sought to overcome the veto power of the ÖGB in the interest of unilateral fiscal consolidation (Tálos and Kittel 2001; Obinger and Tálos 2006). However, they lacked the autonomous reform capacity that was necessary to reject a process of negotiated adjustment that would include unions. This weakness of Austrian governments, I claim, was necessary for the ongoing influence of the ÖGB on the policy-making process, which caused precisely the "solidaristic" elements that define the reform trajectory of smoothed dualization. It is interesting, therefore, that declining union power did not cause a simultaneous decline in union influence on the policy-making process.

The dominant government constellation in the neoliberal era has been that of a grand coalition between two ideologically divided and similarly strong parties. Faced with severe economic challenges, their reform capacity was constrained by intracoalitional divisions, which gave them strong incentives to delegate policy-making authority to a labor-inclusive "social partnership" (*Sozialpartnerschaft*). The "solidaristic" elements of smoothed dualization have therefore not been a product of partisan reform ambitions. Instead, they resulted from trilateral negotiations between unions, employers, and the state. Elections play little role when governments are notoriously divided and can draw on close ties to well-established social partners. We would expect this negotiated reform process to open up opportunities for organized labor to extract concessions from the state. Of course, the character of and trade-offs involved in that political exchange changed over time, but the involvement of unions remained indispensable in this process.

In contrast to employers, unions had a strong stake in the protection of outsiders. The growth of temporary "atypical" workers exerted pressure on the prevailing labor and social security regulations of their core membership, thereby threatening the bargaining power of unions vis-à-vis employers. This pressure was hardest felt by workers in the service sector. In a labor movement where decisions are made by the confederal elite, the demands of the service sector gain stronger attention than in decentralized labor movements, where the interests of the manufacturing unions often prevail (Thelen 2014). With a high level of labor unity, union leaders in Austria could use their policy-making influence to enhance the social protection of outsiders, and not only a shrinking and aging core of insiders.

That the influence of organized labor was not endemic to institutional and cultural legacies of Austrian postwar corporatism was powerfully demonstrated by the formation of a strong government in the 2000s. Drawing on a high level of ideological cohesiveness, the ÖVP-FPÖ coalition was indeed able to impose its policy preference on unions in a range of issues, especially old-age pensions (Obinger and Tálos 2006). In the area of labor market policy, however, the ÖVP-FPÖ coalition failed to pursue its program against organized labor. When confronted with internal turmoil, the FPÖ blocked the ÖVP in its attempt to reinforce status divides in unemployment insurance. Intracoalitional divisions were therefore necessary for the absence of unilateral reform processes that would have excluded the one single actor that incorporated the interests of outsiders in its political priorities: the unions.

My argument proceeds as follows. First, I briefly describe the policy output of smoothed dualization in the area of labor market policy. Second, I show how labor unity gave Austrian unions the strategic capacity to push for outsider-inclusive policy choices, which could materialize in the policy-making process due to the presence of weak governments. Third, I demonstrate my argument through process-tracing and evidence from sixteen semistructured interviews with policy-making elites. In the conclusion, I discuss the main findings of this case study against the backdrop of the general argument of the book.

Smoothed Dualization in a Bismarckian Welfare State

Austria has certainly liberalized its labor market policy, but it has done so in a way that was attentive to the postindustrial demands of unemployed and temporary workers. In other words, the dominant turn to the recommodification of labor was complemented by changes that facilitated transitions to permanent contracts and extended benefit entitlements to workers on the margins of the workforce. In that sense, my definition of smoothed dualization refers to supply-side solidarity in an age of capital liberalization (Baccaro and Locke 1998). Table 3.1 briefly reviews this labor market policy output on the basis of data from chapter 2.

First, the dualistic job security framework was transformed by universalizing entitlement conditions for severance pay entitlements (Abfertigung neu). As Eichhorst and Marx (2012, 84–89) observe, this universalization impeded the growth of temporary employment contracts and preempted rising levels of involuntary fixed-term or part-time contracts. Their study finds that in 2008, Austria displayed the lowest shares of involuntary fixed-term contracts in total fixed-term employment (12.4 percent) and involuntary part-time contracts in total part-time employment (11.2 percent) when compared to Belgium, Germany, France, and the Netherlands (Eichhorst and Marx 2012).

Second, the generosity of unemployment insurance declined from 66 percent in 1987 to 60 percent in 2009. Moderate cutbacks led to a reduction in the net replacement rate for single people to 55 percent, but unemployed workers with dependents receive relatively high family surcharges on top of the basic replacement rate (Lindvall 2010, 161). The Bismarckian welfare state architecture of the Austrian social insurance system disadvantages part-time, temporary, and

TABLE 3.1. Overview of smoothed dualization in Austrian labor market policy.

GOVERNMENT AND PERIOD	POLICY CHANGE	EMPLOYMENT PROTECTION (STRICTNESS OF EMPLOYMENT PROTECTION FOR REGULAR AND TEMPORARY CONTRACTS; OECD STATS.)	UNEMPLOYMENT PROTECTION (NET REPLACEMENT RATE FOR AVERAGE PRODUCTION WORKER AND TWO FAMILY TYPES)	SPENDING ON ACTIVE LABOR MARKET POLICY (AS A PERCENTAGE OF GDP PER UNEMPLOYED)
Grand coalition (1987–99)	Smoothed dualization	– Regular contracts: 2.75 – Temporary contracts: 1.31	– NRR: from 66 to 64 percent – Tightened availability requirements – Extended social insurance coverage	– Spending: from 0.10 to 0.14
Centre-right (2000–2006)	Smoothed dualization	– Regular contracts: from 2.75 to 2.12 – Temporary contracts: from 1.31 to 2.17	– NRR: from 64 to 61 percent – Requalification period: from 20 to 28 weeks – Tightened availability requirements and 'wage protection'	– Spending: from 0.14 to 0.13
Grand coalition (2006–?)	Smoothed dualization	– Regular contracts: no change – Temporary contracts: no change	– NRR: from 61 to 60 percent (2009) – Tightened availability requirements – Extended social insurance coverage	– Spending: from 0.13 to 0.19

Source: See chapter 2.

low-paid employees by reproducing labor market inequalities in the social security system (Esping-Andersen 1990). Access conditions, benefit levels, and maximum durations are tied to the earnings-related contribution record corresponding to the individual employment biography. In addition, the gradual tightening of availability and job-search requirements as well as the growing use of sanctions reinforced the risk of in-work poverty for people on the margins of the workforce (Atzmüller 2009, Fink and Krenn 2014). Access to the form of slightly less generous unemployment assistance (*Notstandshilfe*) for those unemployed who no longer qualify for unemployment benefits remained relatively open (see chapter 2).[1]

At the same time, benefit entitlements were extended to temporary agency workers, quasi-freelancers, and, on a voluntary opt-in basis, to the "new" self-employed. As a result, most "atypical" employees either gained social insurance coverage or a voluntary opt-in choice in the past two decades (Obinger et al. 2012). Notably, despite gradual improvements some divisions between "regular" and "atypical" employment contracts remain with respect to the scope of employment rights (Obinger et al. 2012). Table 3.2 reviews the share and social protection of atypical employment contracts in 2011.[2] It indicates, first, that the predominant form of atypical employment refers to female part-time work, which amounted to a full 44 percent among total female dependent employment in 2011. This high figure reveals the conservative male-breadwinner legacy of both the Austrian welfare state and Austrian family relations.

Second, table 3.2 shows that marginal employment amounts to 9 percent of total employment. Unlike part-time work, marginally employed workers, who are not allowed to exceed a certain income level (€415.72 in 2016), are not covered by unemployment insurance and may opt into pension insurance on a voluntary basis. This segment perhaps reflects the clearest instance of "outsiderness" with respect to wage levels, labor rights, and social insurance coverage in the Austrian welfare state. However, as Riesenfelder et al. (2011) find, the share of involuntary marginal employment amounted to a mere 14 percent in 2010. Accordingly, 44 percent of marginally employed workers had an additional income through a standard contract (19 percent), pension benefits (16 percent), and unemployment benefits (9 percent), whereas high school or university students made up 31 percent of total marginal employment.

TABLE 3.2.   Share and social protection of atypical employment contracts in 2011.

TYPE OF CONTRACT	SHARE IN TOTAL EMPLOYMENT	SHARE OF WOMEN IN TOTAL FEMALE EMPLOYMENT	PENSIONS (1ST PILLAR)	PENSIONS (2ND PILLAR)	UNEMPLOYMENT
Part-time	20.90 percent	44.00 percent	X	X	X
Marginal	9.00 percent	12.30 percent	Opt-in	X	None
Freelancer	0.60 percent	0.70 percent	X	X	X
Temporary agency work	2.30 percent	1.70 percent	X	X	X
New self-employed	0.56 percent (a)	0.60 percent (a)	Y	Y	Opt-in

Notes: X = mandatory insurance; Y = mandatory insurance if income exceeds wage level of marginal employment; (a) share of new self-employed from year of 2008.

Source: BMASK 2010, 2014; Obinger et al. (2012); adjusted by the author.

Finally, table 3.2 shows that the shares of the three remaining atypical employment contracts in total employment—quasi-freelancers, temporary agency work, and the "new" self-employed—are relatively limited. Unlike part-time and marginal employment, the prevalence of these three contract types declined over time, especially quasi-freelancing and new self-employment. This decline might well be related to rising labor costs resulting from extended benefit entitlements, alongside the detrimental impact of the Great Recession on the demand for temporary agency work.

Another reform that extended social security arrangements was the replacement of the territorially fragmented social assistance scheme with the so-called needs-oriented minimum income scheme (*Bedarfsorientierte Mindestsicherung,* or BMS). Although benefit levels remain means-tested, the new scheme entails expansive elements of basic security for the most disadvantaged groups in society (Tálos 2008a). The main political intention behind the legislation of the BMS was to regularize the fragmented social assistance at a higher benefit level for some regions and ease access conditions for various groups such as lone parents. Moreover, the new scheme granted equal access to reintegration measures for minimum income recipients in public employment services. Recent evaluations, however, suggest that its implementation at the regional level has as yet failed to deliver the promised improvements for benefit claimants (ÖKSA 2012; "Mindestsicherung" 2015). The introduction of a collectively negotiated minimum wage at the level of gross €1,000 for full-time employees (about €820 net fourteen times a year) accompanied the reform of social assistance in 2008. The almost universal coverage of collective bargaining ensured an encompassing right to the minimum wage.

Finally, spending levels on ALMP increased from 0.10 to 0.19 percent of GDP per unemployed in the same period. As a result, in 2010 and 2011, Austria achieved the third and fourth highest ALMP expenditure rates, respectively, in proportion to the unemployment rate and GDP in the OECD (BMASK 2012, 2013). The strong focus on training in Austrian ALMP plays an important role in the adult education of low-skilled segments of the labor market (Hofer et al. 2014, 11).

Table 3.1 shows that both grand coalitions *and* the center-right coalition promoted the reform trajectory along the lines of smoothed dualization. The former expanded the coverage of social security and ALMP spending, whereas the latter universalized entitlement conditions to severance pay. It must be highlighted, however, that the absence of radical changes is not a result of a partisan convergence between the political left and right. On the contrary, the government programs of the center-right coalition between the ÖVP and FPÖ did include significant welfare cutbacks to reduce reservation wages and boost the growth of a low-wage sector. However, in the area of labor market policy, the government in large part failed to pursue this agenda, since the final policy output did not reveal radical changes relative to the previous grand coalition. The next section analyses why organized labor remained sufficiently influential to block neoliberal assaults and extract concessions on behalf of "outsiders."

Union Preferences and Government Strength in Austria

In this section, I present my argument about the power-distributional interaction between union preferences and government weakness in detail. First, I describe how labor unity through horizontal concentration and vertical centralization creates an interest in support of the enhanced protection of outsiders. Drawing on density data, I also show a dramatic decline in union power, which limits the political capacity of the ÖGB to assert itself vis-à-vis governments and employers. The fact that declining union power did *not* correlate with declining labor-inclusiveness in the policy-making process points to the role of governments in maintaining labor-inclusive reform strategies. Therefore, I then discuss the underlying weakness of Austrian governments that ruled out a unilateral reform strategy that excludes unions; namely, the inability of ideologically divided and similarly strong coalition partners to formulate a cohesive policy agenda independent from the mitigating influence of a labor-inclusive "social partnership" (*Sozialpartnerschaft*).

Why Austrian Unions Represent the Interests of Outsiders

The Austrian labor movement rests on a nationally distinct cooperation between two different interest organizations: the Chamber of Labor (BAK) on the one hand, and the Austrian trade union confederation (ÖGB) on the other. The BAK represents the whole workforce due to mandatory membership in corporatist parity bodies such as the social insurance and the public employment service. By contrast, the ÖGB relies on voluntary membership and possesses the legal monopoly to conclude collective agreements, but unites with the BAK in advancing the interests of labor within corporatist parity bodies. That one and the same person often holds leadership positions in both interest organizations underlines the popular perception of a united "labor block" in Austrian politics. In fact, however, there is a clear division of responsibilities in the political process: the ÖGB determines the political priorities, whereas the BAK delivers the political expertise to achieve these priorities in the industrial and political arenas (Traxler and

Pernicka 2007, 223). Or, in the terms of the Austrian labor historian Fritz Klenner (1967, 211), the BAK emerged as a subsidiary public-law body in support of the union movement (*Hilfsorgan*), which in addition monitored the implementation of politically achieved and legally binding regulations vis-à-vis the state and capital (*Kontrollorgan*). In response to growing public criticism about mandatory membership, however, the BAK developed a more autonomous profile during the 1990s by advancing individually tailored legal services to employees in a range of different issues at the local level (Karlhofer 2006, 471–472).

The preference for an enhanced protection of "outsiders" has been supported by the ÖGB's perhaps unrivaled extent of labor unity, which it derived from horizontal concentration and vertical centralization. In fact, Austrian unionism has traditionally been the most concentrated and centralized in the OECD (Traxler 1998; Traxler and Pernicka 2007; Gordon 2015). Horizontal concentration refers to the associational monopoly of the ÖGB in covering all unions, which by definition implies a de facto monopoly in representing all workers. Vertical centralization refers to the strong authority of the confederal level in the interest aggregation process within the labor movement. In fact, sector unions are not even independent affiliates, but rather subdivisions under the umbrella of the ÖGB, since they possess no legal personality. Therefore, the ÖGB exercises full control over individual unions' finances and staff. Vertical centralization broadens the representational scope of the interest aggregation process because the confederal level incorporates the voice of the less organized service sectors, thereby empowering them vis-à-vis their more organized counterparts in the manufacturing sector (Gordon 2015, 90–91; see also Thelen 2014). The capacity to shift interest concentration to the highest level sets the ÖGB apart from the classical sectoral model of German unionism. While also displaying a unitary structure, the German union confederation (DGB) lacks the institutionalized hierarchies to overcome cross-sectoral divides in public policy-making (Heinisch 2000, 76). Unlike the ÖGB, therefore, the weak authority of the DGB underpins an unequal distribution of power between different sector unions, which favors a sectoral union framework and codetermination at the plant level.

Labor unity was a clear political postwar choice that arose from historical lessons, whose impact on the ideological outlook of future union generations cannot be overstated. First, the postwar elites of the union movement came to the conclusion that their fragmentation into rivaling factions undermined their mobilizing capacity to resist the Austro-fascist regime in 1933–1934, which then paved the way for the *Anschluss* with Nazi Germany in 1938 (Traxler and Pernicka 2007, 207). In hindsight, this experience led to the conviction that a united organization would be imperative to the future viability of the labor movement and democratic stability alike. To achieve labor unity within a single confederation, the ÖGB internalized all different camps into political factions, which are linked to the parties in parliament (Traxler and Pernicka 2007, 207). The faction of the SPÖ is the strongest among all member unions except for the union of public service employees, which is dominated by the ÖVP. Another important historical lesson for Austrian union leaders was that the country's vulnerability to fascism during the interwar period was inextricably linked to mass unemployment. In consequence, labor unity was considered necessary by union leaders to generate the strategic capacity for the conclusion of "responsible" wage agreements in the interest of full employment and economic growth (Klenner 1967, 178, 200; Katzenstein 1985). With their persecution during Austro-fascism (1934–1938) and National Socialism (1938–1945), the postwar occupation thus marked the turning point from an ideological outlook of class struggle toward class cooperation (Traxler 1998, 272). This commitment was supported by the subsequent integration of the ÖGB into the nationwide economic management of the state, which provided the confederal union level with the associational responsibility and political legitimacy to speak for the entire labor force collectively.

Its representational monopoly and centralized authority across diverse sectors and political factions rules out the externalization of adjustment costs and thus steers the ÖGB to assume an inclusive representational outlook. The hegemonic position of the ÖGB not only made organized labor a "responsible" interlocutor for capital and the state, but also undermined the formation of particularistic public-policy goals driven by powerful sector unions. It thus allowed for an encompassing representational focus when employers discovered the usage of "atypical" employment contracts as a way of boosting flexibility and cost competitiveness. These contracts allow employers to save nonwage labor costs and circumvent legal restrictions enjoyed by workers in "regular" contracts. Therefore, they create pressure on unions' bargaining power as well as the wage levels and working conditions of the firms' core workforce. In particular, the unitary and cross-sectoral white-collar union (GPA-djp) is exposed to (female) part-time employment, "freelance" contracts, and new self-employment (Pernicka 2005). By contrast, unions in the manufacturing sector are mainly confronted with temporary agency work as a deviation from the standard employment relationship (Pernicka 2005). A series of mergers since the 1990s made a growing share of member unions affected by the usage of atypical employment contracts. The number of member unions gradually declined from sixteen in 1978 to seven in 2009. Notably, the powerful blue-collar union of Metal, Mining, and Energy merged with the union of Textiles in 2000, the union of Agriculture and Food in 2006, and the union of Chemistry in 2008 to form the Produktionsgewerkschaft (PRO-GE). As a result, even the traditionally male-dominated industrial union came to include sectors with female part-time workers, albeit to a very limited extent relative to the service sector.

The ÖGB pursued a policy of undermining intralabor competition between "regular" and "atypical" workers by demanding an extension of prevailing labor protections and social security arrangements to those workers who lack coverage in these respects. For example, the inclusion of atypical contracts into social insurance imposes the payment of mandatory benefit contributions on the employer, thereby reducing the cost attractiveness of nonstandard employment relationships as well as expanding the financing base of the welfare state at the same time. In a Conservative welfare regime, the enhanced social protection of outsiders helps union confederations to regain bargaining power vis-à-vis employers, protect their core members from low-wage competition, and reach out to workers at the margins of the labor force. Contrary to Rueda (2007), therefore, the mobilization of political support for "outsiders" can be perfectly compatible with the interest representation of "insiders." That said, the earnings-related nature of benefit entitlements sets institutional constraints on attempts to improve the social security of outsiders.

It is clear that high levels of labor unity not only support a policy *preference* for outsider-inclusive policy choices, but also the *power* to achieve these preferences in the political process. Yet the incredible decline of the density of the workforce that is unionized poses perhaps the greatest threat to the political influence of the ÖGB. Figure 3.1 compares this decline from 63 percent in 1970 to around 25 percent in the early 2010s with the robust levels of unionization found in the Ghent countries of Denmark and Sweden.

There are a number of different reasons for this decline, but the most obvious one appears to be the lack of selective incentives for membership (Traxler and Pernicka 2007). Mandatory membership in the BAK gives non-unionized workers access to individually tailored legal services, whereas collective agreements cover the entire sector irrespective of union membership. As a result of declining density rates, female and service sector workers have become underrepresented in union membership relative to male and manufacturing workers (Traxler and Perknicka 2007). At the level of macro public policy, the organizational structure geared toward labor unity helps counteract the pressure for selective interest representation on behalf of a shrinking and aging core membership.

The decline in union density undeniably weakens the mobilizing capacity of unions to put constraints on unilateral reform ambitions of governing parties. With the decline in organizational power, the political influence of the ÖGB relies to a growing extent on its institutionalized power position, which is derived from participation in corporatist state bodies. The essential question is, then, to

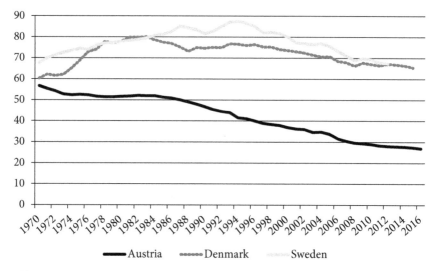

FIGURE 3.1. Union density rates in Austria, Denmark, and Sweden, 1970–2010.

Source: OECD statistics.

what extent governments exploit declining union strength as a political opportunity to swing the balance of political influence away from labor. Faced with the adjustment demands of the liberalization era, governments would have a *structural* incentive to pursue a unilateral approach against the veto of organized labor. But my theory predicts that intracoalitional divides would create a *political* disincentive for the leaders of governing parties to pursue a unilateral policy agenda, because they feel unable to legislate a reform agenda without union involvement. I will now explain why Austria was a case of weak governments in the era of liberalization.

The Weakness of Austrian Governments: Intracoalition Divides

A core feature of the Austrian political system is the close institutional and personal linkage between the two historical major parties and the social partner camps. Vertical coordination in public policy usually takes place between the SPÖ and BAK-ÖGB on the one hand, and the ÖVP and WKÖ-IV on the other. The Austrian Economic Chamber (WKÖ) is the counterpart to the Austrian Chamber of Labor (BAK) in representing every employer due to mandatory membership in collective bargaining and corporatist state bodies. Unlike the WKÖ, the Austrian Federation of Industries (IV) represents large industrial companies but does not form an official part of the Austrian social partnership in corporatist state bodies. Institutional ties between the SPÖ and ÖGB derive from the fact that the strongest trade union faction within the ÖGB, the FSG (Fraktion Sozialde-mokratischer Gewerkschafter), has the right of personal representation in federal party committees and conferences. Election results in the democratic boards of the BAK and WKÖ reveal the party-political orientation of the Chambers. The SPÖ represents the strongest faction in the BAK, while the ÖVP's faction ranks first in the WKÖ. Personal linkages are visible in the phenomenon of multiple mandates (*Ämterkumulierung*): one person may perform the functions of high-ranked politicians and interest group representatives in one of the two camps at the same time. For example, the SPÖ traditionally appoints prominent union leaders as minister of social affairs.

In this highly integrated and corporatist "small state" environment (Katzen-stein 1984), the SPÖ has not only established close personal and institutional ties to the ÖGB, which are important for union leaders to influence the legislature. It has also been willing to grant significant agenda-setting capacity to Social Democratic union elites because the latter can draw on the micro-level information of constitutionally entrenched works councils and the macro-level expertise of the resourceful BAK. Information and expertise are thus important tools deployed by the ÖGB to influence the policy-making action of the SPÖ. Taken together, the ÖGB not only reflects an informal veto-player against unilateral reform initiatives of SPÖ-led governments, but also serves the role of a think tank for the party leadership.

In addition to party-union ties, the reliance of the grand coalitions on trade union support was stabilized by intracoalitional divisions that weakened their reform capacity during the 1990s. To assess the reform capacity of governments in Austria, we can rely on a description of the partisan composition and vote shares of coalition governments as a proxy measure. Table 3.3 shows that Austria has mostly been governed by a grand coalition between two ideologically divided and similarly strong parties, except for a six-year period of a center-right coalition between the ÖVP and FPÖ. Three features are important in this context. First, the challenges posed by the neoliberal era reinforced open distributive conflicts and put an end to the positive-sum game of the booming "golden age" postwar economy (Hemerijck et al. 2000; Tálos and Kittel 2001). Naturally enough, negotiations around sharing the costs of fiscal consolidation between two historically divided camps hardened the political fronts. Second, the relatively balanced distribution of parliamentary seats implied that both parties have been powerful enough to block each other, even though the SPÖ has always been somewhat stronger than the ÖVP in the period of investigation (Obinger 2002). Third, table 3.3 also indicates that both parties came under growing pressure from the

TABLE 3.3.   Elections and governments in Austria, 1983–2016.

COALITION	PERIOD	GOVERNING PARTIES	VOTES (FIRST PARTY)	VOTES (SECOND PARTY)
Centre-left	1983–1987	SPÖ—FPÖ	47.65 percent	4.98 percent
Grand Coalition	1987–1990	SPÖ—ÖVP	43.11 percent	41.29 percent
	1990–1994	SPÖ—ÖVP	42.78 percent	32.06 percent
	1994–1995	SPÖ—ÖVP	34.92 percent	27.67 percent
	1995–1999	SPÖ—ÖVP	38.06 percent	28.29 percent
Centre-right	2000–2002	ÖVP—FPÖ	26.91 percent	26.91 percent
	2002–2006	ÖVP—FPÖ	42.30 percent	10.01 percent
Grand coalition	2006–2008	SPÖ—ÖVP	35.34 percent	34.33 percent
	2008–2013	SPÖ—ÖVP	29.26 percent	25.98 percent
	2013–?	SPÖ—ÖVP	26.82 percent	23.99 percent

Notes: SPÖ = Social Democratic Party; ÖVP = Conservative/Christian Democratic People's Party; FPÖ = Freedom Party (right-wing populist since Jörg Haider's takeover in 1986).

rise of the Green Party and the FPÖ since the grand coalition partners have almost continuously lost vote shares for the past three decades (Pelinka 2005). We would expect all these factors to challenge the ability of a grand coalition to achieve a political consensus on controversial issues.

What added to the conflictual relationship between the grand coalition partners was that the ÖVP became increasingly dissatisfied with its role as the "junior partner" of an SPÖ-led grand coalition. Partly in response to anticorporatist sentiments among the middle class (Heinisch 2001, 36–37), the ÖVP's subsequent shift in orientation away from Austria's pronounced consensus culture and toward neoliberal ideas stimulated political conflicts with the SPÖ in an age of economic turmoil (Fallend 2006, 13–14). Moreover, the rise of the FPÖ buttressed the political credibility of the ÖVP's agenda because the electoral strength of the former opened up an opportunity for the latter to exit from the "eternal" grand coalition in favor of a more cohesive center-right coalition (Müller and Fallend 2004).

This presence of "weak governments" enabled the ÖGB to remain influential through cooperation with the WKÖ. It maintained the leverage of social partner negotiations because reformers of the grand coalition parties faced difficulties in formulating, implementing, and legitimizing unilateral policies. The advantage of delegating policy-making authority away from the grand coalition lies in the low public salience and problem-solving capacity of social partner negotiations. First, unlike the grand coalition partners, the peak-level associations have the organizational capacity to shift conflictual issues to informal and nontransparent elite negotiations that are largely insulated from particularistic member interests and popular electoral demands (Karlhofer 2006, 473–474). Mandatory membership in the Chambers rules out losses of membership, whereas centralization and concentration allows the ÖGB to rein in centrifugal tendencies within the labor movement. Their organizational power gives both sides of the class divide a high level of autonomy vis-à-vis pressure from below, which allows for mutual high-trust relations and "gentlemen's agreements" between union and employer leaders (Heinisch 2000). Following Schmitter and Streeck (1999), the reform capacity of social partnership thus rests very much on an emphasis on the "logic of influence" over a "logic of membership."

Second, the social partners not only help design and implement difficult economic reforms for weak governments, but also broaden the political support base for the legitimization of politically difficult policies. Union consent to controversial austerity packages can be desperately needed by governments under pressure from growing electoral volatility (Hamann and Kelly 2007). Taken together, during the 1990s, the social partners could turn into "modernization brokers" (Heinisch 1999) by mitigating the lack of cohesiveness between the grand coalition partners. That is to say, the low autonomous reform capacity of the grand coalition was the political background against which the transition from demand-side to supply-side corporatism could take place in Austria (Traxler 1998).

The subsequent formation of a center-right "bloc" from 2000 to 2006 suggests a higher intracoalitional cohesiveness relative to previous grand coalitions (Müller and Fallend 2004). Indeed, the ÖVP-FPÖ coalition was united in conservative attitudes on issues such as childcare and immigration. But the neoliberal agenda driven by the ÖVP came under strain from prolonged internal turmoil in the FPÖ. The overwhelming problem for the FPÖ as a governing party was how to reconcile the ideological tension between two opposing wings: the market-liberal government team on the one hand, and the populist grassroots movement on the other (Luther 2003). While sharing the ÖVP's anti-union stance, the electoral success of the populist grassroots movement supporting Jörg Haider rested on its appeal to the social demands of the "little man on the street." Faced with this intrapartisan tension, the center-right coalition had to fall back on the social partners to achieve a durable political consensus at some points in time, even though social partner influence overall declined relative to the previous government (Afonso 2013). With the onset of the Great Recession and the return of another grand coalition, the stage was finally set for a veritable revival of Austrian social partnership (Tálos 2008b). The next section will show that the Austrian liberalization path of smoothed dualization was not simply a reflection of Social Democratic government partisanship or corporatist institutions. Instead, the prevalence of weak governments created the necessary opportunity for unions to extract concessions on behalf of outsiders.

Balanced Power Relationships at the Turn to Liberalization

The core economic problem facing successive Austrian governments during the 1980s was reducing public debt. Fiscal consolidation slowly gained priority in the political goal statements, as the gradual increase of public debt from 20.4 percent in 1970 to almost 50 percent in the early 1980s documented the price of maintaining (almost) full employment during the global turn to monetarism (Obinger et al. 2010, 35–37). Another instance of the gradual erosion of *Austro-Keynesianism* came in 1986, when the collapse of state-run industries revealed the unsustainability of the growing subsidization of public employment in the manufacturing sector. Labor shedding through the opening of early retirement arrangements in response to unemployment aggravated the fiscal problem of the federal state. Alongside structural fiscal pressure, the WKÖ repeatedly called into question the deservingness of unemployed welfare recipients, thereby demanding tightened obligations and benefit cuts for people who were out of work (Tálos and Wörister 1998, 268–270). In line with the WKÖ, prominent party members of the FPÖ and ÖVP initiated various parliamentary debates, in which they alleged welfare recipients to abuse the social security system by refraining to take up paid jobs (Tálos and Wörister 1998, 268–270).

Despite the fiscal problem pressure and populist assaults from the political right, the SPÖ-ÖVP government abstained from unidirectional benefit cutbacks. Instead, the expansion of benefits even outweighed retrenchment in labor market policy until 1993 (Obinger et al. 2010, 44–45). The most significant reason why balanced reforms prevailed in this period was that power sharing between the ideologically divided major parties paved the way for tripartite political exchanges (cf. Tálos and Rossman 1992, 51–52; Tálos and Kittel 2001, 124). Close ties between the SPÖ and the BAK-ÖGB ensured that the interest organizations of labor could play an integral role in the policy-making process. For example, the *amendment of unemployment insurance law of 1989* included the upward homogenization of net replacement rates to the benefit of low-wage earners and eased access conditions to unemployment benefits for young people under the age of 25 by cutting the qualifying period from fifty-two to twenty weeks. The extension of the benefit duration for people with long contribution records benefited insiders with continuous employment relationships, while the integration of foreigners into the unemployment assistance scheme was the product of a Constitutional Court ruling. The amendment also entitled women who were dependent on full-time employed partners to have access to the unemployment assistance. In return, the interest organizations of labor accepted the demands of the ÖVP and the WKÖ for a reduced contribution rate and the tightened use of sanctions.

Policy demands by the SPÖ and the BAK-ÖGB in the subsequent amendment of 1990 show their encompassing representational interests on behalf of the whole workforce, and not only insiders. Both the party and the interest organizations of labor demanded the introduction of statutory minimum benefit standards (Tálos and Rossman 1992, 52; 58–59). Elements of minimum income protection in unemployment insurance would have helped diminish the risk of insufficient welfare entitlements for low-paid workers. The ÖVP and the employers rejected this proposal and instead conceded to the introduction of a uniform net replacement rate of 57.9 percent. The corresponding abolition of wage scales improved the social protection of low-wage earners but the successful attempt of the ÖVP and the WKÖ to block redistributive changes ensured that the principle of earnings-related benefits remained dominant. The amendment also included the retention of the assessment base for males aged 50+ and females aged 45+ to respond to the growing risk of unemployment among elderly employees (Obinger et al. 2012, 181). On the other hand, the ÖVP and WKÖ again managed to obtain measures increasing the pressure on the long-term unemployed to accept jobs and a modest cutback in the level of the unemployment assistance. The subsequent reform of 1993 (*Beschäftigungssicherungsgesetz*) again tightened sanctions and availability requirements on the one hand, and cut the unemployment benefit level from 57.9 percent to 57.0 percent on the other.

EU Accession and Fiscal Austerity

The two major parties and the social partners shared the position that becoming part of the European Union (EU) was necessary to improve the productive capacity of the Austrian economy. On the part of organized labor, the rationale was that small and open European economies have to compete along EU guidelines of the single market anyway. EU membership would thus enable Austria to codesign the guidelines, instead of merely following them (Unger 2003, 102). The social partners therefore joined the government in the mobilization of public support in the public referendum of June 1994; 66 percent voted in favor of EU membership.

EU accession came into force on January 1995 and directly led to the preparation of fiscal adjustment strategies to meet the legal requirements for joining the European Economic and Monetary Union (EMU). The Treaty of Maastricht (1993) ruled out currency devaluations and deficit spending—two options all political actors officially rejected anyway. Austria had traditionally been a coordinated hard-currency regime pegged to the Deutschmark. The political challenge posed by the EMU membership application was the negotiation over the design of fiscal consolidation to combat public debt. Declining economic growth and increasing unemployment rates translated into rising annual public deficits (5.8 percent in 1995), while the debt ratio surpassed the Maastricht threshold of 60 percent in 1993. The following quote from the government program of 1994 is worth reproducing to illustrate the principal aim of the SPÖ and ÖVP to pursue an expenditure-based approach to the consolidation of the federal budget:

> To ensure the attractiveness and stability of the Austrian business location and safeguard our employment policy and high social standards, it is of utmost importance to prioritize the consolidation of the federal budget in the upcoming legislative period. . . . To guarantee the financing of welfare benefits, measures will be taken in particular with regard to the family compensation fund, unemployment insurance, the statutory pension insurance, and the conditions for elderly care benefits. (author's translation, Government of Austria 1994, 22–23)

EU accession changed the domestic distribution of power when the party leaders of the ideologically divided major parties converged around a strategy of welfare retrenchment to meet the Maastricht convergence criteria. Central to this convergence was the conviction of the former bank manager and Social Democratic chancellor Franz Vranitzky (1987–1997) that cost reductions were necessary to ensure the financial viability of the welfare state (Vranitzky 2004, 273). The structural impetus of rising public debt during the politics of EMU adjustment constrained the policy choices of organized labor and provided the WKÖ with an opportunity to demand a political shift to orthodox fiscal adjustment. The politics of EMU adjustment culminated in the adoption of two austerity packages in 1995 and 1996 (Strukturanpassungsgesetze I and II), which reduced the annual public deficit from 5.7 percent of GDP in 1995 to 1.8 percent in 1997.

Proof of the governmental preference for an expenditure-based approach to fiscal consolidation came immediately after the elections of 1994, when the Social Democratic finance minister, Ferdinand Lacina, and the Conservative state secretary for finance, Johannes Ditz, presented a comprehensive package of spending cuts: the "52-point program." For the first time in Austrian postwar history, the social partners were *not* involved in the preparation of an economic policy package. In response, the ÖGB announced "fierce resistance" against the unilateral policy-making style of the government, opposing the distributional profile they considered socially unbalanced at the expense of labor (Sebald 1998, 59). The interest organizations of labor instead demanded the abolition of tax loopholes and the introduction of solidarity surcharges for high-income groups to restore sound public finances, while employers criticized only a few aspects and welcomed the overall direction of the consolidation path (Tálos and Kittel 2001; 85, 127).

The attempt of the government to break with the traditional policy-making logic of pursuing tripartite consent failed when the Social Democratic Party leadership had to renegotiate the austerity package with its affiliated parliamentary trade union fraction to ensure an encompassing support base (Unger 2001, 58; Sebald 1998, 60). Fierce tensions between the party leadership and the ÖGB led the powerful trade union wing, the FSG, to adopt a veto position against the austerity package in the parliamentary group of the SPÖ. In response, Franz Vranitzky invited the ÖGB to subsequent bargaining rounds to obtain consent for the adoption of spending cuts. Various political concessions eventually generated an intrapartisan consensus by smoothing the initially rigorous savings package. The final austerity package (Strukturanpassungsgesetz I) was based on a mixture of political exchanges that amounted to a total savings volume of 15 to 17 billion Austrian schillings (ATS), whereas the 52-point program had proposed fiscal cuts in the amount of 100 billion ATS (Wagschal and Wenzelburger 2008, 102).[3]

The demonstration of veto power by the ÖGB against welfare cuts was a clear response to the government's agenda of fiscal consolidation. A unilateral approach would not facilitate the legislative process unless the government could bet on the support of organized labor. To achieve this support, the two major parties had to fall back on corporatist concertation. As a result, the government attempted to find a tripartite solution to the fiscal adjustment problem of the federal state. The subsequent reform proposal of the social partners, however, was based on flawed calculations from the Ministry of Finance about the extent to which the budget had to be consolidated. Meanwhile, rising tensions between the coalition partners led the new party chair of the ÖVP, Wolfgang Schüssel, to demand a return to the expenditure-based consolidation path along the lines of the government program of 1994. Eventually, this commitment led Schüssel to break off the budget negotiations of 1995 with no result and call for new elections. In fact, Schüssel's strategy was formed with an eye to the opinion polls, which were forecasting an election victory of the ÖVP.[4] The subsequent election campaign took place against the backdrop of two diverging approaches to the problem of reducing public debt: a fifty-fifty ratio of revenue increases and spending cuts (SPÖ) versus spending cuts only (ÖVP). Judging from the election outcome, the approach of the SPÖ proved more popular than the fiscal retrenchment campaign of the ÖVP (Wagschal and Wenzelburger 2008, 104). The 1995 elections extended the share of the SPÖ to 38 percent (+3.0 percent), while the ÖVP remained the second strongest party 28.3 percent (+0.6 percent).

The coalition negotiations between the two major parties reflected the power-conscious party leadership of Schüssel: the ÖVP could either form a coalition with the FPÖ or go into opposition, while the only option left for the SPÖ to remain in office was the formation of another grand coalition.[5] Reflecting their bargaining position, the ÖVP made government participation conditional on the adoption of a savings volume of 100 billion ATS for the next two years—with success. The subsequent formation of another grand coalition in 1995 paved the way for the proposal of a second austerity package (Strukturanpassungsgesetz II) to meet the Maastricht convergence criteria.

Well aware of the electoral dangers of reform deadlocks, the government delegated negotiations about the design of the second austerity package to the social partners. The subsequent compromise between them played an important role in mitigating political conflicts between the grand coalition partners: "With the savings package the social partners proved that they were able to perform their function of 'easing the burden of the state' in a very thorough way" (Unger 2003, 107). Drawing on survey data and press coverage, Reinhard Heinisch notes that the Austrian populace came to trust the reform capacity of the social partners more than that of the grand coalition partners: "The social partnership was seen as delivering an important public good by ensuring overall stability and by diluting painful economic medicine as much as possible—at a time when the government appeared increasingly less effective" (Heinisch 2001, 40).

It is clear that the overall design of the second austerity package in the context of EMU adjustment was more beneficial to capital than to labor. But the labor-inclusive reform strategy of the government created opportunities for the ÖGB to successfully enforce its demand for an extension of the social insurance coverage (Tálos 1999, 274). The second austerity package, for example, therefore included the quasi-freelancers and the dependent self-employed into statutory pension, health, and accident insurance. This extension raised additional contribution payments to the financing of the welfare state and smoothed unequal benefit entitlements across different types of employment contracts. The head of the ÖGB's labor market and education division, whom I interviewed in March 2015, summarized the view of the ÖGB toward the social protection of atypical employment contracts in the following terms: "Atypical employment contracts became an essential question for us, when we recognized that their rapid growth poses a massive threat to regular employment contracts."[6] This view was supported by another high-ranking official in various union posts, who later became the SPÖ's minister of labor market, health care, and social affairs: "We simply recognized that there were ever more of these 'atypical' contracts. Then we realized we can't simply prohibit them. But what we could do was to set framework conditions [Rahmenbedingungen] for the usage of those contracts."[7]

As in previous decades, the SPÖ came to support the demands of organized labor, which sought to stop the rise of unprotected contracts that enable employers to escape from the constraints of labor and employment law. Contrary to the theoretical expectations of partisanship theorists, this support was not based on electoral vote-seeking calculations of party leaders. Instead, the SPÖ delegated its programmatic agenda to the unions, which have a more informed view of the labor market than the party leaders. Eleonora Hostasch, minister of labor market, health care and social affairs from 1997 to 2000, summarized the SPÖ's motivations behind the adoption of the ÖGB's policy demands in the following terms:

> My impression was that the area of social policy has been left to the unions. I cannot remember that the SPÖ has ever advanced its social policy program autonomously. . . . The Chamber of Labor plays a decisive role in this process, because it furnishes the unions' input from the works councils with its intellectual and academic resources. This turns their demands into a solid program, which can sometimes be adopted by the party without any modifications. To solve policy problems in cooperation with unions and employers is for the grand coalition a promising strategy, because the parties as well as the parliament do not have the same level of resources as the Chambers have. In that sense, the SPÖ often uses the interest organizations of labor [ÖGB and BAK] as a think tank.[8]

Comparing the politics of fiscal consolidation of nine countries in the late 1990s, Wagschal and Wenzelburger (2008) come to the conclusion that the reduction of public deficits through the second austerity package was based on "a little bit of savings everywhere." This assessment resonates in characterizing the Austrian corporatist politics of taking small steps in hard times. Rather than seeking transformative change, the cooperation between the social partners reflects a consensual policy-making logic of incremental change. Following this pattern of adjustment, the interest organizations of labor remained sufficiently influential to prevent any large-scale retrenchment initiatives. The final settlement contained in the second austerity package reflected a compromise between the balanced approach of the SPÖ and the cutback agenda of the ÖVP. A subsequent political exchange paved the way for labor's demand for an expansion of training in return for improved social protection of employers in 1998 (Tálos and Kittel 2001, 129).

In the years to come, union influence faced mounting pressure from political forces rather than economic adjustment constraints. From the perspective of prominent representatives of the ÖVP, the power resources of organized labor blocked competitiveness-enhancing policy innovation. In particular, the veto power of the ÖGB under SPÖ-led grand coalitions led to the strategic understanding of Wolfgang Schüssel and his chief ideologue, Andreas Khol, that the disempowerment of organized labor had become imperative for the accomplishment of an economic paradigm change (Khol 2001, 209–210; Schüssel 2009, 53–54).

At the same time, the rise of the FPÖ under its charismatic leader, Jörg Haider, opened up a potential coalition partner that shared the critical stance of the ÖVP against union influence on public policy. Eventually, the FPÖ became the second strongest party in the 1999 elections (26.9 percent; +5 percent) at the expense of the ÖVP (26.9 percent; -1.4 percent), while the SPÖ took the largest vote share in spite of losses (33.2 percent; -4.9 percent). Once again, the strongest party, the SPÖ, invited the ÖVP to form a grand coalition. Unlike in 1995, the failed coalition negotiations between the SPÖ and ÖVP paved the way for the formation of a center-right coalition that aimed at the break with the consensus-oriented past of Austrian social partnership.

Almost, but Not Quite—the Breaking of Union Influence

The "black-blue" coalition between the ÖVP and FPÖ started out as an ideologically cohesive and united front that pushed through a remarkable series of reforms from the beginning of 2000. Cost containment and deregulation were the prime cornerstones of the government's economic agenda. In the area of labor market policy, the WKÖ and the center-right coalition under the Conservative chancellor, Wolfgang Schüssel, advocated the combat of fraud and misuse of unemployment benefit receipt (Afonso 2013, 161). To implement this agenda, the ÖVP-FPÖ government had to rely on its parliamentary majority and suspend the corporatist logic of union involvement in public policy (Obinger and Tálos 2006). The redefinition of labor market policy as a matter of economic competitiveness and efficiency became visible in the organizational transfer of the labor market domain from the Ministry of Social Affairs, which had traditionally been led by Social Democratic trade unionists, to the Ministry of Economic Affairs. At the same time, the government enacted organizational reforms at the level of policy implementation in an attempt to weaken the influence of SPÖ-affiliated officials and trade union members (Obinger and Tálos 2006, 81–84). In late 2000, the government unilaterally legislated the following labor market policy changes: a reduction in the family surcharge and in federal contributions to labor market policy; a reduction of the basic replacement rate from 57 percent to 55 percent; an extension of the qualifying period from 26 to 28 weeks, and the freezing of benefit indexation, as well as tightened sanctions (Fink 2006, 181).

However, the government's reform zeal came under strain from intracoalitional tensions in 2001. Election losses at the regional level in tandem with the ÖVP's neoliberal agenda prompted growing opposition from the populist employees' wing of the FPÖ against welfare state retrenchment (Müller and Fallend 2004, 825). Their fear was that another series of ÖVP-led neoliberal reform initiatives would cause further disaffection among blue-collar workers, a group that had turned into an electoral stronghold of the FPÖ during the 1990s (Luther 2003).[9] Andreas Khol, whom I interviewed in December 2014, highlighted the veto of Herbert Haupt, the FPÖ's minister of social affairs, as a source of reform deadlocks:

> The reform capacity of the ÖVP-FPÖ government was very high in the beginning. It went really well. Every week, another big reform. And we could work through everything we had prepared in the past. However, the main leftist, who prevented a lot of policies, was Herbert Haupt. He was Minister of Social Affairs and Vice Chancellor later on. He always represented the part of the FPÖ that claimed to be the advocate of the "little man."[10]

The politics behind the homogenization of the severance pay scheme, the Abfertigung neu, reveal a great deal about the intracoalitional tensions that ruled out a unilateral reform strategy. By mid-2001, the ÖVP-FPÖ government announced it would transform the severance pay scheme into an occupational pension pillar alongside the statutory public pension insurance—a hot-button issue for organized labor. The old severance pay scheme was the subject of broad criticism for its supposed detrimental impact on labor market mobility and the requirement that the employee be formally dismissed by the employer (EIRO 2001). As eligibility for severance pay required employees to work for three years for one employer and refrain from a notice of employment resignation, the old scheme provided very generous payments for the insiders of the private sector with continuous employment biographies (see table 3.4).[11] In fact, only 15 percent of annual contract dissolutions led to severance pay entitlements (Obinger and Tálos 2006, 91).

However, internal disputes over the minimum duration of employment for entitlement to the accumulation of severance pay marred the autonomous reform capacity of the ÖVP-FPÖ government (EIRO 2002b). The ÖVP under Schüssel demanded strict adherence to the government program, according to which entitlement to severance pay should require one year of employment ("Schüssel verweist auf Regierungsabkommen" 2001). In contrast, the FPÖ contended for entitlement to severance pay from the first day of employment onward ("Abfertigung neu: Koalition weiter uneins" 2001). The center-left opposition and the ÖGB shared the position of the FPÖ. In addition, the ÖVP and WKÖ vigorously opposed the FPÖ's demand for an entitlement for cases of contract dissolutions by employees ("Abfertigung neu: Koalition weiter uneins" 2001).

TABLE 3.4.   Old severance pay and new severance pay since 2001/02.

	OLD SEVERANCE PAY (ABFERTIGUNG ALT)	NEW SEVERANCE PAY (ABFERTIGUNG NEU)
Conditions of entitlement	• Dismissal by employer • 3-year employment relationship for one employer	• Dissolution of employment contract (by employer or employee) • No minimum duration of employment
Options of entitlement	Severance payment	• Severance payment (after 3 years of employment) • Accumulation of occupational pension over different contracts
Levels of entitlement	Dependent on gross wage level and length of service	Dependent on gross wage level and capital market developments
Financing	Individual accrual of entitlement by employer	1.53 percent of gross monthly wage
Coverage (in percent of workforce)	15 percent	100 percent

When the controversial negotiations between the coalition partners appeared to become deadlocked, the ÖVP-FPÖ government delegated the issue to the social partners (Pernicka 2003). In the words of Walter Neubauer, a senior official in the Ministry of Labor Market and Social Affairs, who was involved in the reform process: "The ÖVP and FPÖ did not manage to find an agreement on the basis of the government program. In response, both parties agreed to delegate the Abfertigung neu to the social partners, who developed the so-called 14 cornerstones of the subsequent reform."[12]

This party-political reform deadlock forms one necessary condition for the subsequent policy solution. Another part of the explanation comes from union preferences for outsider inclusion. Since the late 1990s, the BAK and the ÖGB have demanded an extension of the coverage of the insider-oriented severance pay scheme to the whole workforce (EIRO 2001). After long-standing negotiations, the social partners jointly proposed a new scheme, which entitled all private sector employees to accumulate individual savings from the first day of employment onward and across different employment relationships over time. In return, the WKÖ could reduce nonwage labor costs for severance pay provisions through the stipulation of an employers' contribution rate of 1.53 percent of the gross monthly wage. During the final tripartite negotiations, the ÖGB managed to enforce the employees' right to choose between (i) the direct receipt of severance pay after the termination of a three-year employment relationship or (ii) the immediate transfer of the savings in central pension and severance pay funds to accumulate occupational pension entitlements (EIRO 2002b). To set incentives for employees to accumulate pension savings, the ÖVP-FPÖ government imposed a tax rate of 6 percent on the direct payment of severance pay after the termination of a contract. The reform entitles every Austrian employee (including apprentices and marginally employed) to accumulate individual savings—irrespective of the reason for the contract dissolution—but the level of entitlements depends on the fluctuations of capital markets and individual wage levels.

The new severance scheme (*Abfertigung neu*) involved stricter regulation of the use of temporary forms of employment, because it obliged employers to accumulate severance pay provisions for short-term contracts that had not been covered by the previous scheme. At the same time, it translated into slightly reduced employment protection for permanent workers, who had previously enjoyed higher dismissal payments after long job tenure. Unlike the Continental European and Swedish trend of growing dualization, Austria homogenized the conditions job security regulations in favor of discontinuous employment biographies.

In a similar vein, the FPÖ blocked the ÖVP in the area of eligibility conditions for the long-term unemployed. Similar to the German Hartz IV legislation, the Austrian center-right government announced in their 2000 and 2003 government programs to introduce an obligation to work in return for continued benefit receipt and state-financed pay top-ups. In the end, the FPÖ, however, rejected this proposal reminiscent of the German "1-Euro jobs" for the long-term unemployed. Asked about why the government did not implement its government program in this aspect, Andreas Khol responded,

> Because in the end the FPÖ always acted populist and petit bourgeois. So, just as with the ambulance fees, also in the case of the obligation to work in municipal community services for the long-term unemployed— as it is of common practice in Germany with the "1-Euro jobs" of the Hartz IV legislation—the FPÖ came to block us. This was not possible then, as the FPÖ proved too weak to get this passed.[13]

This description about the veto of the FPÖ was confirmed by the head of the Department for Labor Market Policy in the Ministry of Social Affairs.[14] Instead of pursuing a unilateral approach, the government invited the social partners to develop changes for the regulation of the unemployment benefit entitlement (Afonso 2013, 163). The ÖVP and the WKÖ had a common agenda in that they demanded (i) a broadened definition of the kind of jobs that are deemed suitable (*Zumutbarkeitsbestimmungen*) and (ii) the removal of "occupational protection" for job seekers with specific occupational skills (*Berufsschutz*). According to this agenda, the public employment service would have been able to require the unemployed to take up more types of jobs over longer travel distances. To achieve support for this approach, organized labor received two important concessions (Afonso 2013, 163). First, the occupational protection remained in place for a shortened duration of 100 days. Second, the package included the introduction of a "wage guarantee"; that is, a guarantee that the wage level of a proposed job corresponds at least to a certain percentage of the previous job. As a result, a job may be deemed suitable if its related wage amounted to not less than 80 percent of the previous job during the first 120 days of unemployment or 75 percent during the end of the benefit entitlement period. Instead, part-time workers received a wage guarantee of 100 percent for every proposed job placement. In 2005, the government responded to rising unemployment and mounting criticism from the opposition and organized labor with the expansion of ALMP (Afonso 2013, 167).

The "black-blue" era ended with the 2006 elections. Somewhat surprisingly, the SPÖ won the elections with slight losses (−1.2 percent) despite the collapse of an ÖGB-led "red" bank (BAWAG) in the wake of failed speculative transactions. On the other hand, the ÖVP lost a whole 8 percent, whereas the new party of Jörg Haider, the BZÖ, managed to gain entry into parliament (4.1 percent). Eventually, it took the SPÖ more than four months to reach a coalition agreement with the ÖVP in order to form another grand coalition.

Excursus—The Politics of Government Strength in the 2003 Pension Reform

Throughout this chapter, I have argued that the inability of Austrian governments to formulate a common agenda made them fall back on trade union support in the policy-making process. This inability created the necessary opportunity for union leaders to extract concessions from the state by cooperating with organized business in the "social partnership." Unions therefore remained influential because Austria is a case of *weak governments*.

So what happens when Austrian governments become strong? In such a situation, my argument would suppose that they turn their back on unions. Alternatively, one could instead argue that a lack of coalitional cohesiveness does *not* matter for the level of union influence. The relative resilience of labor-inclusive reform processes might well be merely endemic to the incorporation of union elites into a cartelized political establishment of party patronage (Treib 2012). In this perspective, the nationally distinct "small state" environment and institutionalized power position of the social partners would reproduce labor-inclusive elite networks that incorporate the policy demands of unions. This interpretation, however, is wrong (Obinger and Tálos 2006).

The 2003 pension reform provides an illustrative factual scenario showing that under the conditions of a strong government the policy that emerges does not include unions in the reform process—even in *the* "country of corporatism" (Traxler 1998). The strength of the government in the area of pensions rested on two factors. First, the 2002 reelections led to an unprecedented victory of the ÖVP (+15.4 percent) and defeat of the FPÖ (−16.9 percent). Wolfgang Schüssel called for new elections in response to the strong opposition of the FPÖ's populist grass-roots camp against the neoliberal agenda of the "black-blue" coalition. The intrapartisan turmoil within the FPÖ was thus the main cause of this disastrous re-election outcome (Luther 2003). This election victory shifted the balance of power to the ÖVP and made Schüssel more determined than ever to pursue his unilateral reform ambitions against organized labor. Notably, the delegation of the severance pay issue to the social partners took place *prior* to the 2002 elections, which boosted the ÖVP's electoral strength. Second, and unlike the area of labor market policy, the 2003 pension reform was central to the government's priority to consolidate both the federal budget and the public pension system. Cost reductions were therefore an indispensable part of the government's claim to put an end to the "debt policy" of the grand coalition and reach a sustainable fiscal situation (Müller and Fallend 2004, 815).

What was remarkable about the 2003 pension reform was that it came into effect not only despite union protests, but also against the opposition of employers and influential figures within the governing parties. The opposition of the WKÖ can be explained by the reform's detrimental impact on the social protection of small firm owners, which remain their main constituency due to mandatory membership (Paster 2013). The governor of Carinthia, Jörg Haider, who transformed the FPÖ into a populist right-wing party prior to the formation of the ÖVP-FPÖ coalition, also openly attacked his own government team for supporting this draft bill. In a similar vein, the ÖVP's governors of Lower Austria and Upper Austria, Erwin Pröll and Josef Pühringer respectively, demanded a return to trilateral negotiations with employers and unions. Meanwhile, the presentation of the draft bill induced the ÖGB to organize mass demonstrations and industrial actions—a very unusual phenomenon in the consensus culture of Austrian postwar politics (Horaczek 2007). Notwithstanding, the government emphatically rejected a joint request by the social partners to present an alternative proposal.

The ÖVP-FPÖ government presented the draft bill in March 2003, which was legitimized with the objective to ensure the financial viability of the public pension system and the federal budget alike. Its most drastic part was perhaps the gradual extension of the reference period for benefit calculation from the highest paid fifteen years to forty years. This part reinforced the earnings-related character of the public pension system to the detriment of outsiders. In addition, the draft bill phased out the access to early retirement options, increased deductions for early retirement from 3.0 percent to 4.2 percent and decreased the pension credits earned for each year of employment from 2.00 percent to 1.78 percent. In June 2003, the ÖVP-FPÖ government finally passed the bill with a single modification: it capped the amount of pension losses resulting from the extended calculation period to a maximum of 10 percent during the transition period until the late 2020s.

The distributive outcome of the unilaterally legislated 2003 pension reform substantially differed from the labor-inclusive reforms in the area of labor market policy. The former significantly reinforced institutionalized status divisions by extending the calculation period without lifting minimum benefit entitlements for outsiders. The latter, by contrast, lacked any notable departure from the incrementalism of the previous grand coalition and granted concessions to the ÖGB instead. The variation in the reliance of the ÖVP-FPÖ coalition on trade union support best explains the divergent distributive outcome observed between the 2003 pension reform and labor market policy change.

The Rebirth of Union Influence Under the Grand Coalition

The policy performance of the grand coalition since 2007 powerfully demonstrates that union influence increases under favorable political conditions. Announcing its intention to involve (or reinvolve) the peak-level associations in virtually all areas of economic and social policy, the government program of 2007 mentions "the social partners" no less than twenty-one times (Tálos 2008b). The revival of negotiated and labor-inclusive reform reflected a political response to the controversial unilateral reform ambitions of the "black-blue" agenda.[15] Unlike the politics of EMU adjustment during the 1990s, the grand coalition did not set strict policy guidelines along which the social partners helped formulate reforms to consolidate the federal budget. On the contrary, economic growth rates at the level of 3.5 percent of GDP (2006–2007) facilitated the maintenance of sound public finances until the onset of the Great Recession.

The return of the SPÖ to office under Alfred Gusenbauer was one obvious reason for increasing union influence. In fact, however, the grand coalition as a whole benefited from corporatist concertation through the problem-solving capacity of the social partners. During the period of uncertainty that followed the 2006 elections, the interest organizations of labor successfully attempted to find agreement with the WKÖ on a number of policy areas to preempt the emergence of unilateral reform proposals (Afonso 2013, 171). One central lesson of the previous ÖVP-FPÖ government was that the viability of union influence might require the occupation of policy issues in uncertain times. In addition to the proactive strategy of the social partners, the subsequent grand coalition faced difficulties in finding policy compromises. Mutual reform blockages and open confrontations between the coalition partners created tensions that culminated in the call for fresh elections after only one and a half years in office. The interest organizations of labor, however, had an interest in maintaining the grand coalition to sustain their influence through the SPÖ's participation in the ruling coalition. High reform activity in spite of intracoalitional divisions suggests the social partners' stabilizing effect on the reform capacity of the government. Indeed, as the evidence shows, national peak-level associations somewhat offset the government's difficulties in carving out policies by assuming a leading role in the formulation of reforms (cf. "Neue Sozialpartnerschaft" 2008; Tálos 2008b; "Sozialpartnerschaft ist Eliteherrschaft" 2009; Afonso 2013). A senior official of the BAK's Labor Market Policy Division, whom I interviewed in December 2014, described the role of the social partners between 2006 and 2008 in the following terms: "We wanted to make the government appear capable of acting in public policy by allowing them to have a blueprint for reforms they can carry through in the parliament and sell to the public."[16] An expert of the Union of Production (PRO-GE) in social policy and labor law affairs, René Schindler, expanded on this assertion of the unions' influence on the SPÖ's policy-making action:

> The Ministry of Social Affairs, perhaps also the [ÖVP-led] Ministry of Economic Affairs, has hardly any agenda in social policy. The SPÖ simply relies on the trade unions according to the following logic: They will tell us anyway what needs to be done. And if they don't take the initiative by themselves, there is almost nothing we have to do.[17]

The result of this power-distributional configuration—union influence due to a "weak" SPÖ-led grand coalition—was a series of political exchanges that expanded the protection of outsiders in return for tightened activation demands. Table 3.5 provides an overview of changes that improved income minimum standards for the weakest segments of the Austrian labor market.

Proof of the interest group support in the policy formulation of the grand coalition came in October 2007, when the social partners handed a finished joint proposal to the Ministry of Economy and Labor Affairs designed to tackle the rising demand for skilled labor and state support for youth employment. It included the expansion of state-funded apprenticeships and investment into skill

TABLE 3.5. Expansion of social minimum standards—Instruments and measures (2007–2008).

INSTRUMENTS	MEASURES
Unemployment insurance (UI)	• Inclusion of quasi-freelancers into UI • Opt-in possibility for self-employed into UI (since 2009) • Expansion of educational leave (*Bildungskarenz*)
Minimum welfare standards	• Replacement of territorially fragmented social assistance with "needs-oriented minimum income" (third tier unemployment protection scheme) • Modest expansion of unemployment assistance (second tier unemployment protection scheme)
Income support for low-wage earners	• Introduction of collectively negotiated minimum wage (gross €1,000, 14 times a year) • Full exemption of low-wage earners up to €1,100 from contribution payments to UI • Lowering of contribution payments to UI for low-wage earners between €1,100 and €1,350

enhancement in ALMP on behalf of organized labor on the one hand, and the partial opening of the labor market for workers from the new European member states and a new flexible system of financial subsidies for vocational training for organized business on the other (EIRO 2007). Notably, the agreement paved the way for the implementation of the "education guarantee," that is, an entitlement for every young job seeker who does not find an apprenticeship position to attend state-funded training opportunities. At the same time, the WKÖ enforced the employer's right to fire apprentices. By January 2008, the government had unanimously adopted the package, which provided an important basis of legitimation after one year in office (Tálos 2008b, 119).

The amendment of the unemployment insurance law in 2007 revealed once again the strategic capacity of the national peak-level associations to find a compromise around conflictual issues. After long-standing disputes, the agreement followed "a classic social partner deal"[18] involving an extended coverage of unemployment insurance and educational leave (BAK-ÖGB) in return for tightened eligibility conditions and availability requirements (WKÖ). The final reform included the quasi-freelancers into unemployment insurance and entitled the self-employed to opt into unemployment insurance on a voluntary basis. At the same time, the reform entitled quasi-freelancers and the dependent "new" self-employed to occupational pensions, compensation in case of bankruptcy, maternity cash benefits, and sick pay. On the other hand, the interest organizations of labor accepted the demand of the employers to loosen the definition of jobs deemed suitable. Moreover, the WKÖ blocked further steps toward the homogenization of statutory employment rights by labor law for atypical employees (Obinger et al.

2012, 184). When asked about why the ÖGB prioritized the expansion of social rights for quasi-freelancers and the dependent "new" self-employed, the head of the ÖGB's labor market and education division responded,

> Some employers say: "You can either work for me as a freelancer or as a new self-employed. Full stop." What should I do in case I am unemployed? Then I will prefer an offer like this over having nothing. And once I am employed under these conditions, it's hard to regain a regular contract. This is a development we had discovered and we wanted to address. Not because we are the mere representatives of the new self-employed, but rather because we see that these types of contracts lead to a general decline of regular jobs in regular work sectors.[19]

Another political exchange took place against the backdrop of the long-standing demand of the employers for more flexibility in the area of working time. The amendment extended the possibility of finding agreements at the level of the shop floor and liberalized working-time regulations for negotiations at the sector level. In return, the ÖGB won tightened sanctions for employers who breach the working time law and a new 25 percent penalty rate for allowing part-time employees to work overtime (Tálos 2008b, 116). The ÖVP-Minister of Economic and Labor Market Affairs, Martin Bartenstein, concluded that this package "would not have been possible without the social partners" (Stenographisches Protokoll des Nationalrates 2007, 116). The introduction of the "needs-oriented minimum income scheme" (BMS) was based on an initiative of the SPÖ and gave rise to an agreement between the social partners to implement a minimum wage of gross €1,000 (14 times a year). In addition, the government stipulated an exemption from contribution payments to unemployment insurance to the benefit of low-wage earners (see table 3.5).

The election of 2008, which occurred in the wake of internal conflicts, led to the formation of another grand coalition. Immediately after taking office, the SPÖ-ÖVP government under Werner Faymann invited the social partners to design a tripartite policy response to the onset of the Great Recession. Faced with a severe GDP contraction of almost 4 percent in 2009, the three actors were quick to find a consensus around a series of policy changes aimed at: (i) the stabilization of employment and (ii) reintegration of people out of work. Perhaps the most prominent change was the extension of short-time work, first to eighteen and then to twenty-four months. This was tailored to similar measures in Germany, given Austria's strong trade relationship with its larger neighboring country, especially in automobile production. Overall, the short-time work strategy was considered effective in retaining qualified staff, thereby mitigating the corrosive effects of the Great Recession on employment levels.

In addition to the short-time work extension, the policy response to the Great Recession included an expansion of training arrangements such as labor foundations in tandem with eased access to partial retirement. To finance these changes, the grand coalition increased ALMP spending by €400 million (44 percent) in 2009 (Atzmüller et al. 2012, 27). According to the Ministry of Labor, Social Affairs, and Consumer Protection, this investment saved or created 97,000 jobs in the same year (Atzmüller et al. 2012, 28). Moreover, with a significant loosening of eligibility criteria in 2008, the recipient rate of the educational leave scheme (Bildungskarenz) more than tripled from 2,621 to more than 9,000 employees in 2013. Further upskilling investments came into force in 2013: the qualified employees' grant (Fachkräftestipendium) and educational part-time work (Bildungsteilzeit) (EIRO 2013). The former eases access conditions on retraining for low-skilled employed and unemployed workers. The latter addresses employed workers who pursue a reduction in working time to attend training activities by offering a monetary compensation for wage losses. Overall, the crisis response thus simultaneously involved both instruments to keep existing jobs (e.g., short-term work) and combat unemployment (e.g., training).

Conclusion

The case of Austria illuminates two points about the politics of labor market policy in the era of liberalization. First, in situations where unions are united, they are able to support the social demands of outsiders. The virtue of labor unity is that it gives voice to member unions, which are hit hardest by the competition from atypical employment contracts. This institutionalized hierarchy of the ÖGB sets Austrian unionism apart from the classical sectoral model of German unionism (Heinisch 2000). Counterfactual reasoning lends additional credibility to my claim. *If* the ÖGB had not demanded concessions for the enhanced protection of atypical employment contracts, there would have been no interest representation of outsiders. On the part of the employers, the WKÖ advocated cuts in labor costs through wage subsidies, lower reservation wages, and exemptions from contribution payments (see Tálos 1999). The SPÖ under Franz Vranitzky (1987–1997) and Viktor Klima (1997–2000) prioritized fiscal consolidation in the first place, while in large part relying on the unions in the area of labor market policy. By contrast, the ÖVP was the main partisan force pursuing a strategy of pronounced dualization. The FPÖ was somewhat inconsistent and changed positions over time, with the result that it came to block some of the ÖVP's policy proposals.

Second, however, the causal significance of union preferences is not determinative. On the contrary, a decline of the workforce that is unionized might well legitimize a unilateral reform strategy that excludes the preferences of unions from the policy-making process. Policy proposals for stronger insider-outsider divides were on the table in Austria, given that the government program of the ÖVP-FPÖ coalition was very much in line with the German Agenda 2010 of Gerhard Schröder's "red-green" government. Strong pressure to reduce public debt and low de facto institutional barriers to reform would have been conducive to political attempts shifting the costs of adjustment on to the least well-off (Obinger 2002).

However, a path of pronounced dualization would have required the capacity of governing parties to find a durable consensus independent from trade union support. When governments lack this cohesiveness in the policy formulation process, they resort to extraparliamentary channels of consensus mobilization. This weakness best explains why Austrian governments granted concessions to organized labor despite fiscal constraints (1990s), neoliberal policy platforms (2000–2006), and the onset of the Great Recession (post-2008). Let us recall that the grand coalition of the 1990s started out with a common agenda to reduce public debt in accordance with the Maastricht convergence criteria. In theory, a unilateral reform strategy would have facilitated the legislation of fiscal cutbacks to consolidate the federal budget. Yet in reality, the ÖVP called for early elections in response to a reform deadlock around the negotiation of austerity packages. This was a point in time where social partner negotiations played an essential role in brokering intense political conflicts between the grand coalition partners who came under growing pressure from the rise of the FPÖ. Union involvement was thus a way of overcoming intracoalitional divides and broadening the political support base around controversial austerity policies.

This argument about weak governments extends to the grand coalition as well as to the center-right coalition from 2000 to 2006. In spite of its anti-union platform, the ÖVP-FPÖ government also delegated reforms of the labor market to a labor-inclusive social partnership. Again, this was a political choice resulting from intracoalitional divisions. If the ÖVP had been supported by the FPÖ, there would have been a clear parliamentary majority in favor of changes along the lines of the German Hartz IV reform (e.g., the introduction of "1-Euro jobs") on the one hand, and the exclusion of temporary workers from job security regulations (Abfertigung neu) on the other. A counterfactual case can also be made with respect to the subsequent grand coalition. If the SPÖ and ÖVP had not suffered from growing political conflicts, they would not have benefited from the reform capacity of trilateral negotiations. Tellingly, the grand coalition produced a remarkable number of reforms despite open political conflicts (Tálos 2008b; chap. 5), which culminated in the call for fresh elections in 2008 after less than one and a half years in office. Finally, a unilateral reform strategy in response to the Great Recession was not even considered.

Another factor that deserves attention is the role the WKÖ played in maintaining cooperative relations with the ÖGB. The principle of mandatory membership was undeniably central to its commitment to the "social partnership." This institutional compulsion on employers implied that owners of small firms could not defect from corporatist arrangements in favor of a market-clearing adjustment strategy at the firm level. It therefore ruled out the full neoliberal reorientation characteristic of business associations in countries with similar corporatist legacies (Paster 2013).

My findings are consistent with a core claim of the social pact literature; namely, that weak governments have a powerful incentive to pursue a labor-inclusive reform strategy (Baccaro and Lim 2007; Baccaro and Simoni 2008; Hamann and Kelly 2007). But the kind of weakness characteristic of Austrian governments was not one of electoral instability and hung parliaments, as in most cases within the social pact literature. The defining feature of the Austrian weakness was a reliance on well-established social partners in the policy-making process. This mutual reliance historically evolved through close ties between the grand coalition and the social partners, but it was stabilized by mounting intracoalitional divisions during the era of liberalization. Elections and vote-seeking calculations play little role when governments share policy-making authority with organized interests to improve their reform capacity. This political choice of weak governments provides trade unions with the opportunity to resist increased inequality. When that political choice shifts to a unilateral reform strategy, the result excludes that opportunity to the detriment of outsiders.

STRENGTHENED GOVERNMENTS AND THE EROSION OF DANISH FLEXICURITY

Introduction

The 2000s was the decade during which academic and policy-making circles discovered the egalitarian distributive outcomes produced by Danish labor market reforms of the 1990s. Welfare state and political economy researchers attributed this outcome more specifically to the maintenance of Social Democratic–like unemployment protection and Anglo-liberal "hiring and firing" arrangements in tandem with a strong expansion of human capital formation through ALMPs (e.g., Martin and Thelen 2007; Palier and Häusermann 2008; Martin and Swank 2012; Bredgaard 2013; Thelen 2014). This triangular policy formula came to be known as the Danish Flexicurity model, and it served as an important role model for European progressive reformers of the 2000s (Clasen and Viebrock 2009). Scholars who observed the dynamic political processes underlying Danish capitalism have, in this perspective, attributed its policy output to sustained macrocorporatist coordination between encompassing peak-level associations and the state (Martin and Thelen, 2007; Martin and Swank, 2012; Thelen, 2014).

This chapter raises doubts about the viability of the Danish Flexicurity model by highlighting the gradual changes that led to an erosion of its security-related components during the 2000s. In that sense, my claim is that academic scholarship came to recognize the egalitarian quality of the Danish Flexicurity model at a time when it had already started to erode. Three interrelated patterns of erosion can be identified. First, restricted access to training, tightened benefit obligations, and the institutional disempowerment of the trade unions in the implementation of ALMP accelerated the recommodification of labor. Second, retrenched benefit entitlements in tandem with the onset of the Great Recession excluded a significant number of unemployed workers from receiving benefits. Third, and even more importantly, legislative interventions curtailed the long-term power basis of organized labor by reducing workers' institutional incentives to become a union member. The breaking of the de facto union monopoly in the administration of voluntary unemployment insurance (the Ghent system) gave rise to expanded membership in "alternative unions" that do not take part in collective bargaining and reject industrial action. Rapidly falling membership rates among the traditional "red" unions caused damage to the viability of the tripartite concertation on which policy intervention in the Danish Flexicurity model was built. Although I concede that the Danish Flexicurity model may well reflect the egalitarian variety of liberalization from an international comparative perspective (Thelen 2014), I argue that the literature so far has failed to recognize its significant erosion in the 2000s and early 2010s. This chapter explores the reasons behind this temporal variation in the social protection of outsiders in Denmark.

So how can we explain the rise and erosion of the Danish Flexicurity model? The most commonsense explanation is linked to partisanship. Between 2001 and 2011, the political right managed to gain a clear and united parliamentary majority for the first time since 1929, as the right-wing populist Danish People's Party supported the Liberal-Conservative minority government for ten years. This parliamentary majority enabled the Liberal Party (Venstre), which was the dominant party in government, to undermine the institutional position of union power in order to liberate its voters from the Social Democratic–friendly union movement in favor of alternative unions. Attacks on union power were thus a clear instance of right-wing partisanship (Jensen 2014; chap. 6). However, my diachronic research design allows me to question a hypothesis derived from differences in partisanship with respect to unemployment support (Klitgaard and Nørgaard 2014). If anything, in fact, the center-left coalition under the auspices of the Social Democrats (2011–2015) went *further* than the political right by legislating modest welfare cuts for benefit recipients to cofinance tax cuts for people in employment (Goul Andersen 2012a). What is puzzling is that welfare cutbacks for the unemployed took place under both center-right *and* center-left governments, despite egalitarian welfare attitudes among the electorate (Larsen 2008; Larsen and Goul Andersen, 2009). In nationwide, representative surveys conducted in the years 2000 and 2008, three quarters of the respondents in both surveys stated that access to unemployment benefits should be a universal social right (Goul Andersen 2011c, 16). Moreover, postelectoral survey data from 2011 show that 71 and 79 percent of the electorate rejected welfare and tax cuts, respectively (Stubager et al. 2013, 37–39). That partisan reformers obviously did not respond to the demands of the overwhelming electoral majority is not consistent with a claim based on partisanship.

While partisanship lost causal significance over time, the reform trajectory of Danish Flexicurity also may not be attributed to political deals between unions and employers in macrocorporatist institutions, as suggested by producer group approaches (Martin and Thelen 2007; Martin and Swank 2012; Thelen 2014). On the contrary, the Scandinavian literature identified a decline in corporatist policy integration in favor of a more pluralized pattern of interest articulation and policy deliberation (Christiansen and Rommetvedt 1999; Blom-Hansen 2001; Klitgaard and Nørgaard 2010; Jørgensen and Schulze 2011; Öberg et al. 2011; Klitgaard and Nørgaard 2013; Rommetvedt et al. 2013). As Rommetvedt et al. (2013) argue, political lobbying supplemented, and to some extent substituted for, the representation of organized interests in corporatist policy-making because political decisions have been increasingly prepared by the government of the day, without any formal tripartite deliberation. This finding is consistent with the analysis of Jørgensen and Schulze (2011), who observed a gradual exclusion of the unions from the policy-making process in the past two decades. More specifically, table 4.1 reviews the declining importance of corporatist committees with union involvement in the preparation of labor market policy-making across the past five decades.

While the unions were not formally involved in any of the major labor market reforms of the 2000s, they also lacked a strong influence over the regular reform commissions. While in the 1960s and 1970s, the unions participated in fifty-three labor market commissions, in the 2000s, they were present in only eighteen. It follows that the inclusion of organized interests, and not least the unions, has become a politically contingent choice of governments, and not an institutionalized constant by virtue of corporatist legacies.

Thus, I contend that the erosion of the Danish Flexicurity model did not result from partisanship or producer group coalitions, but rather from the political

TABLE 4.1. Inclusion of trade unions in preparation committees in labor market policy-making.

	1960s AND 1970s	1980s	1990s	2000s
Number of corporatist committees with union involvement	53	17	20	18

Source: Klitgaard and Nørgaard 2010, 23.

capacity of strong governments to exclude organized labor from the policy-making process. The rise of Flexicurity began during the late 1980s as an exhausted center-right minority coalition between four different parties under Poul Schlüter (1982–1993) shifted to a labor-inclusive reform strategy in the area of labor market policy. Unable to receive a parliamentary majority for its preferred policy output, the Schlüter cabinet delegated the negotiation over a turn to "welfare-to-work activation" to a commission dominated by unions and employers. The appointment of this commission created opportunities for unions to extract concessions from the state because the government was reliant on an extraparliamentary channel of consensus mobilization. Union influence was instrumental in forcing the Schlüter cabinet to drop its preference for benefit cutbacks and connect the activation of the unemployed to an expansion in training. This political exchange led to Labor Market Reform I in 1993, which triggered the rise of the Danish Flexicurity model during the 1990s. It is clear why the Danish Confederation of Trade Unions, or LO (Landsorganisationen i Danmark), which is the peak union confederation, used this opportunity to mobilize political support for outsiders. Thanks to the unions' administrative responsibility over the Ghent system, the LO integrated the margins of the workforce into its membership base (Rothstein 1992). With the decentralization of collective bargaining, the LO thus found in the social protection of outsiders its new raison d'être to reach out to union members who were at high risk for unemployment (Ibsen 2013; Thelen 2014).

Despite this position, as of the late-1990s, Danish governments have gradually turned their back on the trade unions and have, instead, appointed experts and civil servants to formulate changes to labor market policy (Christiansen and Klitgaard 2010; Klitgaard and Nørgaard 2010; Jørgensen and Schulze 2011). This political choice, I argue, can be attributed to the growing independence of governments from trade union support in the policy-making process. First, the center-left minority government of the 1990s successfully enhanced its capacity for autonomous reform through flexible majority-building processes in the parliamentary arena, which are difficult for unions to influence (Blom-Hansen 2001). Second, the subsequent formation of a Liberal-Conservative minority government was supported by the right-wing populist Danish People's Party (DPP). Unlike in the 1980s, the political right therefore had a united parliamentary majority from 2001 to 2011, which allowed it to liberalize and retrench the Ghent system despite opposition from organized labor. That the erosion of Danish Flexicurity cannot be attributed to partisan left-right differences was powerfully demonstrated by the subsequent center-left minority government under Helle Thorning-Schmidt (2011–2015). Neoliberal problem definitions induced her cabinet to prioritize employer demands with the support of the nonsocialist opposition, and not the social protection of outsiders.

The temporal variation we can observe between the rise and erosion of Danish Flexicurity supports my claim that union influence rests on the presence of weak governments. When the parliamentary arena allows minority governments to find majorities for its preferred policy output, organized interests do not dominate the policy-making process. It is instead the key leaders of political parties that negotiate over the content of legislation. In a historically distinct context where parties of the right and left prioritize employer demands while trade unions lose the power to resist their ambitions for reform, the policy output of unilateral government action produces growing inequality in employment and welfare standards.

My argument proceeds as follows. First, I give a descriptive overview of changes in labor market policy, which shows that the Danish Flexicurity model has eroded during the 2000s. Second, I present my argument explaining this erosion, which is grounded on the power-distributional interaction between governments and organized labor. Third, I show through process tracing that governments shared policy-making authority with the unions in the late 1980s and early 1990s, but not during the 2000s and explain how this temporal variation led to the rise and subsequent erosion of Danish Flexicurity. Methodologically, the empirical section draws on data from official documents and secondary literature as well as from twenty-one semistructured interviews with policy-making elites that I conducted in Copenhagen in December 2013 and August 2014. In the conclusion, I discuss the further implications of this case study.

Still Egalitarian? Unionization and State Support for Outsiders

The specific features of the Danish labor market are the result of an evolutionary historical process that has only recently been identified as a distinctive institutional set reconciling flexibility and security in postindustrial capitalism (Emmenegger 2010). As of the early 2000s, the interrelationships between the different institutional arenas of the Danish labor market have been seen as constituting a "golden triangle" of employment-promoting flexibility, universal and generous unemployment protection and training-based ALMP (Madsen 1999). The Anglo-American component of liberal "hiring and firing" arrangements as well as the Scandinavian component of universal and generous unemployment protection are part of the Danish welfare state legacy and are thus far from new.

By contrast, the expansion of ALMP with a strong emphasis on training was the novel response to the economic crisis of the early 1990s and completed the "golden triangle" (Torfing 1999). Thelen (2012, 147) therefore comes to the conclusion that Danish Flexicurity reflects the egalitarian variety of liberalization through the combination of market-promoting recommodification with strong social protection and reintegration programs intended to ease the adaptation of employees' social circumstances and skill levels to changing market demands.

Following Thelen (2012), I regard universal and generous unemployment protection and training-based ALMP as the constitutive pillars of Danish welfare-to-work activation and define Flexicurity through the lens of the "golden triangle" (Madsen 1999) to operationalize its development. Based on this definition, I argue that the retrenchment of unemployment benefits and restricted access to training-based ALMP have led to an erosion of the security-related components of the Danish Flexicurity model. Table 4.2 summarizes this erosion in detail. First, it shows that the strictness of employment protection for regular workers somewhat increased from 2.13 to 2.20 (due to a collective agreement in 2010), whereas regulations on temporary contracts remained stable at 1.79, according to the revised OECD database. Therefore, the differentiation between permanent and temporary workers somewhat widened, albeit remaining relatively small. Second, as of the early 1980s, the benefit generosity of unemployment insurance has continuously declined over time, although the formal benefit level remains at 90 percent. In fact, however, net replacement rates for average production workers declined from 82 percent in 1983 to 60 percent in 2009 (Van Vliet and Caminada 2012).

Moreover, the Social Democratic–led government (1993–2001) halved the benefit duration from eight to four years in three steps and doubled the contribution record necessary to be entitled for benefit receipt from twenty-six to fifty-two weeks (Goul Andersen and Pedersen 2007). The subsequent Liberal-Conservative government, with the support of the DPP, further halved the benefit duration from four to two years and doubled the requalification period from twenty-six to fifty-two weeks in 2010. This cutback retrenched the most generous aspect of the system, given that net replacement rates for average and high-income groups have gradually declined over time (Goul Andersen 2011b). Unlike in Austria and Sweden, benefit eligibility may not be extended via participation in ALMP programs. Another vulnerability for the inclusiveness of the Danish Ghent system is declining membership of voluntary unemployment benefit funds: statistical evaluations registered a gradual loss of from almost 80 percent in 1995 to 71.5 percent in 2012 (Due et al. 2012, 4). As a consequence, in 2012, almost one third of the workforce was not entitled to income replacement in the event of unemployment. A further change that was brought in by the Liberal-Conservative government was

TABLE 4.2. Overview of rise and erosion of Danish Flexicurity model.

GOVERNMENT AND PERIOD	POLICY CHANGE	EMPLOYMENT PROTECTION (STRICTNESS OF EMPLOYMENT PROTECTION FOR REGULAR AND TEMPORARY CONTRACTS)	UNEMPLOYMENT PROTECTION (NET REPLACEMENT RATE FOR AVERAGE PRODUCTION WORKER AND QUALIFICATION CRITERIA)	SPENDING ON ACTIVE LABOR MARKET POLICY (IN PERCENT OF GDP PER UNEMPLOYED)
Center-right (1982–1993)		– Regular contracts: 2.18 – Temporary contracts: 1.38	– NRR: from 82 to 69 percent	– Spending: from 0.21 (1986) to 0.18
Center-left (1993–2001)		– Regular contracts: from 2.18 to 2.13 – Temporary contracts: no change	– NRR: from 69 to 63 percent – Qualification period: from 26 to 52 weeks – Benefit duration: from 8 to 4 years – No re-qualification or extended receipt via ALMPs possible	– Spending: from 0.18 to 0.42
Center-right (2001–2011)		– Regular contracts: no change – Temporary contracts: no change	– NRR: from 63 to 60 percent (2009) – Benefit duration: from 4 to 2 years – Requalification period: from 26 to 52 weeks – Tightened activation demands	– Spending: from 0.42 to 0.27 (2010)
Center-left (2011–2015)		– Regular contracts: from 2.13 to 2.20 – Temporary contracts: 1.79 (OECD data revision)	– Modest benefit cut through reduced indexation mechanism	– Spending: no significant change

Source: see Chapter 2.

the de facto abolition of the early retirement scheme (*efterløn*) that was legislated in May 2011. As Goul Andersen (2012b) argues, this cutback constituted another instance of deuniversalization at the expense of older workers because Danish senior workers do not enjoy seniority dismissal protection clauses and social inequality in health and life expectancy is increasing.[1]

Third, it is well known that Denmark expanded ALMP spending to very high levels during the 1990s. The subsequent Liberal-Conservative government

(2001–2011) gradually reduced spending on training and tightened the work-first approach of activation demands (Jørgensen 2009; Goul Andersen 2011b). Declining spending went hand in hand with the full transfer of the administrative responsibility over ALMP from corporatist bodies to the municipalities, thereby breaking the institutional capacity of Danish unions to influence the regional design and local implementation of labor market programs. Although high levels of spending persisted from a comparative between-case perspective (Bonoli 2010), the within-case direction reveals a significant decline in spending during the 2000s.

Table 4.2 also shows that both center-right *and* center-left governments retrenched the generosity and inclusiveness of unemployment insurance during the past three decades. In the area of ALMP, the rise of spending during the 1990s was not merely a product of center-left partisanship, but rather was based on a political compromise worked out by the previous center-right coalition with the unions. It is also clear that the center-left Thorning-Schmidt cabinet (2011–2015) did not reverse the spending cuts that had been made by the previous center-right government. Regardless of partisanship, I claim that declining union influence undermined the power-distributional coalition on which "solidaristic" policy intervention rested. The next section analyses the causes of this gradual shift to a unilateral reform strategy that excluded unions.

Union Preferences and Government Strength in Denmark

In this section, I will sketch out my argument about the interaction between organized labor and governments in Denmark. First, I describe why Danish unions had the strategic capacity to incorporate the policy demands of outsiders into their policy priorities. Then I discuss the increased reform capacity of minority governments, which allowed them to design and implement reforms independent of union support.

Danish union preferences and the Ghent system

The strategic capacity of the Danish labor movement to advocate outsider-oriented policy demands results from the institutional function of the Ghent system for membership recruitment on the one hand, and the encompassing representational focus emerging from high density rates on the other. Both factors of interest formation are closely intertwined, as the Ghent system per se facilitated the direct incorporation of outsiders into the membership base of Danish unions (Rothstein

1992). The same institutional connection can be found in the case of Sweden (see chapter 5).

To begin with, the Ghent system refers to a voluntary and state-regulated system of unemployment insurance, but it is the trade unions that administer it by paying out the cash benefits.[2] In the Keynesian postwar era, growing state subsidization of unemployment benefits implied increased potential benefits and decreased concentration of membership costs, thereby enlarging unionization and unemployment insurance coverage alike (Goul Andersen 2012b, 172). Unlike in other countries, the rise of mass unemployment did not result in declining density rates because the union-run administration of voluntary benefit funds integrated unemployed workers into the labor movement. Therefore, the Ghent system appealed to the margins of the workforce in particular since it established a clear link between trade unions and unemployed workers. It is well known in the scholarly literature that the attractive cost-benefit ration involved in joining the union-run unemployment benefit funds strongly contributed to high levels of union membership in countries with a Ghent system (Rothstein 1992; Western 1997; Scruggs 2002; Ebbinghaus et al. 2011; Gordon 2015).

It might appear somewhat puzzling that in practice almost all workers in Ghent countries choose the more expensive option of dual membership in unemployment insurance and trade unions, although both institutions are formally separated from each other. However, as Clasen and Viebrock (2008) point out, there are both informal traditions and selective benefits that incentivize this choice. First, the strong identification with the trade unions turns dual membership into a question of collective loyalty. Second, the posttax financial costs of dual membership are still relatively low, even in Sweden, where the center-right government differentiated and increased the fees of unemployment insurance in 2006 (see chapter 5). Third, the public perception of a dual package gained by joining a trade union somewhat undermines the awareness of a formal institutional separation between trade unions and unemployment insurance. Finally, in the case of Denmark, unemployed union members receive potentially more effective job-search support from their corresponding union-run benefit fund. In sum, the political mobilization of support for universal and generous labor market protections served as an incentive for workers to become members of a union.

Danish Union Power and the Liberalization of the Ghent System

Partisan reformers of the political right were well aware of the institutional connection between high union density rates and the Ghent system. To weaken the veto-power of Social Democratic–friendly "red" unions, the political right had to find a way to undermine their *de facto* monopoly in the administration of unemployment insurance without stimulating a forceful countermobilization. This context called for a strategy of "layering" (Streeck and Thelen 2005, 22–24), whereby the agents of change leave an established institution formally untouched while actually exposing it to competition from newly created alternative institutions. This line of action preempts a counter-mobilization of vested interests attached to the established institution at the same time as crowding out its coverage through measures that foster the growth of alternative institutions.

Immediately after taking office in 2001, the Liberal-Conservative government pursued precisely this strategy of "layering" with support of the DPP. It liberalized the union monopoly over the administration of unemployment insurance by enabling private and cross-occupational benefit funds to compete for members with the LO-affiliated benefit funds. This institutional reform gave rise to growth in the membership of the alternative unions to the detriment of the recognized union movement. Unlike the traditional "red" unions, the alternative "yellow" unions do not take part in collective agreements with employers' associations and reject industrial action, which enables them to provide a cheap dual-membership package, which includes unemployment insurance and individual services across all sectors and occupations (Ibsen et al. 2013). Hence, they provide an ideological alternative to the traditional unions that is also less expensive, while their members still benefit from the collective-bargaining system as sector agreements cover all employees, irrespective of union membership (Ibsen et al. 2013).

Figure 4.1 traces the changing membership structure of Danish unions from 1985 to 2012. It shows that the total number of members in alternative unions tripled, although the number of unorganized employees grew by 28 percent between 1995 and 2011. In the same period, LO-affiliated unions lost almost every fourth member and covered only one third of all Danish employees, even though the total number of all employees and unemployed has grown by 108,000.

This transfer away from the LO has partly to do with occupational changes but the competitive pressure from the alternative unions reinforced declining membership numbers, since this development was closely connected to declining membership in the LO's union-run benefit funds (EIRO 2010). According to the most recent evaluation, between 2000 and 2014 the overall level of unionization among the traditional unions dropped from almost 69 percent to 60 percent, while the alternative unions registered a steady membership increase from 2.5 percent to 9 percent of the workforce over the same period (Ibsen et al. 2014).

Despite a decline in density rates and labor unity, Danish unions continued to be strong from an international comparative perspective during the era of lib-

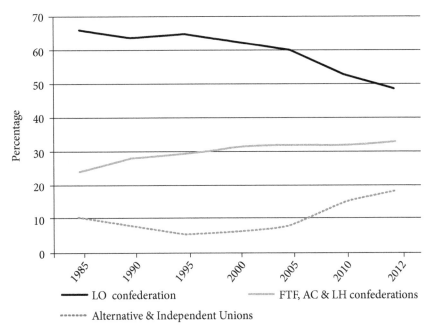

FIGURE 4.1. Trade union membership structure: membership share of LO (Danish Confederation of Trade Unions); FTF (Confederation of Salaried Employees), AC (Confederation of Professional Associations), and LH (Association of Managers and Executives); alternative and independent unions, 1985–2012.

Source: Due et al. (2012); C. Ibsen (2013), F. Ibsen et al. (2013).

eralization. This example cannot be causally sufficient to explain a decline of union involvement in the policy-making process because a number of much weaker unions in noncorporatist economies gained formal policy influence through the conclusion of tripartite social pacts in the 1990s and 2000s (e.g., Baccaro and Lim 2007; Baccaro and Simoni 2008; Avdagic 2010). The rise of alternative unions to the detriment of the LO must therefore be placed in the context of the significant shrinking of union confederations elsewhere (Ebbinghaus et al. 2011). In fact, a decline in union power merely points to an increased relevance of governing parties in maintaining cooperative relations with organized labor. Even though union exclusion became less risky for successful economic management and reelection over time, European governments continued to pursue deals with unions when it corresponded to their interest in enhancing their capacity for reform. I will now explain why governments in Denmark gradually lost this interest as of the mid-1990s.

The Rise of Autonomous Reform Capacity in Denmark

Weak governments are more likely than strong governments to pursue a labor-inclusive reform strategy because they lack the capacity to formulate or pass a common reform agenda independent of union support. As we saw in the case of Austria, this capacity can be constrained by intracoalitional divisions between ideologically divided and equally strong governing parties because they are often not able to achieve a consensus inside the government. When the governing parties inside a coalition achieve no consensus, they have powerful incentives to delegate policy-making authority to unions and employers under the supervision of the state.

But what happens when governments are united but lack the majority to pass their preferred policy output in parliament? The case of Denmark gives us insight into this question by pointing to the relevance of flexible majority-building processes for the autonomous reform capacity of minority governments. Since the early 1970s, the country has always been governed by a minority coalition, except for a single eighteen-month period. We would expect the autonomous reform capacity of minority governments to depend not only on the number of parliamentary seats required to receive a majority, but also on the willingness of the opposition to enter a deal with the government. Labor-inclusive reform negotiations are unnecessary when minority governments can "choose" support from a number of different opposition parties. Under this condition, the minority government can pursue an agreement with the party that is closest to its ideal policy preference. By contrast, however, when the minority government is confronted with an adversarial opposition in a context of bloc-oriented party competition, it is more likely to face difficulties in finding a majority for its preferred policy output. This difficulty creates a powerful incentive to mobilize an extraparliamentary channel of consensus mobilization that includes unions. To assess the autonomous reform capacity of Danish minority governments, we will look at their partisan composition and vote share in the era of liberalization, as shown in table 4.3.

In 1982, the so-called four-leaf clover center-right minority government under Poul Schlüter took office without winning any election, but rather because the previous Social Democratic single-party minority government had collapsed due to a lack of support. The center-right minority government significantly enhanced its vote share two and a half years later, in 1984, increasing its support from 36.4 percent to 42.8 percent. Therefore, it was no longer reliant on support from the populist and antitax Progress Party, which was considered to be a nonresponsible actor at that time. It could instead build a majority by reaching out to one of two different parties: the Social Liberals from the nonsocialist bloc or the So-

TABLE 4.3. Elections and governments in Denmark, 1981–2015.

COALITION	PERIOD	GOVERNING PARTIES	TYPE	VOTE SHARE
Center-left	1981–1982	SD	Minority	32.9 percent
Center-right	1982–1984	K, V, CD & KrF	Minority	36.4 percent
	1984–1987	K, V, CD & KrF	Minority	42.8 percent
	1987–1988	K, V, CD & KrF	Minority	38.5 percent
	1988–1990	K, V & RV	Minority	37.1 percent
	1990–1993	KV & V	Minority	31.8 percent
Center-left	1993–1994	SD, RV, CD, KrF	Majority	48.3 percent
	1994–1996	SD, RV & CD	Minority	42.0 percent
	1996–1998	SD, RV	Minority	39.2 percent
	1998–2001	SD, RV	Minority	39.8 percent
Center-right	2001–2005	V, K (& DF)	Minority	40.6 percent
	2005–2007	V, K (& DF)	Minority	39.3 percent
	2007–2011	V, K (& DF)	Minority	36.6 percent
Center-left	2011–2014	SD, SF, RV	Minority	43.5 percent
Center-left	2014–2015	SD, RV	Minority	34.3 percent

Notes: SD = Social Democrats; K = Conservative Party; V = Liberal Party; SF = Socialist People's Party; RV = Social Liberals; KrF = Christian Democrats; CD = Centre Democrats; DF = right-wing populist Danish People's Party.

cial Democrats from the socialist bloc. The 1987 election, however, was a serious defeat for the government and thereby created a hung parliament involving the two opposing blocs. As a consequence, the nonsocialist bloc's thin majority relied on the support from the Progress Party. Somewhat surprisingly, the center-right government stayed in office even though this instable majority situation was aggravated by the 1990 election outcome, in which a two-party coalition of the Conservatives and the Liberals won only 31.8 percent of the vote. We would expect the presence of this weak government to create opportunities for unions to influence the policy output because the 1987 elections impeded the formation of reliable majorities in the parliamentary arena. Labor-inclusive negotiations would mobilize an extraparliamentary channel for consensus mobilization to the benefit of a government haunted by instable majorities.

In the subsequent two decades, the reform capacity of minority governments gradually increased, independent of union support. A crucial source of this gain was a decline in the polarization between the two opposing party blocs through the implementation of new patterns of flexible majority building. As Green-Pedersen (2001a, 63) points out, the center-left minority government of the 1990s not only connected a growing set of policy changes to the negotiation of annual budget laws, it also built majorities with different combinations of parties for different elements of the budget law. These negotiations were thus used as a forum to pass a growing set of different legislative changes in connection with the budget, which were retrospectively called "patchwork agreements." Handled this way, the minority government could pursue flexible and pragmatic cross-bloc agreements, which are hard for organized interests to influence (Blom-Hansen 2001).

Flexible majority building as of the 1990s was underpinned by a mutual convergence between the two strongest parties of the political center on welfare state issues. On the one hand, the Social Democrats of Denmark were a forerunner party of the "Third Way" by endorsing market-conforming positions and thereby opening up to the Liberals in the parliamentary majority-building process (Green-Pedersen et al. 2001; Larsen and Goul Andersen 2009). On the other hand, the Liberals replaced former open calls for the direct dismantling of universal welfare with the proclamation of tax freezes to adjust their electoral platform to egalitarian welfare attitudes (Klitgaard and Elmelund-Præstekær 2013; Arndt 2014). This ideological convergence facilitated the majority-building process across formally divided electoral blocs.

As a result, we would expect the policy output of the center-left minority government to correspond in important respects with its first-best policy preference, as it could seek a parliamentary majority either with support from the left-wing opposition parties (Socialist People's Party and Red-Green Alliance) or with one of the two strongest parties of the nonsocialist bloc (Liberals or Conservatives). Unlike in the 1980s, the political right of the 2000s managed to gain a clear and united parliamentary majority for the first time since 1929, as the right-wing populist DPP supported the Liberal-Conservative minority government. This implied a significant strengthening of the center-right government relative to the instable majorities of the late 1980s and early 1990s.[3] The center-left government that took over from 2011 to 2015 could either build a majority with the left-wing Red-Green Alliance or the support from one of the two dominant center-right parties, the Liberals or the Conservatives.

We should expect unions to lose influence in a party system where the flexibility of the majority-building process increases and ideological divisions between parties of the center-left and center-right decrease. This contrasts with the case of Austria, where governments are notoriously divided between two historically evolved political camps. In that sense, the growing flexibility of the parliamentary majority-building process in Denmark acts as a functional equivalent to the ongoing reliance of Austrian grand coalitions on the problem-solving capacity of the social partners. The next section illustrates my claim that governments in Denmark dismissed the unions from the policy-making process, once they were no longer reliant on the mobilization of an extraparliamentary channel of consensus mobilization.

Liberalization "on the Brink of the Abyss"

Denmark was hit hard by the second oil price shock in the late 1970s. The Social Democratic minister of finance, Knud Heinesen, had signaled the public crisis awareness in the face of inflation and unemployment levels at the levels of 10 percent, his view being that the country was standing "on the brink of the abyss" (Obinger et al. 2010, 95). However, the Social Democratic single-party minority government of Anker Jørgensen failed to find a majority in parliament for the introduction of its economic policies, which were designed in close cooperation with the trade unions. As a consequence, Jørgensen had to give way to a center-right minority coalition that stayed in office for more than ten years under the conservative Poul Schlüter (1982–1993). The dissolution of a single-party minority government after a year and a half demonstrated the hardened political fronts between the two blocs. Unlike in Sweden, the Social Democratic Party of Denmark was simply not strong enough to impose its policy program on the nonsocialist bloc (Esping-Andersen 1985).

The subsequent center-right government under Schlüter achieved the parliamentary majority necessary to introduce austerity measures in response to wage-inflation spirals by opening up toward the populist right-wing Progress Party—which had up to that point been discredited politically—and successfully exploiting the public's perception of the crisis; both these factors enabled it to implement unpopular spending cuts. Schlüter's government strategy undermined the influence of the unions in the policy-making processes to impose welfare cutbacks and state-led wage settlements on organized labor (Scheuer 1992, 188; Green-Pedersen 2001a, 59). The center-right coalition curtailed the number of policy preparation committees with corporatist interest group representation from 188 in 1980 to 117 in 1985, and down to 59 in 1990 (Christiansen et al. 2010, 31).

The reform profile of the early 1980s initiated the transition to a monetarist hard-currency regime against the protests of the Social Democrats and the unions. After taking office in 1982, one of the first austerity measures was the retrenchment of welfare benefits (except for old-age pensions) by an effective freeze on benefit levels for three years and the abolishment of benefit indexation in relation to wage increases. Given the high inflation rate of around 10 percent at that time, the nonindexation led to a substantial decline in the benefit ceiling for the insured unemployed. The public crisis awareness of the early 1980s and the support of the Progress Party enabled the Schlüter government to refrain from corporatist power sharing without electoral punishment. With its 1984 election victory, the government could rely on parliamentary support from the Social Liberals (RV) to have a majority without having to please the Progress Party (Green-Pedersen 2001, 59).

Labor Inclusion and the Rise of Flexicurity

In the late 1980s, Denmark faced a resurgence of high unemployment (8–10 percent) and concerns about the "passive" nature of its labor market policy. The Danish Economic Council and the center-right coalition under Prime Minister Schlüter criticized the permissive granting of welfare benefits. In the spring report of the Economic Council (1988) and the government's "White Paper on the Structural Problems of the Labor Market" (1989), unemployment was presented as structural, being caused by a lack of financial work incentives, a surplus of low-skilled labor, and high minimum wages (Larsen and Goul Andersen 2009, 244–248).

Unlike the early 1980s, however, the Schlüter cabinet faced difficulties in reaching compromises in the formulation of structural reforms of the labor market and social security. The election loss of 1987 meant that the support of both the Social Liberals and the Progress Party would be required to assemble a nonsocialist majority for its economic policies. At the same time, the Social Democrats proved unwilling to compromise with the Conservative-led minority government on reforms that would restrict the rising costs of unemployment benefit receipt. In response, Schlüter appointed two commissions to propose institutional changes to the labor market. The Labor Market Commission (Zeuthen Udvalg) consisted of representatives from the employers' and union's associations, municipalities, ministries, and parties, while the Social Commission (Sociale Udvalg) included experts only. The national peak-level associations of the employers (DA) and unions (LO) formed a majority on the Zeuthen Commission.

The first significant reason why Poul Schlüter appointed the labor-inclusive Zeuthen Commission was the lack of parliamentary support for the adoption of structural reforms. Goul Andersen (2011c, 13) underscored the political stalemate of the late 1980s in the following terms: "There was an abundance of neoliberal ideas, but no political majority to carry them through." Jørgen Rosted, who was state secretary in the Zeuthen commission, told me in an interview that a negotiated reform strategy with the LO was conceived as the most viable option to achieve a consensus with the Social Democrats.[4] Faced with a nonsocialist coalition for almost a decade, the LO preferred negotiations with the bourgeois bloc over a potential reform deadlock, while the Social Democrats could not refrain from supporting a proposal that received the consent from its allied union wing. Second, Schlüter sought labor acquiescence having concluded that the prospect of unilateral austerity policies with support from the nonsocialist opposition would not generate sufficient electoral appeal. The central lesson of the 1987 election defeat was that the legislation of unpopular reforms on social security and the labor market without the consent of the Social Democrats and the unions was electorally dangerous (Green-Pedersen 2001, 59). Party-political considerations in the face of insufficient parliamentary support proved to be more influential than the ideological first-best policy preferences of the minority government. Thus, the weakness of the center-right coalition and the willingness of the LO to negotiate with the nonsocialist coalition gave the unions the novel opportunity to gain policy-making influence under Poul Schlüter.[5]

Despite the recommendations made by the Economic Council and the Conservatives, the involvement of the unions at the bargaining table prevented any further cuts in unemployment benefit levels. After lengthy and controversial negotiations both between and within the labor market organizations, the political exchange inside the commission implied stricter eligibility criteria and the reduction of benefit duration to seven years in return for social investment for the (long-term) unemployed in the field of ALMP (Torfing 1999; Schulze 2011). As Jørgen Rosted recalls, the unions made their support for the welfare-to-work activation paradigm conditional on the state's credible commitment to expanding training-based ALMP spending.[6] This description is consistent with a number of existing studies that underline the unions' strong support for an enabling human-resources approach that would focus on individual training and choice rather than on sanctions and coercion only (e.g., Torfing 1999; Jørgensen 2009; Lindvall 2010).

The Schlüter coalition, however, had to resign in the wake of a scandal in the Ministry of Justice and thus could not legislate the tripartite compromise reached in the Labor Market Commission. Instead, the dissolution of the center-right coalition led to the formation of a Social Democratic–led government under the leadership of Poul Nyrup Rasmussen. Once again, the change of government was not the result of an election but rather the result of an exhausted minority government after many years of an unstable majority situation in the parliament. The new center-left majority government immediately adopted the policy recommendations of the prelegislative commissions through the legislation of Labor Market Reform I in 1993–1994. In the process of preparing the labor market reform, unions and employers not only played a pivotal role but were also supported in their institutional responsibilities through the establishing of fourteen tripartite regional labor market boards to administer and design the regional activation of the unemployed (Etherington and Jones 2004, 29; Martin and Thelen 2007, 26). This institutionalized power in the implementation of ALMP secured labor acquiescence in the paradigm change toward activation, as it gave unions a strong foothold in the protection of the insured unemployed. The combination of retrenching benefit duration and tightening eligibility criteria while expanding social investment in the realm of activation policies on the one hand, and a classical Keynesian economic recovery plan including temporary leave options on the other, created a labor-inclusive consensus around issues that were initially very controversial. The overall generosity of the income-security system was left untouched, although benefit duration was cut to a still very generous period of seven years and participation in activation became mandatory. People on unemployment benefits had the right, but also the obligation, to take part in activation programs after two years.

Losing Ground: Unions in the Reform Process

The Social Democratic–led minority government adhered to the previously reached consensus of the Labor Market Commission that activation strategies were needed to combat what was deemed "structural" unemployment; that is, a mismatch between the supply of and demand for labor due to insufficient qualifications, work incentives, or employment-matching procedures (Larsen and Goul Andersen 2009). Contrary to the unions, however, the government's activation strategy came to consider cuts in the benefit duration as a necessary instrument to increase the labor supply once unemployment began to decline (Larsen and Goul Andersen 2009, 249–251). As economic recovery proceeded rapidly, unemployment figures went down from almost 10 percent in 1993 to 6.7 percent in 1995 and then 4.9 percent two years later.

Being well aware of the unions' opposition to cuts in the benefit duration, the government delegated the preparation of policy changes to civil servants and policy experts without the formal participation of the unions (Goul Andersen and Pedersen 2007, 13). Perhaps not surprisingly, the Liberals and Conservatives supported the idea of a reduced maximum duration of benefits, alongside tightened activation demands to reinforce work incentives. Unlike in the late 1980s, the government therefore did not need the consent of the unions to mobilize an extra-parliamentary channel of consensus for cuts in the benefit duration. It could instead pursue cross-bloc agreements with the center-right opposition rather than a negotiated reform strategy with the unions. In addition to this partisan convergence, the government bundled subsequent labor market reforms into annual budget laws that were negotiated between a few party leaders and thus precluded open discussions in the parliament (Larsen and Goul Andersen 2009, 251–253).

Labor Market Reform II (1995) was negotiated with the Conservatives as part of budget negotiations in 1995, and the unions were not even invited to take part in informal discussions (Larsen and Goul Andersen 2009, 248). The benefit duration was cut from seven to five years and the job-search requirements were tightened. In addition, the Conservatives "compelled" the Social Democrats to increase the length of the employment record necessary to be entitled to unemployment benefits from twenty-six to fifty-two weeks (Klitgaard and Nørgaard 2014, 10).

Labor Market Reform III (1998) was also prepared by civil servants and experts, and it was legislated with support of the Conservatives and the Liberals through a compromise over the annual budget for 1999. Employers and the unions had a common interest in advancing their institutional authority in the regional labor market boards and, as a result, successfully persuaded the Social Democrats to strengthen their role on the labor market boards (Mailand 2006, 378; Klitgaard and Nørgaard 2014, 11). As Larsen and Goul Andersen (2009, 251) document, the unions had no realistic chance of gaining a foothold in the formal preparation of the reform and faced widespread criticism for not preventing the government from reducing the benefit duration once again. The LO had to accept the cutback in any case and successfully obtained expanded social investment for the unemployed in return. It must be stressed, however, that the cutback in the maximum duration of benefit receipts did not yet threaten any job seeker from losing benefit entitlements, while the power position of the unions was strengthened due to the consolidated process of tripartite governance in regional labor market councils and consultative bodies.

The most controversial instance of union exclusion was the unilateral retrenchment of the early retirement scheme (*efterløn*) as part of Labor Market Reform III. In the election campaign in the same year, the Social Democratic prime minister, Poul Nyrup Rasmussen, promised to leave the popular benefit scheme untouched, thereby securing his reelection. However, the Social Democrats aimed at increasing the labor supply in the face of expected labor shortages due to rapidly declining unemployment and the rising costs associated with increased numbers moving into the *efterløn* system. In contrast, because the unions administer the early retirement scheme as part of the union-run unemployment benefit funds, benefit eligibility for early retirement required membership in their benefit funds (Clasen and Viebrock 2008). Thus, the unions had a strong interest in defending the generosity of the benefit scheme. In secret and closed negotiations between the minister of finance, Mogens Lykketoft, and the party leader of the Liberals, Anders Fogh Rasmussen, the center-left coalition decided, with support of the Conservatives and the Liberals, to tighten the access criteria for the early retirement scheme directly after the election of 1998 (Larsen and Goul Andersen 2009, 255).[7]

The reform took the public by surprise and led to a halving of support for the Social Democrats in the opinion polls compared to the election result nine months later, while Poul Nyrup Rasmussen calculated that there would be enough time left to recover from public protest until the next election (Larsen and Goul Andersen 2009). This turned out to be a miscalculation. Disaffection with the government's welfare policy and the successful exploitation of the immigration issue by the DPP led to the landslide victory of the political right in 2001 (Goul Andersen 2003, 192; Larsen and Goul Andersen 2009, 242; Obinger et al. 2010, 103–104; Arndt 2013). In response, the LO distanced itself from its traditional parliamentary ally and eventually removed any reference to the Social Democratic Party in its constitution of 2002 after 130 years of unity (Allern et al. 2007, 614).

Union Exclusion and the Erosion of Flexicurity (2001–2007)

In contrast to the center-right and center-left governments of previous decades, the subsequent Liberal-Conservative minority government (2001–2011) under Anders Fogh Rasmussen was supported by the right-wing populist DPP and was thus able to legislate de facto independently of the opposition. As the Social Liberals, a party that would have come closest to the Liberals on economic issues, was committed to cooperate with the left-wing bloc, the Liberals opted for an alliance with the DPP to gain a parliamentary majority (see Goul Andersen and Pedersen 2007, 15). The government thus pursued a shift to the center on welfare state issues while implementing restrictive immigration policies to attract working-class voters and the support of the DPP (Rydgren 2004, 496–497; Goul Andersen 2011a, 29; Jupskås 2015, 29–30). In response to the Liberal Party's electoral defeat in 1998, Anders Fogh Rasmussen additionally sought to avoid any explicit assault against the Danish welfare model that could have provoked unfavorable discussions about the distributive effects of welfare retrenchment (Klitgaard and Elmelund-Præstekær 2014).

Unlike the Austrian ÖVP-FPÖ government, the Danish political right was thus united enough to pursue a common labor market policy agenda independent of union support. Its unilateral reform strategy was accomplished through the strategic appointment of independent expert committees without any representation by the unions.[8] But its shift to the center on welfare state issues in tandem with a favorable economic development ruled out an open attack on universal social security arrangements. Given this vote-seeking strategy, the government refrained

from implementing welfare cutbacks in unemployment insurance in the beginning of its tenure, but rather shifted the focus to less salient demands such as more
competition ("free choice") in the unemployment protection system and stronger work incentives for people receiving social assistance.

Immediately after taking office in 2001, the minister of employment and chief
ideologue of the Liberals, Claus Hjort Frederiksen, proposed a state-run and politically neutral unemployment insurance system to run alongside and compete
with the union-run Ghent system. The idea of breaking the union monopoly in
its responsibility for the unemployment benefit funds had long been on the agenda
of the Social Liberals and the Liberal Party. However, various "practical considerations"[9] advanced by civil servants in the Ministry of Employment about the
bureaucratic and economic costs of a state-run unemployment insurance convinced the Liberal Party to abandon this ambition.

Instead, Claus Hjort Frederiksen came to an agreement with the Danish
People's Party, which enabled private and cross-occupational unemployment
insurance funds to compete for members with the LO-affiliated benefit funds.
The LO resorted to informal lobbying activities targeted at Claus Hjort Frederiksen to prevent any legislation in this direction,[10] while the employers took no
part in that discussion.[11] This institutional liberalization undermined the
"Ghent effect" for the recognized union movement, as the alternative benefit
funds broke the monopoly of the LO-affiliated unions in the provision of voluntary unemployment insurance. This reduction of incentives became evident
in the effect of rapidly falling membership rates, which were closely connected
to declining membership in the union-run unemployment benefit funds (EIRO
2010).

The subsequent reform, entitled "More People to Work" (Flere i arbejde), in
2002 allowed private providers to offer activation programs that used cost containment as a preferred strategy due to their profit-orientation; this outsourcing
strategy tended, however, to downgrade the qualitative aspects of the reintegration measures used in the "activation industry" (Jørgensen and Schulze 2011,
212). In addition, the reform tightened activation demands for the unemployed
and social assistance recipients alike. Notably, it also introduced benefit cuts for
different family types on social assistance that were followed by a series of further restrictions in the social assistance scheme at later stages.[12] Following demands
from the DPP, the retrenchment of the social assistance scheme was targeted at
family types in which non-Danes constituted the majority of recipients to reduce
the influx of immigrants and refugees.[13] On top of this, the government stipulated a new benefit scheme for immigrants from non-EU countries, who had not
satisfied the criteria of legal residence in the country for a minimum of seven out

of the last eight years. According to Anker et al. (2009, 13), this so-called "start assistance" scheme was 35 to 50 percent less generous than ordinary social assistance rates. The parliamentary socialist bloc and the unions protested against the introduction of the "start assistance" program, whereas employers supported the government. Overall, targeted cutbacks for social assistance recipients on the one hand, and the liberalization of the Ghent system with stronger work-search requirements for the unemployed on the other, gained momentum in the first half of the 2000s (Goul Andersen and Pedersen 2007, 15–20).

But how did the government manage to attack the unions and win the elections of 2005 at the same time? The answer to this question begins with the fact that "free choice" in the unemployment protection system was simply not an issue of high salience among the public during this period of economic boom. In the words of Jan Birkemose, chief editor of the union-affiliated magazine *Ugebrevet A4*: "It wasn't a big question. It wasn't a question people on the streets would talk about."[14] Second, in the election campaign of 2005, the Liberal prime minister, Anders Fogh Rasmussen, announced the establishment of an advisory multipartite board, which would formulate reforms in response to the challenges posed by globalization: the so-called Globalization Council. In this council, the government developed reform proposals together with the national peak-level associations, experts, and ministries on a broad range of issues. Some commentators interpreted this strategic maneuver by Anders Fogh Rasmussen as part of his electoral calculus to co-opt the center of the party system in the run-up to the elections of 2005.[15] Nevertheless, the council initiatives indeed materialized into concrete investments that were negotiated between the government and the peak-level associations on lifelong learning (2006) and public-sector employees (2007), both of which can be viewed as positive outcomes for the unions. In line with his vote-seeking calculations, Anders Fogh Rasmussen did not take up the recommendation by an expert commission on welfare (Velfærdskommission) to reduce the duration of unemployment benefit to two and a half years in order to avoid any electoral risks caused by the high salience of unemployment insurance in Danish politics. Thus, the government only followed the recommendations to legislate stricter activation demands, employment-matching procedures, and sanction possibilities for the unemployed with the aim of speeding up job placement. In principle, however, the government was in favor of the recommendation to cut the benefit duration.[16] The employers and the unions could only comment on the expert proposals after the expert commission had finished its work. The subsequent successful election in 2007 ensured another period in office for the government.

The Policy Window of the Great Recession (2008–2011)

The period between 2008 and 2011 marked the final break with the consensual tradition of Danish politics. The reliable support of the Danish People's Party continued to be a crucial property providing the Liberal-Conservative government with the necessary strength to eschew labor acquiescence. Unlike the crisis-ridden period of the late 1980s, the political right was thus not reliant on a labor-inclusive reform strategy at a time when the climate between the government and the trade unions deteriorated in the wake of the Liberals' turn toward a policy-oriented reform strategy. *But why, then, did the Liberal Party shift from a vote-maximization strategy to a neoliberal policy path and thereby break with its "winning formula" of the elections of 2005 and 2007?* What is sure is that the onset of the Great Recession in autumn 2008 was perceived as a window of opportunity to legitimize cuts in unemployment protection as a matter of "economic responsibility." The gradual deepening of the financial crisis and media campaigns about the scope and depth of fiscal crises in southern Europe and Ireland were conducive to the government's attempt to exploit public crisis consciousness in order to ease the legitimization of an austerity package that shifted the costs of adjustment to the unemployed. The Liberals therefore turned the crisis from vice into virtue and realized their policy preferences through a unilateral reform strategy that excluded unions. By contrast, the DPP supported this unilateral reform strategy, partly in return for concessions in the areas of immigration, border controls, and investments for the elderly.[17] In the words of Claus Hjort Frederiksen, minister of employment (2001–2009) and minister of finance (2009–2011) for the Liberals:

> Politics has also something to do with the timing of your policies and at that time the economy was booming [2001–2007] and we had very big surpluses at the national budgets, we had enormous surpluses and at that moment it is very difficult to ask for savings because people would ask: "Why do we have to save here with all these surpluses?" . . . But after 2008, the crisis changed the perception of people.[18]

Nationwide representative survey data corroborate Claus Hjort Ferderiksen's description of a rising awareness of crisis in the wake of the Great Recession is in line with nationwide survey data (figure 4.2). Between July 2009 and the general election in November 2011, the share of respondents stating that the Danish economy faced a "quite serious" crisis more than doubled from 29 percent to 60 percent, while 14 percent were of the opinion that the economy faced a "very serious" crisis.

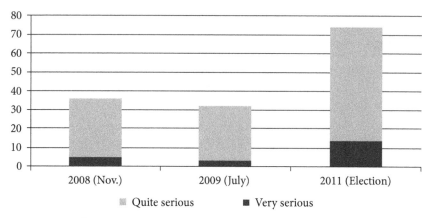

FIGURE 4.2. Voter's perception of the seriousness of the crisis (Nov. 2008–Nov. 2011).

Source: Goul Andersen and Hansen (2013, 140–143)

Another situational factor was the inauguration of the new prime minister, Lars Løkke Rasmussen, in April 2009. After his third consecutive election victory in 2007, Anders Fogh Rasmussen decided to leave Danish politics and, thus, not to run in another election campaign. According to his close advisers, this decision might have changed his political calculations and led to a shift in emphasis to policy considerations over vote seeking (Christensen 2013, 200).

It was at this point, then, that negotiated reform between the government and the LO ended. In the words of Jan Kaeraa Rasmussen, chief economist of the LO:

> You could say the first six years or maybe even the first seven years, but let's say the first six years of the center-right government from 2001 to 2011, I would say we had a pretty terrible relationship with that government. . . . We didn't think it was good but it could certainly have been worse, but what happened with that budget law made in 2008 for the year of 2009, there was no negotiations after that and the government just ran over the social partners, especially LO.[19]

In contrast to the LO, employers shared the assessment of the government that the economic crisis was a welcomed window of opportunity. According to Thomas Qvortrup Christensen, senior adviser to the Confederation of Danish Industries (DI), the Great Recession led the government to legislate every single labor market policy demand that was advocated by them throughout the 2000s: the reduction of marginal taxes on labor (2009), the reduction of benefit duration for the unemployed (2010), and the phasing-out of the early retirement scheme (2011).[20]

In the annual budget negotiations of 2008, the government broke its promise to wait for the end of an evaluation period testing the employment performance of fourteen municipal pilot job-centers to decide about the future reform of the public employment system (PES). Instead, the government decided to transfer the full administrative responsibility of the PES from the labor market organizations to the municipalities without waiting for the final report on the performance indicators of the municipal job-centers. The idea of breaking union influence in its institutional responsibility over the implementation of activation programs has long been on the agenda of the Liberal-Conservative government (Christiansen and Klitgaard 2010). Claus Hjort Frederiksen justified the "municipalization" of the PES with the government's aim to harmonize the employment service for the unionized insured unemployed and the non-unionized uninsured unemployed in the job-centers.[21] As a result, employers and unions were no longer policy-makers in the administration and implementation of regional ALMP. The financing of unemployment benefits was now dependent upon performance indicators that were aimed at steering the municipal administration toward rigorous activation and rapid job placement. If anything, this involved financial incentives for the municipalities to prioritize disciplinary work-first activation (Goul Andersen 2011b, 198). Thus, the insured unemployed lost the membership bonus they had previously had, as they are enrolled into the same municipal employment agencies as the noninsured social assistance claimants.

In June 2010, the government passed an austerity package that amounted to a spending cut of 24 billion Danish kroner (3.21 billion Euro). The government justified the "recovery plan" with its aim of signaling economic stability and meeting the criteria of the European Growth and Stability Pact, as the projected budget deficit amounted to 5.4 percent of GDP in 2010 (European Commission 2010). In response, the LO organized a mass demonstration with an estimated 80,000 participants in front of the parliament in opposition to the government's austerity package under the slogan, "No to the austerity package—Yes to jobs and education." The package included the following changes for the unemployed (Ibsen et al. 2013, 453): (i) the benefit duration was cut from four to two years and the period for calculating the benefit level was extended from thirteen weeks to twelve months; (ii) the requalification period to obtain access to unemployment insurance was doubled, to fifty-two weeks. The period of the so-called adult education support for unskilled or uneducated persons was halved, from eighty to forty weeks. The reform took effect as of January 2013 and excluded a significant number of the unemployed from benefit entitlements. A study of the umbrella organization of unemployment benefit funds (AK-Samvirke) shows that 33,900 insured unemployed workers lost their benefit entitlements in 2013 (Klos 2014).

In addition, the austerity package entailed the virtual abolishment of tax deductions for trade union membership fees, to the detriment of the traditional "red" unions. The ceiling over the tax deduction for union fees was set precisely at the level of 3000 Danish kroner, so the members of the cheaper "alternative unions" were not affected by the change. This meant that traditional union membership became more expensive compared to the alternative unions. Finally, in his New Year speech of 2011, Lars Løkke Rasmussen announced the phasing-out of the early retirement scheme (*efterløn*) and a gradual increase of the statutory retirement age from sixty-five to sixty-seven years.

In response to the cutback in unemployment insurance, the trade unions demanded stricter job security regulations in the subsequent collective bargaining round of 2010. Although the attainment of a new severance pay scheme in the collective negotiations had only a modest impact on the overall strictness of employment protection, the demand for job security still pointed to a strategic departure from the Flexicurity formula that used to serve as a common reference point for the national peak-level associations.[22] In the words of Anita Vium Jørgensen, of the LO-affiliated blue-collar workers' union 3F (Fagligt Fælles Forbund): "The demand for a severance pay scheme was a way to signal that if you actually deteriorate the Flexicurity model, we will have something instead, so it was directly connected to the savings on the unemployment benefits."[23]

In a polarized election campaign in November 2011, the Social Democrats and the Socialist People's Party united with the LO and promised to roll back the welfare cutbacks in their election program entitled "Fair Solution" (En Fair Løsning). This plan involved a declaration to find a negotiated crisis response with unions and employers. Contrary to the employers, the unions supported the opposition parties in their proclamation to prevent people from losing benefits as unemployment had more than doubled from 3.5 percent in 2007 to 7.5 percent in 2011. The socialist bloc won the election with a narrow majority in October 2011.

The Broken Promise of Union Inclusion

In the government program, the center-left minority government under the Social Democratic prime minister, Helle Thorning-Schmidt, stated that it would continue the economic reform policy of the previous Liberal-Conservative government.[24] Therefore, immediately after taking office, the Social Democrats and the Socialist People's Party broke their election promises. *But what was the calculation behind this programmatic turnaround?* Social Democratic spokespeople pointed to the pivotal position of the market-liberal Social Liberals within the center-left coalition, arguing that they made government participation conditional on this written declaration. Indeed, the Social Liberals had already pointed out that they were in favor of the cuts that had been made by the previous government in the election campaign, and they thereby outmaneuvered the promises of the "Fair Solution" campaign already prior to Election Day. However, this argument about the influential role of the Social Liberals is unsatisfactory for the simple reason that the Social Democrats remained the key political operators of the government. If anything, in fact, the Ministry of Finance was under the Social Democratic leadership of Bjarne Corydon and carved out the entire economic reform policy in close cooperation with his civil servants.

Rather than reflecting a divided coalition, I claim that the Social Democrats and the Social Liberals started out with a common policy agenda: to continue the reform strategy of orthodox economic adjustment despite its popular campaign against austerity. The electoral calculus was to generate economic growth and subsequent votes through the adoption of neoliberal reforms. Asked about the calculations behind their neoliberal reform path, the campaign director in the elections of 2011 and political adviser of the Social Democratic Party, Jens Christiansen, responded as follows:

> The strategic idea of Bjarne Corydon and Helle Thorning-Schmidt was to start off with unpopular reforms in order to get us out of the recession and then receive credit from the voters in the elections of 2015. That's the calculation. . . . It's a bad excuse to say they only do this due to the pressure from the Social Liberals. They do it because they think it is the right strategy. They think they will fix the country and then get the credit from the voters.[25]

Proof of their autonomous reform capacity came in June 2012, when Bjarne Corydon closed down tripartite negotiations with no result as the powerful metalworkers' union (Dansk Metal) and other LO-affiliated unions opposed his proposal to eliminate two public holidays. The Social Democratic leadership demanded an increase in working time in order to finance future investments in education, job creation, and welfare. The unions, however, were only willing to agree to an increase of working days under the condition of rising labor demand, but not at a point in time with an unemployment rate of more than 7 percent. In the words of Jan Kaeraa Rasmussen, chief economist of the LO:

> Everybody knew, even the government knew and the employers knew that we just lost 200,000 jobs, so there wasn't any need for a higher

working time. And that's why we didn't have that on the table as an immediate part of the deal. You could say that there would be some agreement . . . that maybe after 2015, one could start on having a longer working time if unemployment had fallen drastically.[26]

In response, the Social Democrats attributed the failure of the talks to the high expectations of the trade unions to a new Social Democratic–led government. Arguably, falling membership rates and competition from alternative unions weakened the political assertiveness of the recognized union movement. In the words of a political consultant of the Social Democrats, who was involved in the tripartite deliberations:

> The trade unions overestimated themselves, definitely. . . . And the picture they have of themselves is to some extent absurd sometimes; that they think this is 1950s where they can propose a general strike and paralyzes the country or decide who is going to be Prime Minister. Those days are over; like it or not, it's over. And their demands within the negotiations were too harsh.[27]

Instead of continuing any further negotiations with the unions, the center-left government turned to the Liberals and Conservatives to introduce tax cuts for those in employment, partly financed through welfare cuts that were legislated through a reduced indexation mechanism of all cash transfers for the nonemployed, except for pensioners. The official idea behind it was to increase labor supply by reducing taxes on labor income. On June 21, the tax reform was supported by the Liberals and the Conservatives, while the employers' association welcomed the reform to the disappointment of the trade unions and the left-wing Red-Green Alliance.

In 2015, a Liberal single-party minority government came to power with a vote share of 19.5 percent. Its weak support base not only resulted from the election outcome per se, but also the unwillingness of the center-right bloc's remaining parties—the DPP, the Liberal Alliance, and the Conservative People's Party—to form a coalition with Venstre. Whereas the past Liberal-Conservative minority government (2001–2011) had been able to rely on backing from the DPP, the Liberal government (since 2015) has seen itself dependent on parliamentary support from all three center-right parties or cross-bloc agreements with the left-of-center parties. The apparent job of Lars Løkke Rasmussen has therefore been to administer a political compromise, and not unilateral government intervention.

Against this fragmented balance of power in parliament, the Liberal government refrained from pursuing another attack on the union-run unemployment insurance, but instead relied on recommendations flowing from a commission of experts and social partner representatives. In consequence, the LO successfully extracted one notable concession from the government; that is, the possibility to accumulate benefit eligibility up to one additional year by performing minor jobs during the unemployment benefit period for those unemployed who exhausted the maximum benefit duration of two years (Denmark Government 2016). Still, the core tenets of the 2010 cutback remained in place. This measure was also accompanied by moderate cuts in the benefit levels for university graduates and the stipulation of three waiting days for each year of unemployment benefit receipt. The reform was adopted with support from the DPP and the Social Democrats. In addition, the government signed a tripartite agreement on the integration of refugees into the labor market. Its key compromise came in April 2016, with the unions blocking what they considered wage dumping through a "phased-in wage" (*indslusningsløn*) and extracting resources for skill development, while the employers received the possibility to put refugees into short-term jobs at an apprentice level for up to two years (EIRO 2015, 2016).

Unlike in the area of unemployment insurance, however, the government was able to muster a right-wing majority for the legislation of social assistance cuts against fierce protests from the opposition and organized labor. The package reinstated a general ceiling on the level of social assistance, targeted cutbacks for residents who had not been in Denmark in seven of the past eight years ("integration allowance"), and an employment requirement of at least 225 hours a year to gain eligibility for social assistance benefits (Denmark Government 2016). It came into effect in October 2016 and led to an immediate reduction in benefit levels for 33,000 recipients (Neue Sozialhilfeobergrenze: 33.000 Dänen ab 1. Oktober betroffen, 2016). While the DPP welcomed the cutback as a way of reducing the attractiveness of Denmark as a host country for refugees, the Liberal Alliance and Conservative People's Party shared the government's ambition to reinforce work incentives. By contrast, the LO chairwoman, Lizette Risgaard, reacted strongly against this legislation and demanded its reversal from the Social Democrats when assuming office again.

In sum, the policy outcomes of union exclusion involved a restructuring of labor market institutions to reduce the generosity and coverage of unemployment and social assistance benefits, make the receipt of benefits contingent on tightened availability and job-search demands, reduce state support for training, and shrink the collective organization of labor. Even though Danish Flexicurity might well remain the egalitarian variety of liberalization from an international comparative perspective, it is clear that unilateral government action of the right well as the left tilted the balance toward less security for workers while leaving untouched the flexibility for employers.

Conclusion

The claim of this chapter is that (i) the erosion of the outsider-oriented security elements of Danish Flexicurity was not inevitable, and (ii) that this erosion was caused by the strength of governments to pursue a unilateral reform strategy that excludes unions. The first assertion rests on the observation that Austria *did* enhance the protection of outsiders during the 2000s (Obinger et al. 2012), while the rise of Danish Flexicurity emerged at a time where fiscal constraints were more severe than during the Great Recession. Thanks to remarkable budget surpluses during the 2000s, the Danish welfare state appeared fiscally more sustainable than ever (Haffert and Mehrtens 2015). It would also be questionable to attribute the detrimental impact of the Great Recession on the Danish economy to the presence of universal welfare arrangements. If anything, the economic downturn was stimulated by a burst of credit and housing bubbles, which caused a credit squeeze with falling investment and consumption rates (Goul Andersen 2012a). Therefore, the functionalist argument that the Great Recession as an exogenous shock inevitably prompted welfare cutbacks does not hold.

The second assertion rests on the observation that the unions were the one actor that supported universal labor market protection over the entire period. Employers advocated cuts in marginal taxes, unemployment benefits, and public pensions, while the Liberal-Conservative government used the crisis to legitimize its demands. The DPP, by contrast, successfully demanded social assistance cuts for immigrants in the early 2000s, while prioritizing restrictions in immigration and border controls over unemployment support during the Great Recession and in 2015. Even though the Social Democratic Party officially supported the unions' demands in the election campaign of 2011, it emphatically rejected a reversal of the cuts that had been made by the previous government. Notably, a mere relaxation of the qualifying conditions for the insured unemployed was neither fiscally burdensome nor electorally unpopular. Recall that, as shown at the start of this chapter, survey data documented popular support for universal welfare for the unemployed. Moreover, voters reacted negatively against the 2012 tax reform, which combined cuts in taxes and welfare, revealed by a decline of 4 percent, on average, in the first five opinion polls conducted after the presentation of the reform (Goul Andersen 2012a, 10). When the reform was legislated with support of the political right, the Social Democratic–led government lost once again at the polls, by 2 percentage points (Goul Andersen 2012a, 10). It was thus a political choice by the Social Democratic Party leadership, which was motivated by the government's perception of competitiveness pressures *against* popular demands from voters and unions. This finding is consistent with existing studies from scholars of Danish capitalism, which point to an ideational convergence between the parliamentary center-left and center-right on welfare state issues (Larsen and Goul Andersen 2009; Goul Andersen 2012a; Arndt 2013).

However, the presence of neoliberal policy preferences was not causally sufficient because the rise of Flexicurity took place *despite* the neoliberal reform agenda of the Schlüter cabinet in the first place. Let us recall that there was a center-right minority government that tried to impose unilateral welfare cuts on outsiders but was vetoed in the parliament. The absence of a parliamentary majority ruled out the legislation of its policy preference. A view that restricts its focus on neoliberal policy preferences assumes away the temporal variation in the autonomous reform capacity of governments. *If* the center-right government had not been supported by the DPP, there would have been no parliamentary majority for the liberalization and retrenchment of the Ghent system on the one hand, and the "municipalization" and retrenchment of ALMP spending on the other. When in opposition, the left bloc, including the Social Democrats, did not support these changes. Similar to the Schlüter cabinet, the Liberal-Conservative minority government of the 2000s would have needed an extra-parliamentary channel of consensus mobilization to find a majority for the legislation of its preferred policy output. If invited to tripartite deliberations, the LO would have had a powerful incentive to protect outsiders from welfare retrenchment, because it integrated them into its membership base. A counterfactual case can also be made with respect to the subsequent center-left government in the early 2010s. *If* the Socialist People's Party (for the first time in government) had been willing to veto the Social Democrats and Social Liberals, the government would not have been able to legislate the 2012 tax reform against the protests of the LO. In other words, my argument about the strength of governments to cause the exclusion of outsider-inclusive unions is therefore one that extends to the right as well as to the left. Regardless of partisanship, the difference in the strength of governments best explains why the LO was more successful to protect outsiders in the late 1980s and early 1990s than in the late 2000s and early 2010s.

An additional way of underscoring my claim is to point out the inconsistencies between conventional explanations and the evidence at hand. Against the producer group claim, this chapter showed that organized interests were not influential in the formal policy-making process. This finding calls into question the position of Cathie Jo Martin and Duane Swank about Danish Flexicurity, that even when the "right parties gained power in recent decades, the consensus orientation of coalition governments has limited the viability of neoliberal attacks on coordination" (Martin and Swank 2012, 171). As of the late 1990s, institutional changes were increasingly determined by informal negotiations between party leaders, and not tripartite deliberations in corporatist committees. It also showed that employers were not reliant on a corporatist channel of policy-making action because the unilateral reform ambitions of partisan actors served them well. It was clear that the unions demonstrated against welfare cuts that had been demanded by the employers in the first place. Conventional producer group claims cannot explain why the policy-making process shifted away from the corporatist arena because they fail to recognize the autonomous policy choices of strong governments in the neoliberal era.

In theory, the policy response of the political right to the Great Recession is consistent with a theory based on partisanship. However, in reality, the role of electoral vote-seeking strategies is not borne out by the evidence because governments of the right *and* left retrenched unemployment support *despite* the presence of egalitarian welfare attitudes. Contrary to Rueda's theory (2007), this chapter showed that Social Democrats and unions were not united allies in this process. Unlike the Social Democrats, the LO had clear stakes in the social protection of "outsiders" due to the institutional incentives of the Ghent system. Consistent with previous accounts on Danish labor market reform during the 1990s (Larsen and Goul Andersen 2009, Arndt 2013), my interview evidence suggests that the Social Democrats under Thorning-Schmidt (2011–2015) followed the political right's economic policy outlook *although* it compromised with the preferences of its voters. In this way, the Danish case illustrates that the center-left's motive for endorsing labor market inequality is not necessarily a response to voters' policy demands. More accurately, the party leadership believed that neoliberal reform would stimulate economic growth, which they considered an important precondition for subsequent re-election. Otherwise, so the logic went, economic recovery would fall behind, followed by the party's electoral fortunes. Understanding this policy choice requires taking into account how governments have come under enhanced pressure to respond to employer demands in the historical context of liberalization (see chapter 1).

The defining political feature of the rise and erosion of the Danish Flexicurity model is not the action of cross-class coalitions or vote-seeking parties, but the growing independence of governments from union support in the policy-making process. In short, this is a story of minority governments that became stronger over time. The crucial weakness of the Schlüter cabinet in the late 1980s was not one of intracoalitional conflicts, as in the case of the Austrian governments. Instead, it was a lack of electoral support for a multiparty minority government, which was compounded by the polarization between the left and right bloc of the party system. The problems faced by the Schlüter cabinet resonate in characterizing the weakness of governments in Ireland, Italy, and South Korea at a similar point in time, which used the conclusion of labor-inclusive social pacts to mobilize a consensus around controversial issues (Baccaro and Lim 2007). Faced with the persistence of minority governments (since the "earthquake election" of 1973), however, party leaders changed the parliamentary norms in the reform process. The flexibility emerging from so-called patchwork agreements created the leeway for elite negotiations between party leaders to the detriment of union influence. A united right-wing majority was then electorally powerful enough to refrain from political exchanges with the opposition or unions. The subsequent change in government did not change the direction of the policy output. To understand this temporal variation, we have to recognize the shift in partisan preferences towards employer demands in the overall direction of labor market reform and the increase in the autonomous reform capacity of governments in Denmark. Only when governments were weak did they work with unions. When they were strong, they pursued their preferred policy output to the detriment of outsiders.

GOODBYE TO SWEDISH SOCIAL DEMOCRACY AND UNIVERSAL WELFARE

Introduction

Sweden is the least likely case for a "Bismarckian" dualization in important theoretical respects: the dominant position of the Social Democratic party, the SAP (Sveriges socialdemokratiska arbetareparti), in tandem with the strongest union movement in the world appears crucial to the political interest representation of outsiders (Huo 2009; Pontusson 2011; Thelen 2014). In addition, universalist welfare state legacies, low tax burdens for business, and broad public sector employment are conducive to egalitarian welfare attitudes by appealing to different electoral constituencies (Svallfors 2011; Beramendi et al. 2015). In theory, therefore, the nationally distinct coalitional background underlying Swedish capitalism creates opportunities for the successful reconfiguration of institutional postwar arrangements to new social needs, while putting constraints on the reform ambitions of neoliberal policy entrepreneurs at the same time. Against this backdrop, international scholars continue to highlight the relative success of Sweden in its attempts to reconcile successful economic performance with egalitarian distributive outcomes (Steinmo 2010, 2013; Lindgren 2011).

In the area of labor market policy, however, this chapter demonstrates that Sweden no longer represents the paradigmatic case of universal solidarity. On the contrary, broad spending cutbacks and marketization efforts in public security arrangements have underpinned a significant risk shift from the public to the individual (Haffert and Mehrtens 2015, 140). Institutional dualisms are particularly acute relative to the cases of Austria and Denmark: permanent workers continue to enjoy relatively high levels of security, while fixed-term and unemployed workers faced the burden of labor market adjustment through cuts in benefit entitlements, job security, and training provisions (Davidsson 2011; Davidsson and Emmenegger 2012; Lindvall and Rueda 2012). This labor market policy output seems to be part of a larger systemic trend toward social segmentation (Mehrtens 2014), and the OECD (2011, 2013, 2015) has observed this change being experienced by the weakest segments of Swedish society ever since. In the past two decades, Sweden displayed the fastest growing inequality and poverty rates in the OECD, as the share of people having less than half of the median income in 2010 (9 percent) was more than twice what it was in 1995 (4 percent) (OECD 2013, 5). As a result, Sweden slipped down from the most poverty-free country to the fourteenth place in terms of relative income poverty levels, ranking behind Germany and Ireland (OECD 2013, 5). Unlike most countries, this steep increase appears to have been a product of inactivity and (long-term) unemployment, and not wage dispersion (OECD 2011, 150). Labor market policy, therefore, seems to be the right avenue for studying the sources of growing poverty in Swedish capitalism (Thelen 2014, 174–175).

The apparent contrast to smoothed dualization in Austria and Flexicurity reforms in Denmark poses crucial insights into the conditions under which political actors reinforce inequality in labor markets and welfare. *So what explains the demise of Swedish universalism, given the resilience of encompassing unionization and egalitarian welfare attitudes?* A functionalist explanation would be linked to the economic crisis of the early 1990s. Financial turmoil, currency speculation, and the deepest recession in Swedish postwar history led party and interest group elites alike to agree on a path of orthodox economic adjustment. It is clear that the immediate adoption of spending cuts was an attempt to combat skyrocketing public debt levels while shifting resources away from public welfare and unemployment support (Lindvall 2004). Yet a functionalist claim about the impact of the economic crisis does not hold for the simple reason that Sweden produced continuous budget surpluses as of the late 1990s, which made it one of the most fiscally sustainable political economies in the OECD (Haffert and Mehrtens 2015). In contrast to Austria, the remarkable decline of gross public debt would have allowed increased spending on outsider protection and fiscal consolidation at the same time (figure 5.1).

The Swedish case, however, also puts conventional political explanations to the test. A classic partisanship explanation attributes Swedish dualization to the erosion of Social Democratic hegemony and the corresponding formation of center-right governments (Pontusson 2011). Yet in reality, Social Democratic governments (1994–2006) did not counteract dualisms in the first place (Bergmark and

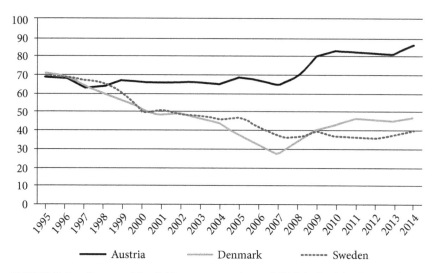

FIGURE 5.1. Gross public debt as a percentage of GDP in Austria, Denmark, and Sweden, 1995–2014.

Source: OECD statistics.

Palme 2003), while the proceeding center-right coalition (2006–2014) simply reinforced an ongoing trend (Obinger et al. 2012). A correlation between Social Democratic governments and dualization would be more in line with Rueda's labor dualism theory (2007) than classic partisanship notions. Accordingly, the rational vote-seeking strategy of Social Democrats targets insiders, and not outsiders. Yet the claim of Rueda is unconvincing from a comparative perspective, as Austrian Social Democratic–led grand coalitions and Danish center-left governments did support outsider protection at various points in time. Even more important, a view that puts elections front and center misses the essence of the Swedish decision-making model. Scholars of Swedish political economy have highlighted the rationalistic and technocratic nature of institutional change, which grants high levels of policy autonomy to administrative elites and policy experts (Eichhorst and Wintermann 2005; Lindvall and Rothstein 2006; Bergh and Erlingsson 2008; Steinmo 2013; Svallfors 2015). In the words of Sven Steinmo (2013), the political culture of Swedish governing should thus be conceived of as an "engineering problem," which tends to insulate policymakers from the popular demands of the citizenry.

Another coalitional explanation would link Swedish dualization to the demise of macrocorporatism (Martin and Thelen 2007, Martin and Swank 2012). At its most basic, the most obvious problem with this explanation is its benign view of employers. Accordingly, centralized and encompassing employers' associations develop an interest in maintaining cooperative relations with outsider-inclusive trade unions. In fact, however, Swedish employers forcefully withdrew from corporatist policy forums in an attempt to undermine the privileged policy-making influence of the Swedish Trade Union Confederation (LO) (Pontusson and Swensson 1996; Lindvall and Sebring 2005). Moreover, a coalitional explanation focusing on producer groups ignores the direct access the LO used to have on the policy-making action of the SAP (Anthonsen and Lindvall 2009). Formal linkages remained strong, given that the LO provided the SAP with votes and money (Allern et al. 2007). High levels of class organization and strong party-union ties could have provided trade unions with robust policy-making influence. However, the Social Democratic single-party minority governments gradually refrained from acquiescence to labor, relying instead on the policy prescriptions of neoliberal economic ideas (Blyth 2001) and parliamentary support from among different opposition parties (Bale and Bergman 2006). The election victory of a united center-right bloc reinforced unilateral reform patterns, thus further pushing the LO out of the reform process.

The variation in government strength, as I will show, is theoretically important: Austrian governments, even the neoconservative "black-blue" coalition, lacked the autonomous reform capacity to impose unilateral labor market reforms on organized labor. During the late 1980s, Danish center-right minority governments also desperately sought political exchanges with unions to mobilize extra-parliamentary support for controversial reforms. Confronted with a strong government, by contrast, the LO gradually lost the political capacity to protect a growing share of its membership base; that is, the outsiders. In sum, I contend that it is not the economic crisis, partisanship, or eroding macrocorporatism per se that explain outsider-oriented cutbacks. Instead, I argue that the strength of Swedish governments to formulate and pass labor market policy change independent of union influence precluded outsider-oriented concessions to organized labor. Similar to the Austrian and Danish cases examined before, the Swedish union movement would have benefited from the enhanced protection of outsiders. First, from a representational point of view, its encompassing membership scope incorporated the interests of outsiders into the union movement. Second, from an organizational point of view, its administrative monopoly over inclusive and generous unemployment insurance (Ghent system) acted as an institutional bulwark against losses of membership or influence in the neoliberal era (Clasen and Viebrock 2008). Therefore, the viability of union strength rested on the solid mobilization of political support for "solidaristic" patterns of liberalization. It comes as no surprise, then, that organized labor was the strongest supporter of the weakest segments of labor, especially the LO. Yet the Swedish LO was much less successful than the Austrian ÖGB or the Danish LO in receiving concessions from different governments.

This chapter explores how Swedish governments managed to turn their back on the policy demands of organized labor. Faced by the collapse of the Swedish postwar model in the early 1990s, the SAP party elite lost faith in the policy-making authority of the LO. Instead, the Social Democrats became receptive to the recommendations advocated by neoclassical economists, declaring sound public finances as the ultimate precondition for economic growth and job creation (Blyth 2001). The chapter also demonstrates that Social Democratic single-party minority governments (1994–2006) were in a strong position to legislate this policy priority in parliament, because they could seek parliamentary support from among different opposition parties. This autonomous reform capacity of the SAP facilitated the relegation of the LO from pivotal agenda-setter to mere veto-player. While reducing public debt successfully, the SAP, however, faced problems in responding to the growing emergence of labor market exclusion, especially among immigrants, young people, and single parents (Palme et al. 2009). In light of the decentralization of collective bargaining, the most viable macroeconomic tool of boosting job creation would have been increased public spending (Iversen 1998). Yet, to the great disappointment of the LO, the SAP placed more emphasis on fiscal discipline than on full employment (Lindvall 2004). Paradoxically, the novel formation of a united center-right front advocated the targeting of precisely this problem, which had been pointed out by the LO in the first place. Job creation, therefore, was the central policy issue on which the center-right could mobilize electoral support for a union-hostile agenda along the mantra of "make work pay" (Lindvall and Rueda 2012).

I will proceeds as follows: The next section provides an overview of labor market policy change to describe the path of dualization in Sweden. In the subsequent theory section, I present my argument for this outcome, grounded on the political capacity of governments to diminish the policy-making influence of organized labor. Then I empirically show through process-tracing and interview evidence from nine interviews with policy-making elites that an enhanced autonomous reform capacity made Swedish governments strong enough to eschew labor acquiescence, and how this precluded outsider-oriented concession to the LO. In the conclusion, I discuss the findings of my case study.

Dualization in the Social Democratic Welfare Regime

As chapter 2 showed, institutional change in the Swedish labor market policy evolved across all three dimensions at the cost of outsider protection. First, employment protection remains strong for permanent workers, whereas governments of all partisan complexions gradually deregulated temporary forms of employment. Second, the generosity of public unemployment insurance substantially declined due to nonindexation and direct cutbacks, while tightened qualifying conditions restricted access to benefit entitlements. Third, active labor market policy—a cornerstone of the traditional Rehn-Meidner model of the postwar era—became subject to gradual spending reductions and work-first strategies, shifting emphasis from upskilling training schemes toward fast job placement and subsidized employment. Table 5.1 summarizes the dualization of Swedish labor market institutions in the past three decades.

From 1991 onward, it shows a decline in the strictness of regulations on temporary contracts from 4.08 to 0.88 (OECD statistics), a decline in net replacement rates for average production workers from 88 to 62 percent (Van Vliet and Caminada 2012), and a decline in spending on active labor market policy from 0.43 to 0.13 percent (measured in percent of GDP and divided by harmonized unemployment rates). By contrast, the strictness of employment protection for permanent contracts remained quite robust, decreasing marginally from 2.80 to 2.61.

It could be argued that the decline in net replacement rates hit the whole workforce, and not only outsiders. Yet this reading would ignore the emergence of new insider-outsider divides resulting from the rapid rise of private provision of unemployment protection. In response to declining benefit levels, the academics' union confederation, the Swedish Confederation of Professional Associations (SACO), and the white-collar union confederation, the Swedish Confederation of Professional Associations (TCO), started to introduce private security arrangements to provide their members with the possibility of qualifying for supplementary benefit payments in the event of unemployment (Rasmussen 2014, 48). When handled in this way, union members can top up their unemployment benefits to levels above the state-regulated maximum ceiling through the private payment of additional contributions. To receive access to increased benefit levels, benefit claimants must be union members and eligible for public unemployment benefits. Between 2002 and 2012, the number of workers covered by supplementary unemployment protection increased from below 200,000 to more than 1.8 million (Rasmussen 2014, 51). In relative terms, more than one third of the Swedish workforce were members of private benefit schemes in 2012

TABLE 5.1.   Overview of dualization in Swedish labor-market policy.

GOVERNMENT AND PERIOD	POLICY CHANGE	EMPLOYMENT PROTECTION (STRICTNESS OF EMPLOYMENT PROTECTION FOR REGULAR AND TEMPORARY CONTRACTS)	UNEMPLOYMENT PROTECTION (NET REPLACEMENT RATE FOR AVERAGE PRODUCTION WORKER AND QUALIFICATION CRITERIA)	SPENDING ON ACTIVE LABOR-MARKET POLICY (IN PERCENT OF GDP PER UNEMPLOYED)
Post-war era until 1991	Expansion	– Regular contracts: 2.80 – Temporary contracts: 4.08	– NRR: 88 percent – Qualification period: 4 months	– Spending: 0.43
Center-right (1991–94)	Dualization	– Regular contracts: no change – Temporary contracts: from 4.08 to 1.77	– NRR: from 88 to 82 percent – Qualification period: from 4 to 5 months	– Spending: from 0.43 to 0.34
Social Democrats (1994–2006)	Dualization	– Regular contracts: from 2.80 to 2.61 – Temporary contracts: from 1.77 to 1.44	– NRR: from 84 to 72 percent – Qualification period: from 5 to 6 months – Tightened suitability criteria – Re-qualification through ALMPs no longer possible	– Spending: from 0.34 to 0.20
Center-right (2006–2014)	Dualization	– Regular contracts: no change – Temporary contracts: from 1.44 to 0.88	– NRR: from 72 to 62 percent (2009) – Tightened suitability criteria – Differentiated and increased fees	– Spending: from 0.20 to 0.13 (2010)

Source: see Chapter 2.

(Rasmussen 2014, 51). By contrast, the share of unemployed workers receiving public unemployment benefits fell from 80 percent in the early 2000s to 43 percent in 2014 (LO Sweden 2015, 339). The onset of the Great Recession and the increased proportion of labor market entrants with low attachment to the labor market (young, unemployed, immigrants) in tandem with the 2006 reform of the center-right government substantially curtailed the coverage of Swedish unemployment insurance (IAF 2009, Sjöberg 2011). Taken together, in the early 2010s, one third of the workforce was entitled to public and private provision of unemployment insurance, while more than one half of the actual unemployed were reliant on family members or means-tested social assistance.

Table 5.1 also shows that both center-right and Social Democratic governments promoted the dualization of Swedish labor market policy. Faced by the deep economic crisis of the early 1990s, the problem of reducing public debt became central to the political agenda of the SAP government (1994–2006). The immediate retrenchment of social security benefits and active labor market policy spending was thus motivated by the principal objective to rein in public spending and reduce large deficits. To tighten up the process of fiscal consolidation, the SAP subsequently stipulated a new budgetary process, including an annual expenditure ceiling, a structural surplus target, and a prohibition of municipal deficits (Haffert and Mehrtens 2015, 136). From a fiscal point of view, the SAP was indeed remarkably successful in reducing public debt, since Sweden produced continuous budget surpluses as of the late 1990s. Despite the onset of the financial crisis and the Great Recession, the gross public debt level remained at around 40 percent of GDP in 2014.

While the fiscal indicators for Sweden's adjustment path look quite impressive (robust budget surpluses and low public debt levels), behind these aggregate figures the labor market is perhaps more segmented than ever. Arguably, the liberalization path of deregulating fixed-term contracts and retrenching unemployment support while broadening the definition of jobs deemed suitable contributed to rising levels of labor market segmentation (Thelen 2014, 173–175). Immigrants, young people, and single parents are the core groups hit by growing inequality in employment and welfare standards (Palme et al. 2009, 48). At the same time, Sweden displayed relatively high unemployment rates after the economic crisis of the early 1990s, both from a diachronic perspective and in comparison to Austria and Denmark (Thelen 2014, 174). Figure 5.2 illustrates the development of unemployment rates in Sweden from 1990 to 2014.

As a result of the economic crisis of the early 1990s, unemployment reached a peak of 10.0 percent in 1997, before declining to 5.6 percent in 2000. During the 2000s, however, unemployment remained relatively high, floating between 6 percent and 9 percent. Again, especially young people (aged between 15 to 25 years) are seriously affected by the demise of full employment—almost one in four were unemployed in the early 2010s. In fact, the rate of youth unemployment is only exceeded by those in the crisis-ridden countries of the Eurozone, whereas in both Austria and Denmark they sit at around 10–11 percent (OECD statistics). A glance at unemployment rates, however, underestimates the problem of economic inactivity resulting from the number of sickness benefit recipients, which turned into an issue of "great concern" in the early 2000s (Lindvall 2010, 172). The increase in sickness absence until 2002 was in part related to the

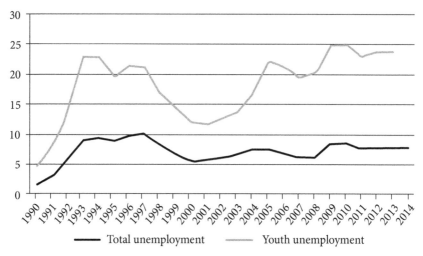

FIGURE 5.2.   Harmonized unemployment rates in Sweden (in total and youth unemployment), 1990–2014.

Source: OECD statistics.

transfer of the long-term unemployed from unemployment benefit and social assistance programs to the sickness insurance system (Lindvall 2010, 172). In fact, since the early 1990s, it seems that unemployment rates decreased only when sickness absence rates increased at the same time, and vice versa (Sjöberg 2011, 215–216). Moreover, the long-term increase in the number of people with reduced work incapacity (e.g., temporary disability benefit recipients) additionally contributed to high rates of economic inactivity (Sjöberg 2011, 215). Overall, it seems thus fair to say that the twin objectives of social cohesion and labor market participation were much less successfully pursued than reducing public debt.

Conventional approaches, I claim, are inconsistent with the Swedish reform trajectory because they fail to recognize the power-distributional interaction between a weakened peak union confederation (LO) and a strengthened government. A decline in union power decreases the potential costs governments face from unilateral government action, whereas government strength provides parties with the capacity to formulate and pass institutional change independent of union support. While confirming the crucial relevance of organized labor for outsider protection, my argument places less emphasis than the account of Thelen (2014) on the variable of state capacity along the logic of the "shadow of hierarchy." According to Thelen, the constitutional tools to coerce unions and employers into an agreement lacking in the Swedish state undermined the political reconfiguration of an outsider-inclusive producer group coalition. By contrast, I will show that Swedish governments did in fact not even push for a labor-inclusive reform strategy once they became strong enough to pursue a unilateral reform path.

Union Preferences and Government Strength in Sweden

The liberalization path of pronounced dualization in a Social Democratic welfare regime could be called a product of the strength of governments to undermine the policy-making influence of organized labor. This strength refers to a high level of autonomous reform capacity, which enables partisan actors to eschew the problem-solving support of trade unions in the politics of labor market adjustment. If invited to political exchanges, I claim, organized labor would have extracted concessions on behalf of outsiders. In this section, I will sketch out my argument about the interaction between union preferences and government strength in detail. First, this section describes the organizational and representational calculations of Swedish unions behind support for improving the social protection of outsiders. Second, drawing on membership and industrial conflict data, it shows a decline in union power, which limits the political capacity of the LO to assert itself vis-à-vis governments and employers. Although this decline must be seen relative to remarkably high levels of union power in the Keynesian postwar era, it does point to the increased relevance of governments in maintaining cooperative relations with organized labor. Third, it discusses the twin elements of Swedish government strength that were necessary for successful unilateral reform strategies; namely, the political capacity to (i) formulate cohesive policy preferences and (ii) get them passed in parliament independent of trade union support.

Swedish Union Preferences: A Voice for Outsiders

As in Denmark, the core institutional recruitment mechanism of unions in Sweden is the Ghent system. Low direct costs and relatively generous benefits for every member were its core features, which contributed to the member-based strength of Swedish unions and thus shaped their policy preference for universal benefit entitlements. In addition, union membership allows workers to top up their public unemployment benefit entitlements with private union-run group insurance schemes through the payment of additional contributions. This latter option gained relevance over time because the gradually declining generosity of public unemployment benefits induced union leaders to establish private benefit arrangements for their members (Rasmussen 2014). Obviously, this private element of unemployment protection added an incentive for union membership primarily among affluent workers, who can afford the costs of private welfare coverage. Given this powerful membership recruitment function of the Ghent system, it comes as no surprise that the unions had a vested interest in mobilizing political support for universal labor market protections on the one hand, and active labor market policies on the other. In consequence, the Ghent system was necessary in order to have high density rates, which in turn broadened the representational focus of organized labor to workers at high risk of unemployment. Despite gradual membership losses, in fact, Sweden is still the most unionized country in the world. Naturally enough, the more encompassing unions become, the more they reach out to disadvantaged workers to recruit members (Becher and Pontusson 2011; Gordon 2015).

Within the union movement, the LO has the highest representational stakes in the protection of outsiders, because it primarily organizes less privileged workers at high risk of unemployment (Svallfors 2015, 4). By contrast, the white-collar confederation, TCO, and especially the academics' confederation, SACO, are less concerned with questions of inequality, as their members have relatively stable jobs and high incomes on average. This applies to SACO in particular, which strictly adheres to political independence, whereas TCO traditionally supported the LO in shaping universalist wage earner coalitions.

Swedish Union Power: The Eroding Hegemony of the LO

The power of the Swedish unions has rested on a number of historically specific and nationally distinct characteristics; that is, high levels of membership, centralization, concentration, and administrative involvement in public policy (the Ghent system). The historical absence of ethnic, religious, and regional cleavages on the one hand, and late but rapid industrialization on the other, contributed to the exceptional strength of reformist unionism in Sweden (Korpi 1978, 74–75). Despite a general decline in union density from the top level of 85 percent in the mid-1980s to 68 percent in 2013, the Swedish union movement continues to be remarkably strong from an international comparative perspective.

Yet unlike in Austria and Denmark, the mobilization of union support for the margins of the workforce came under strain with growing labor fragmentation between the three different union confederations (Thelen 2014, 185–186). In particular, the decline of the LO implies a decline in the power of the voice for workers hit hardest by dualism, which in turn loosens the structural constraints on neoliberal reform ambitions of partisan policy entrepreneurs. The traditionally hegemonic position of the confederal LO level came under pressure not only from significant decentralization in collective bargaining (Iversen 1996), but also from gradual membership shifts to TCO and SACO (Kjellberg 2015). The growth of independent unions outside the three confederations pulled in the same direction. Membership away from the LO points not only to growing interunion fragmentation, but also to a decline of the politically active wing of the union movement, which is grounded on a tradition of mobilizing members for public campaigns and Social Democratic votes (Aylott and Bolin 2007; see also Thörnqvist 2007, 327; Kjellberg 2015). With the LO losing members and power, therefore, the mobilizing capacity to resist unilateral government action also declined. Figure 5.3 illustrates this development by tracking change in the membership shares of the three different confederations and independent unions ("Others") between 1975 and 2013.

It shows that the share of LO-members among the union movement declined from 63 percent in the mid-1970s to 44 percent in 2013. In the same period, the membership shares of SACO and TCO increased from 4 percent to almost 17 percent and from 32 percent to almost 36 percent, respectively. As a result of deindustrialization, transfers in membership from blue-collar to white-collar unions reflect primarily structural changes in the workforce. Notably, however,

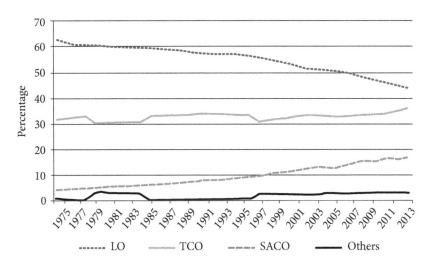

FIGURE 5.3. Membership share of union confederations in percentage of total union membership, 1975–2013.

Source: Kjellberg (2015); author's own calculations.

political intervention reinforced this development, as the center-right government in 2006 differentiated and raised fees for unemployment insurance. This change in the funding mechanism made eligibility to unemployment benefits more expensive for workers in sectors with high unemployment risks. Given the close relationship between unionization and membership of voluntary benefit funds, this institutional change accelerated membership losses in the LO-affiliated unions in particular (Kjellberg 2011). As table 5.2 shows, the membership loss of the LO was particularly acute over the past two decades, while SACO and independent unions continued to gain members.

Between 1990 and 2013, the LO lost as many as 690,000 members, whereas SACO and, to a lesser extent, the independent unions continuously grew in size. The TCO, on the other hand, remained relatively stable, albeit also losing members in that period. In sum, the conclusions we can draw from membership data are clear-cut: while the union movement as such declined, the LO in particular suffered from membership losses. Unlike membership data, industrial conflict data may shed some light on the development of union power at the workplace level (Baccaro and Howell 2011, Culpepper and Regan 2014). Figure 5.4 portrays the number of work stoppages in the period from 1975 and 2014.

Despite some outliers, the overall direction demonstrates an incredible decline in work stoppages. In particular, the dramatic economic crisis of the early 1990s went hand in hand with a sudden drop in strike activities, especially among LO-affiliated unions (Thörnqvist 2007, 335). It would be difficult to contend that decreasing industrial conflict levels reveal union strength, and not weakness, in the sense that the mere threat of work stoppages would induce employers to give in. Against the general background of capital liberalization (growing unemployment, decreasing wage growth relative to productivity, and growing economic inequality), the drop in industrial conflict rates should rather be interpreted as another indicator of declining union strength (Baccaro and Howell 2011, 9).

TABLE 5.2. Membership numbers of Swedish union confederations, 1990–2013.

	1990	1995	2000	2005	2013	CHANGE
LO	1.962.416	1.926.404	1.753.075	1.586.927	1.272.424	−689.992
TCO	1.144.218	1.131.207	1.045.473	1.039.870	1.018.296	−125.922
SACO	260.127	298.537	355.074	418.648	474.725	+214.598
Others	20.977	33.984	78.512	87.407	100.636	+79.659
Total	3.387.738	3.390.132	3.232.123	3.132.852	2.866.081	−521.657

Source: Kjellberg (2015).

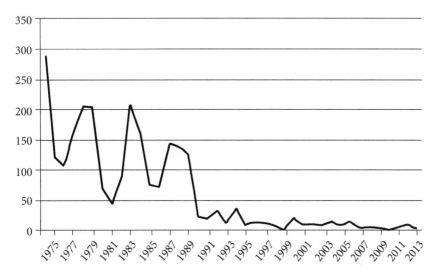

FIGURE 5.4.   Annual number of work stoppages in Sweden, 1975–2014.

Source: Medlingsinstitutet (Swedish National Mediation Office).

While a decline in labor unity and industrial conflict points to a general weakening of union power, perhaps the absent tradition of political strikes or mass demonstrations additionally impedes an activist approach against unilateral reform ambitions. In fact, political strikes aiming to influence parliamentary decisions are strictly forbidden in the public sector (Thörnqvist 2007, 323). Despite the forceful withdrawal of employers from corporatist state agencies in the early 1990s, political processes remained consensus-oriented in style through a renewed reliance on the appointment of ad hoc government commissions (Eichhorst and Wintermann 2005; Bergh and Erlingsson 2008; Steinmo 2013). The privileged integration of experts helps generate legitimacy for government commissions, thereby making the preparation of policy changes open to new actors (Christiansen and Klitgaard 2010). Given this postcorporatist and rationalistic political culture, the LO faces difficulties in mobilizing social support for a shift to conflictual patterns of interest intermediation. Seen in this way, the formal inclusion of the LO in the policy-making process has become a politically contingent choice of governments. The government can work with unions when it corresponds to their interest in mobilizing extraparliamentary consensus, but a unilateral approach appears much less risky for successful economic management and re-election than in the Keynesian past of Swedish corporatism. I will now turn to the properties of Swedish government strength that allowed for the exclusion of the LO from the policy-making process.

Swedish Government Strength: Dissolving Party-Union Ties and Center-Right Unity

My argument implies that the LO, the main union confederation, had the political preference to protect outsiders, but not the political capacity to assert itself. The question is, why? It is clear that the decline of the LO loosened the structural constraints on unilateral reform ambitions to the detriment of outsider representation. Yet this shift in the balance of class power was not nationally unique at all. The decline of the Swedish LO must be placed in a comparative context, and particularly in the context of the striking shrinkage of peak union confederations elsewhere (Ebbinghaus et al. 2011). From a comparative perspective, therefore, the empirical observation that the Swedish LO lost power is definitely not sufficient to explain the cross-national variation in union influence between Austria, Denmark, and Sweden. On the contrary, it could be argued that higher levels of class organization should pose stronger incentives for labor-inclusive policy compromises in Denmark and Sweden than in Austria. In reality, however, the medium-sized (and rapidly declining) Austrian union movement was much more successful than its powerful Scandinavian counterparts in striking policy deals on behalf of outsiders. While also coming under intense pressure from the unilateral reform ambitions of the political right (Obinger and Tálos 2006), the Austrian governments were simply too weak to eschew labor-inclusive concertation in labor market policy (Afonso 2013).

My argument is that the active rejection of labor demands by national governments requires a high level of autonomous reform capacity. This brings me to the role of governments in the political economy of Swedish dualization. While confirming the significant agency of Swedish employers in the transition to post-corporatism (Pontusson and Swensson 1996), I argue that a crucial factor of union exclusion was the strength of Swedish governments to formulate and pass policy changes independent of union support. As in the previous chapters, we look at the partisan composition and vote share of governments in the period of dualization to assess their reform capacity. Table 5.3 illustrates that Sweden was governed by a center-right coalition from 1991 to 1994, a Social Democratic single-party minority government from 1994 to 2006, and a center-right coalition from 2006 to 2014.

Over this entire period, there was never a single ideologically divided coalition government in office. To begin with, between 1991 and 1994, the four-party center-right government was set to unite around spending cuts in response to the dramatic economic and fiscal crisis of the early 1990s. The subsequent Social Democratic single-party minority government was in a very strong position to find support for its preferred policies. With a vote share of 45.25 percent from

TABLE 5.3. Elections and governments in Sweden in the dualization period, 1991–2014.

COALITION	PERIOD	GOVERNING PARTIES	TYPE	VOTE SHARE
Center-right	1991–1994	M, CD, L, KD	Minority	46.6 percent
	1994–1998	SAP	Minority	45.3 percent
Center-left	1998–2002	SAP	Minority	36.4 percent
	2002–2006	SAP	Minority	39.9 percent
Center-right	2006–2010	M, L, CD, KD	Majority	48.3 percent
	2010–2014	M, L, CD, KD	Minority	49.3 percent
Center-left	2014–?	SAP, MP	Minority	37.9 percent

Notes: SAP = Social Democratic Party; M = Conservative Party; L = Liberal Party; CD = Center Party; KD = Christian Democrats; MP = Green Party.

1994 to 1998, the party was in a hegemonic position and it needed support from only one party among a diverse set of opposition parties. It is clear that the ideological distancing between the SAP and LO in the 1980s allowed the party leadership to formulate policy priorities independent of union support (Blyth 2001). A consequence of this electoral strength is that party leaders—even of Social Democratic parties—have expanded capacity to push back the influence of affiliated unions on policy output. We would therefore expect this four-year period to reveal the lowest level of union influence under the Social Democratic single-party minority governments from 1994 to 2006. Between 1998 and 2006, the SAP was in a less powerful position, albeit still dominating the legislative process.

The subsequent four-party center-right government had a majority of seats from 2006 to 2010. Their capacity to formulate a common agenda came with the unification process of the four traditionally divided bourgeois parties into the so-called Alliance for Sweden (Allians för Sverige) (Aylott and Bolin 2007). Notably, this government did not rely on support from a populist right-wing party that was attached to the blue-collar working class, as was the case in Austria and Denmark. This absence of a right-wing populist party underpinned the neoliberal profile of the center-right bloc. That a united center-right majority may be strong enough to marginalize a relatively strong labor movement was powerfully demonstrated in the policy performance of the Allians during the late 2000s.

These two constellations—Social Democratic single-party minority government and a united center-right majority government—were the driving forces underlying the political capacity of Swedish governments to eschew labor acquiescence. To be sure, during the 1990s, European Social Democratic parties across the continent moved to market-conforming positions along the lines of the "Third Way" in an attempt to adapt their welfare states to the demands of globalization and deindustrialization (Green-Pedersen et al. 2001). However, the renewal of the SAP was distinct in that it also retrenched precisely the "employment-friendly policies" (Huo et al. 2008) characteristic of the "Third Way"; that is, active labor market policies and short-term unemployment benefit rates. While fiscal retrenchment was in large part a response to the public debt crisis of the early 1990s, the subsequent establishment of a strict fiscal policy regime significantly constrained spending choices in the long run (Mehrtens 2014; Haffert and Mehrtens 2015). Of course, this is not to say that partisan differences disappeared completely. On the contrary, the novel formation of a united center-right front in 2006 was crucial to the reinforcement of institutional dualisms. However, the overall reform trajectory of Swedish dualization reveals partisan differences mainly in degree, and not direction. My argument that union exclusion by strong governments paved the way for dualization will be illustrated through process-tracing in the next section.

Strong Party-Union Ties: The Rehn-Meidner Model

Named after the two main labor economists of the LO, the famous Rehn-Meidner model was the central reference point for the successful macroeconomic policy mix of consecutive SAP-led governments during the 1950s and 1960s (Meidner and Hedborg 1984). In short, the ambition of Gösta Rehn and Rudolf Meidner was to ensure high levels of social solidarity without undermining the productive capacity and monetary stability of Swedish capitalism. Its normative starting point was a "solidaristic wage policy" delivered by centralized and nationwide deals between the peak union confederation, the LO, and the peak employers' association, the Swedish Employers Association (SAF). Centralized collective bargaining oriented wage increases around average productivity increases of the entire economy, thereby rewarding the cost competitiveness of high-productivity firms while imposing demands for restructuring on low-productivity firms. To curb wage pressure and inflation alike, the state had to eschew introducing expansive fiscal policies as a means to provide full employment. Instead, the compensation for the massive "productivity whip" of wage equalization came from the expansion of active labor market policies; that is, measures to avoid structural unemployment by facilitating the adaptation and mobility of labor to competitive areas of the economy.

The successful elaboration of the Rehn-Meidner model demonstrated two important conditions underlying the egalitarian legacy of the Swedish postwar political economy. First, the "solidaristic" outlook of the LO in designing macroeconomic policy priorities revealed its encompassing representational focus on behalf of labor as a whole. Its centralized structure and mobilizing strength were crucial to the strategic capacity of the LO to pursue an equalization of primary incomes within the constraints of a capitalist economy. Second, the adoption of the Rehn-Meidner model in political practice showed the central role played by the LO in designing the policy agenda of the SAP. Holding office with more than 40 percent of the vote between 1936 to 1976, the SAP did not merely accept free collective bargaining between the two peak-level associations, as in corporatist economies elsewhere. Rather, the Rehn-Meidner model also implied a shift in the policy-making authority over virtually all economic affairs from the SAP to the LO in the interest of viable wage solidarity (Scharpf 1987, 230; Pontusson 1992, 313). In other words, to ensure the functioning of the Rehn-Meidner model, the LO had to take control of the state through close ties with the SAP (Korpi 1978, 1983; Esping-Andersen 1985).

Proof of the SAP's adherence to the demands of the LO came in the early 1970s, when the unions' rank and file pushed for the democratization of working life in general and more job security in particular.[1] Even though the Swedish wildcat strike movement was not nationally unique in this period, the imperative of labor mobility in the Rehn-Meidner model generated distinctly strong demands for greater employment stability. Various societal changes— growing female employment, dual earner couples, homeownership, and falling wage differentials—undermined the willingness of workers to shift their job to successful high-productivity firms, which were predominantly located in the manufacturing sector of southern Sweden. While the willingness of workers to move to prospering firms decreased, the mobilizing strength of the labor movement reached its historic top. Faced by mounting pressure from below, the LO leadership had to realize that the SAF would block any serious attempt in collective bargaining to constrain the managerial prerogative of hiring and firing workers. Eventually, the opposition of the SAF induced the LO to break with the consensual tradition of Swedish corporatism by turning to the legislative arena instead. Central to the subsequent introduction of the Employment Protection Act of 1974 was the direct access of the LO to the policy-making action of the SAP: "Their political partner, the ruling Social Democratic Party, was willing and able to find a majority in favour of public regulation" (Emmenegger 2010, 283). Notably, even the Liberal People's Party supported the bill with a view to attract votes from the politically neutral TCO, which lined up with the LO in pushing for legislation in job security (Emmenegger 2010, 283).

The Employment Protection Act of 1974 (LAS) marked a "critical juncture" for both the policies and politics of Swedish labor market reform. First, from a policy point of view, the LAS imposed a number of restrictions on the managerial prerogative to set the terms and conditions of employment (Gordon 2012, 235–236). It privileged employment contracts of an unlimited period by allowing fixed-term contracts only for trainees and substitutes or labor that required temporary employment for explicitly work-related reasons (e.g. seasonal work in agriculture or tourism) (EIRO 1997). Therefore, the unlimited contract became the legally binding "regular" type of employment, albeit with the provision that employers may deviate from these restrictions in collective negotiations with the trade unions. Moreover, the LAS stipulated a seniority principle for dismissals entitled "last-in, first-out." Employers were therefore obliged to find alternative employment or privilege the reemployment of now-redundant senior workers, thereby prioritizing functional over numerical flexibility at the workplace. In addition, the length of the notification period depends on work and age history, ranging from a minimum of one month to a maximum of six months. Notably, the LAS also required employers to consult local union representatives in order to receive consent for important changes in the company such as mergers or dismissals. As a result, local union representatives may demand concessions from the employer in exchange for deviations from the LAS framework, including expanded training provisions or redundancy payments, for example. It thus provided another incentive for union membership, since local union officials gain a say over the selection of redundancies within a given enterprise. Taken together, the LAS provided the unions with a strong organizational foothold at the workplace level.

It is interesting that the introduction of the LAS favored the employment stability of older workers in particular (the "last-in, first-out" principle). As Davidsson (2011, 134–135) pointed out, the reason for this significant age bias in the LAS framework lay in the perception of union leaders that conventional retraining instruments are not effective for the reemployment of older and handicapped job seekers, as their ability to adapt to structural economic changes is generally limited. Therefore, both the Danish and Swedish LO confederations called for tightened job security regulations (Emmenegger 2010). Given higher levels of societal pressure and labor unity, the LO managed to put these demands in legislative action, whereas the Danish LO failed with similar attempts (Emmenegger 2010). Ironically, it seems that the recognized limits of lifelong learning induced union leaders to reject the contemporary notion of Flexicurity, the idea of providing employment security through human capital formation on the

terms of a highly volatile labor market, before it had become popular in contemporary political discourse (Streeck 2008, 12). After the LO had successfully
mobilized political support for the LAS framework, Rudolf Meidner himself
called for an expansion of state support for disadvantaged labor market groups
in order to undermine a segmentation of the Swedish labor market (Meidner
and Hedborg 1984, 102).

Second, from the point of view of politics, the LO showed that it is not dependent on the consent of the SAF to pursue its political ends. The state not only inter-
vened into issues previously reserved for collective bargaining, but also acted in a
way that decisively expanded union power at the workplace level. Party-union ties
provided the LO with a direct channel of interest mediation without having to
place any reliance on lengthy and costly bargaining procedures with the employers. This move provoked resistance on the part of the SAF ever since. In the words
of Patrik Karlsson, labor market policy expert of Swedish business:

> It is correct that this legislation [Employment Protection Act of 1974]
> has always been questioned by the employers since the beginning and
> the reason for this—and I think this is important to realize—is that since
> 1938 there was a treaty between the employers and the unions to keep
> legislation out and deal with rules and regulations via collective bargain-
> ing. But in the early 1970s, this was abandoned by the unions, as they
> asked for legislation.[2]

This power demonstration implied a substantial loss of trust by the SAF in the
reliability of the LO within corporatist institutions. To the SAF, the LO-led political initiatives of the early 1970s toward economic and industrial democracy
strongly violated the Swedish model of consensual exchange between the peak-
level organizations of labor and capital. Perhaps the clearest expression of business
resistance came with the organization of unprecedented mass demonstrations
in response to union demands for the introduction of "wage earner funds,"
which were essentially planned "as a mechanism to socialize the economy and
reverse the trend toward the concentration of economic power in private hands"
(Steinmo 1988, 431). While successfully constraining the scope of collective
profit-sharing with the 1983 reform (Pontusson 1993, 555), the SAF arrived at
the conclusion that the LO-led push for legislative action would call for a
conflict-oriented shift in the strategic outlook of interest mediation (Blyth 2001,
9–10). Rather than restricting its action repertoire to collective bargaining, the
SAF initiated an impressive mobilization of public campaigns to resist the hegemonic alliance of the SAP and LO (Blyth 2001, 9–10). Faced by the counteroffensive of the SAF, the political assertiveness of the LO became ever more tied

to its cooperation with the SAP (Svensson and Öberg 2002, 311–312; Anthonsen and Lindvall 2011, 128–129).

To the great disappointment of the SAF, the formation of a series of bourgeois governments between 1976 and 1982 did not result in a neoliberal policy turn-around. Ideological divisions and a narrow parliamentary majority between three equally strong parties—the Center Party, the Liberals, and the Conservatives—undermined the capacity of the center-right bloc to challenge the position of the LO (Scharpf 1987, 130; Mehrtens 2014, 97). Starting with a majority of eleven seats, the coalition broke down after two years due to a disagreement over the issue of nuclear energy, leading to a single-party minority government of the Liberals. With the 1979 election, the three parties formed another coalition with a majority of only one seat, which once again fell apart after less than two years following the withdrawal of the Conservatives (Moderaterna). In addition to this coalitional instability, the popularity of the welfare state and the crucial role of the LO in moderating wage growth undermined the strategic capacity of the political right to deviate from Social Democratic strategies of economic adjustment (Mares 2006, 105). As of 1980, however, the center-right coalition faced mounting budget deficits and the "aggressive neoliberal posture" of the SAF (Huber and Stephens 2001, 241). In response, the government passed a set of very small entitlement reductions for part-time pensioners and sick-pay recipients (Huber and Stephens 2001, 241). For our purposes, one change of interest was a modest amendment to the LAS in 1982, which allowed employers to offer fixed-term contracts "for six months over a period of two years, when necessitated by a temporary accumulation of work; and for a probationary period of six months" (EIRO 1997). Still, despite the emerging constraints of fiscal austerity, the absence of a strong center-right bloc led to contin-ued strong union influence, which in turn was crucial to the resilience of universal employment and welfare rights.

Taking the "Third Way" (1980s)

In office from 1982 until 1991, the SAP single-party minority governments also left the overall thrust of labor market and welfare regulation intact, while still fol-lowing full-employment policies and expanding parental leave and public day-care provisions (Huber and Stephens 2001, 243). Therefore, the reform path of dualization did not start off directly during the 1980s. But this period certainly paved the way for this outcome, as it marked the emergence of growing interun-ion divides and the ideological emancipation of the SAP from the LO. Once the dramatic economic crisis of the early 1990s hit the Swedish economy, both factors eventually contributed to an unraveling of the LO's hegemonic policy-making influence, on which high levels of social solidarity rested.

During the 1980s, the LO came under pressure from both without and within. First, the SAF came to the conclusion that the LO failed to moderate wage demands, while industrial employers in particular demanded greater bargaining flexibility (Pontusson and Swensson 1996). Therefore, as of 1983, the engineering employers (VF) successfully convinced the metalworkers union (Metall) to defect from centralized wage bargaining and pursue autonomous sector-level agreements instead. This initiative of engineering employers reflected their preference for stronger wage differentiation in response to the rise of post-Fordist production arrangements (Pontusson and Swensson 1996, 235–239), whereas Metall was in large part seduced to follow suit by sector-related concessions (Mares 2003, 113–114). Second, the intralabor authority of the LO was challenged by the demand to link pay hikes to productivity increases by manufacturing unions on the one hand, and the growing membership strength of the white-collar confederation, TCO, and the academics' confederation, SACO, on the other. As indicated by the defection of Metall, the former became critical to the imperative of "wage solidarism," whereas the latter questioned the hegemonic interunion position of the LO and successfully pursued various compensation clauses (Mehrtens 2014, 94, 110). As a result, a gradual decentralization in collective bargaining took place, which impeded the capacity of the LO to moderate economy-wide wage growth.

In addition to growing labor fragmentation, the SAP developed a more autonomous policy outlook, which no longer adhered closely to the demands of the LO (Blyth 2001; Lavalle 2008). To be sure, the gradual emancipation of the SAP in the policy-making arena was in part a response to the political failure of the LO to mobilize sufficient support for the introduction of wage earner funds, which were intended to resolve the internal contradictions of the Rehn-Meidner model (Pontusson 1992, 321). Moreover, the declining capacity of the LO to deliver sufficient wage restraint in exchange for favorable policy results pulled in the same direction (Mares 2006, 114). However, the weakening of the LO did not automatically give rise to a new and distinct policy approach. It took the agency of key players within the party and the advice of economists to push the SAP into a neoliberal direction (Blyth 2001). Notably, the minister of finance, Kjell-Olof Feldt, was the central figure in this regard (Steinmo 2013, 92), designing a new policy mix entitled the "Third Way," which was a combination of a Keynesian-like currency devaluation (as pursued by the Socialists in France) and monetarist fiscal austerity (as pursued by Margaret Thatcher in the United Kingdom).

Given the problem of growing public debt, the SAP refrained from another expansion of state spending and instead tailored its recovery strategy to the productivity demands of the manufacturing-dominated export sector. Accordingly, a devaluation of the Swedish krona by 16 percent in 1982 was expected to boost the cost competitiveness of exports, while it was envisaged that fiscal moderation and wage restraint would undermine the reemergence of inflationary wage-price spirals. While leaving strong labor market protections untouched, the reform path of cutting public spending, privatizing state enterprises, introducing market mechanisms in public sector service provision, and intervening into a number of wage bargaining rounds implied an undeniable redistribution of income from labor to capital (Huber and Stephens 2001, 242–243). Perhaps the clearest expression of this neoliberal turnaround came with the deregulation of financial markets, which was pursued more radically in scope and speed relative to that of other countries (Ryner 2004, 98–99; Schnyder 2012, 1132; Mehrtens 2014, 121–125). The distributive profile of the "Third Way" created tensions between the SAP and the LO, which came to be known as the "War of the Roses," fought out between the LO chairman, Stig Malm, and the minister of finance, Kjell-Olof Feldt. Unlike in the heyday of the Rehn-Meidner model, the "overall thrust of government policy after 1982 conformed closely to the prescriptions of Feldt and his advisors and thus must be considered a defeat for LO and its allies within the government" (Pontusson 1992, 314–315).

At first, the "Third Way" was relatively successful in generating economic growth and reducing public debt during the 1980s. However, the deregulation of credit markets without raising exchange controls and the stimulus from the "tax reform of the century" (1989–1990) in tandem with real wage growth contributed to the bursting of an enormous inflationary bubble. By 1990, the SAP had to respond to the most dramatic economic crisis of the postwar era, where a steep increase in unemployment rates from 2 percent to 11 percent translated into a budget deficit of 12 percent in 1993. In response, the SAP followed the European mainstream by declaring the combat of inflation, and not full employment, as the ultimate goal of Social Democratic state policy (Lindvall 2004). Given the long-standing legacy of full employment and robust growth, this economic turmoil created a widespread crisis awareness among both the party system and the populace.

Consistent with its radical shift in ideological outlook, the SAF reacted strongly to the onset of the economic crisis by drawing the curtain on centralized bargaining with the LO (1990) and permanently withdrawing all of its representatives from corporatist state agencies (1991). The disruptive strategy of the SAF added a political crisis to the economic turmoil and shifted the full policy-making authority away from producer groups to the state. Aided by massive campaigning on the part of the SAF, the public perception came to attribute the recession to the economic policies of the government, which then led to an unprecedented election defeat of the SAP in 1991 (Huber and Stephens 1991, 243–244). In consequence, from 1991 to 1994, the Conservatives (Moderaterna) under Carl Bildt formed a center-right minority coalition with the Center Party, the Liberals, and the Christian Democrats. The depth of the economic crisis helped to mobilize political support for two austerity packages in 1992, which included spending cuts in various social security arrangements (sick-pay, accident insurance, etc.). Notably, these two packages were supported by the SAP as part of a general transition to a hard currency regime and in response to skyrocketing public deficits.

Recognizing the economic crisis as a "window of opportunity" for neoliberal reform ambitions, the Bildt cabinet pursued controversial reforms in the area of labor market policy. The major point of discord was the idea of "nationalizing" the Ghent system; that is, converting the union-run benefit funds into a state-administered benefit system. Faced by the fiscal overburden of unemployment insurance, the SAP was indeed willing to support the retrenchment efforts of the center-right coalition to rein in the costs of the system (Anderson 2001, 1081). Yet the proposal of the Bildt cabinet actively linked cost containment measures (reduction in the replacement rate from 90 to 80 percent, extended qualification period, increased membership fees) with the elimination of the Ghent system. In spite of protests from the SAP and the unions, the government achieved a majority for this package combining benefit cutbacks and the "nationalization" of unemployment insurance. Most notably, the package also deindexed benefit levels from inflation, thereby effectively cutting future entitlements by default. Yet after the election of 1994, the new SAP government immediately reversed the "nationalization" of unemployment insurance to the benefit of union membership recruitment.

In addition, drawing on recommendations from the Lindbeck Commission, the Bildt cabinet extended the maximum duration of fixed-term contracts and trial periods from six to twelve months, while also allowing employers to exempt two employees from the dismissal restrictions of the LAS as well as legalizing temporary work agencies (Van Peijpe 1998, 68–69; Gordon 2012, 238). The most far-reaching recommendation of the "Lindbeck Commission"—the abolition of the "last-in, first-out" principle—was blocked by resistance from the Center Party inside the coalition.[3] Judging from official announcements, the SAP supported the LO in opposing the flexibilization of temporary contracts (Van Peijpe 1998, 68–69; Gordon 2012, 238). However, the memoirs of the minister of finance (1991–1994), Anne Wibble, indicated that her Social Democratic successor, Göran Persson (1994–1996), considered these changes "quite reasonable" in the first place (Wibble 1994, 64, cited in Davidsson 2011, 141–142).

Accordingly, the opposition of the LO led the SAP leadership to reject reductions of job security for temporary workers (Wibble 1994, 64, cited in Davidsson 2011, 141–142).

Taken together, the SAP clearly protested against the "nationalization" of the Ghent system to protect the organizational strength of the trade unions, but at the same time consented to cost-saving retrenchment efforts in a number of benefit schemes. Its position in the area of job security was less clear—official announcements and the memoirs of Anne Wibble contradicted each other. I will now turn to the period of the Social Democratic politics of dualization, which was grounded on the ideological distancing of the SAP from the policy preferences of the LO.

Dualization: The Dissolution of Strong Party-Union Ties (1994–2006)

"We didn't manage to convince them [the SAP]. The leadership and the people working for them were overconfident that sound public finances are good for employment. Instead, we were saying that high employment is good for public finances."

Interview with Dan Andersson, Chief Economist of the LO
(2000–2008), May 5, 2015

"We must remember that sound public finances are the most fundamental conditions for growth and development."

Pär Nuder, chief of staff to the prime minister (1997–2004) and
minister of finance (2004–2006), at a party meeting of
the SAP in 2004 (cited in Lavalle 2008, 146)

The 1994 elections raised strong hopes of the LO. After a short bourgeois interlude, the return of the SAP brought the "political arm of the labor movement" back in power. Certainly, formal party-union ties remained relatively strong in Sweden, given that the SAP derived a considerable share of its votes and funding directly from the LO (Allern et al. 2007). The chairman of the LO was a member of the SAP's executive committee, whereas connections between both organizations remained particularly close at the local membership level (Aylott 2003). At the same time, the SAP received a whole 45.25 percent of the vote, which allowed the formation of parliamentary majorities with the support from a single party among five alternative opposition parties. Therefore, partisanship theorists and trade union representatives alike would have expected labor market policy to shift in the preferred direction of the LO; that is, toward the expanded protection of outsiders (Huo 2009; Pontusson 2011). Indeed, these expectations seemed to come true at the beginning of their tenure, since the SAP adhered to its election promises and reversed two pieces of legislation introduced by the previous center-right government. First, the SAP single-party minority government repealed the "nationalization" of the Ghent system by effectively reinstating the administrative monopoly of the unions over unemployment insurance. Second, it undid a large part of the previous job security reform by reintroducing restrictions on the usage of fixed-term contracts.

Despite these apparent concessions to the LO, the SAP undeniably turned into a party that was committed to the rapid achievement of sound public finances via moderate cuts for the weakest segments of the labor market. After having contributed to the outburst of a severe economic crisis, the SAP sought to regain economic credibility by vigorously tackling the inflationary public debt crisis through a strategy of orthodox economic adjustment. In fact, thanks to rigorous crisis packages, the SAP turned a budget deficit of 12 percent in 1993 into an impressive surplus of 2.7 percent of GDP by 1997, according to OECD statistics. As roughly illustrated by the quotations above, the prioritization of fiscal consolidation as an end in itself almost invariably relegated the influence of the LO's agenda of an "active working line"; that is, the combination of stringent work requirements with expanded spending on labor market policy to stimulate employment growth and undermine social exclusion (Andersson 2005, 2008). Faced by the governing strength of the SAP in the historically distinct context of liberalization, the LO had a much weaker grip on its political ally than in the past.

Proof of the capacity to eschew labor acquiescence came in 1995, when the SAP for the first time established cross-class cooperation with the bourgeois Center Party to obtain support for unilateral reforms in the areas of: (i) job security and (ii) unemployment insurance. In both cases, the SAP moved in the preferred direction of the SAF, and not the LO. First, the SAP provided for more flexibility in the in the hiring of temporary workers. This legislation allowed employers to conclude fixed-term contracts for an increased period of twelve months (eighteen months for first-time hires) without requiring a particular reason. Notably, it allowed employers to deviate from restrictions of the LAS framework via agreements with union representatives at the workplace level, thereby abandoning the veto-power of the confederal level. Tellingly, this liberalization was put into law precisely after the LO had openly rejected this proposal at its annual congress (Henkes 2006, 294). The concern of the LO was that the option to deviate from the LAS framework via collective negotiations would allow employers "to bully certain weaker local branches to adopt changes with the threat of lost jobs" (Gordon 2012, 239). According to OECD statistics, the strictness of regulations on temporary forms of employment temporary thus decreased from 1.77 to 1.44.

Second, the SAP concluded an austerity package with the Center Party, which included a moderate cut in the replacement rate of a number of welfare benefits (from 80 percent to 75 percent in unemployment benefits). This cutback must be placed in the context of the SAP's previous refusal to reindex the unemployment benefit ceiling to inflation, thereby effectively accepting the ongoing decline of benefit generosity. In addition, the law extended the time for which workers may lose access to unemployment benefits if they resigned from a job "without good cause" from twenty to forty-five days (Gordon 2012, 257). This possibility to restrict access to unemployment benefits also applied to workers who refused various job offers in a row (Gordon 2012, 257).

In response to these changes, the LO mobilized, for the first time in its history, a mass demonstration, together with a social movement against the policy performance of the SAP (Davidsson 2011, 144), and openly sided with the Left Party in its opposition to the government (Henkes 2006, 293). Faced with pressure from the LO and its rank and file, the SAP leadership revoked its plan to restrict eligibility requirements, which initially included an increase in the qualification period to nine months and a limitation of the maximum benefit duration to 600 days (EIRO 1997). The TCO and SACO particularly opposed tightened qualification criteria to keep the system open to university graduates, while the LO rejected the proposed fixed time limit on benefit receipt (Gordon 2012, 257). The SAP then delegated this issue to a commission, which incorporated these union demands and thus paved the way for a compromise between the government and the unions in 1997. Aided by an economic recovery, the SAP consented to a return of the top replacement rate to 80 percent on the one hand, and an extension of the qualification period to 6 months on the other. However, the issue of a fixed time limit had to be dropped

By 1996–1997, the SAP had followed the recommendations of the Lindbeck Commission in pursuing a far-reaching structural reform of fiscal policy, which restricted the control over the budgetary planning process through expenditure ceilings and an annual surplus target of 1 percent of GDP (Mehrtens 2014, 175–179). Fueled by long-standing academic deliberations and the crisis awareness of the early 1990s, the reform effectively insulated policymakers from the popular demands of the electorate and organized labor by placing legally binding limits on future spending choices. By 2000, the government additionally imposed a de facto debt break on the municipalities, which implied a raise of the sur-

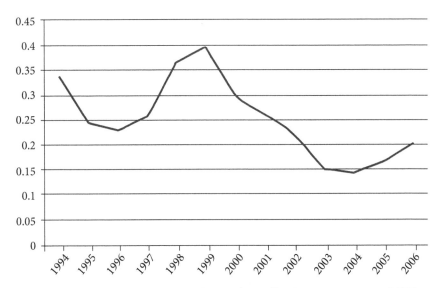

FIGURE 5.5.   Spending on active labor-market policy (as a percentage of GDP per unemployed) under SAP single-party minority governments, 1994–2006.

Source: OECD statistics.

plus target to 2 percent of GDP (Mehrtens 2014, 175–179). Naturally enough, the new fiscal policy framework ruled out any investment choices via discretionary deficit spending.

The stipulation of the fiscal policy framework went hand in hand with a gradual decline of spending on active labor market policies (ALMP) (figure 5.5). Notably, the spending reductions in ALMP observed after 1999 must be placed in the context of a simultaneous rise of fiscal surpluses (Calmfors 2012). As economists from the LO criticized the cuts (Andersson 2008), the share of participants in active labor market programs went down, especially among the unemployed who were not members of a union-run benefit fund and thus are in the "weakest position on the labor market." While two thirds of this group attended labor market programs in 1992, this figure fell to a mere one third in 2005.

Figure 5.5 shows that in the governing period of the SAP, the spending level measured as a percentage of GDP per unemployed more than halved within five years, declining from almost 0.40 percent in 1999 to 0.14 percent in 2004. Despite a modest increase between 2004 and 2006, the spending pattern, as compared to the beginning of their tenure in 1994, was strongly contractive. A critic of this development was Dan Andersson, the former chief economist of the LO

(2000–2006). In an interview with the author, he attributed this spending decline to the policy recommendations of liberal economists:

> There was an enormous influence of new liberal economists, more than in other countries. They were saying that ALMP is a bad idea. Lars Calmfors and senior policy advisors of the University of Stockholm said that we should take down ALMP and now they continue to say that we need to make labor even more flexible.[4]

Sture Nordh, the former chairman of the TCO (1999–2008), shared this assessment, but also added that membership shifts within the labor movement reduced the electoral relevance of policy demands from the LO for the SAP during the leadership of Göran Persson (1996–2006):

> Being in an open economy, the government and especially the Prime Minister himself believed in the more liberal theories we have now, especially with your reference to Lars Calmfors and others. That is important. But you also have to see the structural change in the labor market. LO is not as big as it was. LO is not as strong an organizing force as it was in the election campaigns. . . . . To win elections, it is not enough to have support from the LO.[5]

By 2000–2001, the SAP had passed the most significant labor market reform of its tenure (Lindvall 2010, 168). The SAP's autonomous reform capacity, however, was inhibited by a change in the parliamentary balance of power. Unlike in the period from 1995 to 1998, the electoral loss of the SAP in 1998 did not allow for the conclusion of another cooperation agreement with the bourgeois Center Party. Therefore, the political priority *remained* the same—"sound public finances"— but the capacity to pass this preference in the legislative process was weakened by the SAP's reliance on the support from the Left Party, which certainly would not have accepted another round of cuts (Aylott and Bolin 2007, 624).

The 2000–2001 reform raised the benefit ceiling twice and placed higher demands on the active job-search of unemployed workers, while abolishing the possibility to requalify for unemployment benefits through participation in active labor market programs. Instead, the reform introduced an "activity guarantee" for the long-term unemployed, which was intended to strengthen work incentives and provide access to reintegration measures. Unlike in the previous reform, the SAP did not take up the issue of a fixed time limit. The rationale behind this reform was based on calculations from experts showing that tightened work obligations would allow for a cost-neutral raise in the benefit ceiling. At that time, Dan Andersson, who later became chief economist at the LO, had been state secretary in the intradepartmental committee that prepared the reform in the Ministry of

Industry, Employment, and Communications. When I asked him about the role of the 2002 elections in the choice to lift benefit levels, he responded as follows,

> The raises of the benefit ceiling in 2001–2002 were not due to elections. In the Ministry of Employment, we were able to outmaneuver the Minister of Finance and the Prime Minister's office, so it was an internal power struggle inside the government. It was as simple as that. We could show them with calculations that additional restrictions in the control of the unemployed will decrease costs. . . . Our argument was then that we can afford an increase of benefit levels by strengthening the control over the unemployed, so it wasn't due to the election of 2002. It was the clever work of people inside the Ministry. It was a single one-time shot against the system! . . . The Prime Minister was very much against it, because he thought that if we raise the unemployment benefits, we will increase unemployment, which is a very crude way of thinking, but still conservative people think like that.[6]

This view was corroborated by Mats Wadman, a senior official at the Ministry of Employment from 1988 to 2007: "It resulted from work inside the Ministry. Dan Andersson was the main architect behind this."[7]

Judging from the interview evidence, the SAP leadership wanted to keep the reform cost-neutral in the first place. Technocratic arguments from the intradepartmental committee, and not popular demands from voters or trade unions, eventually convinced the SAP leadership that the tightened control of the unemployed would allow for a rise in unemployment benefits without reinforcing open unemployment (see also Lindvall 2010, 168).

Drawing on the dataset of Van Vliet and Caminada (2012), figure 5.6 describes the development of net replacement rates for average production workers during the tenure of the SAP from 1994 to 2006. It shows that the 2000–2001 reform raised the net replacement rate for average production workers from 70 percent in 2000 to 79 percent in 2002, but the subsequent nonindexation of the benefit ceiling led to a gradual trend back to 72 percent at the end of the SAP's tenure in 2006. To be sure, the redistributive design of the Ghent system maintained higher replacement rates for low-income earners. Yet, as described above, the erosion of the income-replacing generosity for middle-income earners induced SACO and TCO to provide private supplementary benefits alongside the public insurance in the early 2000s (Gordon 2012, 259–260). Between 2002 and 2012, the number of workers covered by private unemployment protection increased from below 200,000 to more than 1.8 million (Rasmussen 2014, 51). In relative terms, more than one third of the Swedish workforce were thus members of private arrangements in 2012 (Rasmussen 2014, 51).

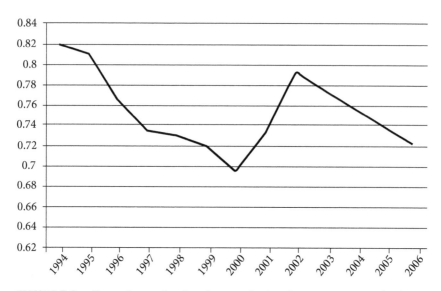

FIGURE 5.6. Unemployment net replacement rates for an average production worker (mean of two family types: single people and one-earner couple with two children) under SAP single-party minority governments, 1994–2006.

Source: Unemployment replacement rates dataset (Van Vliet and Caminada 2012).

It might appear ironic that the "solidaristic" design of the SAP's retrenchment efforts resulted in a new insider-outsider divide in unemployment protection; that is, a divide between workers who were entitled to private supplementary insurance and those who were reliant on public unemployment benefits only. After all, Göran Persson considered his reforms necessary to protect the Social Democratic credentials of the benefit system (Fichtelius 2007). However, the retrenchment of the public unemployment insurance clearly incentivized the demand for private provision of unemployment protection among middle-income and high-income earners. From a political point of view, the growing popularity of private benefits calls into question the electoral support for universal risk protection, since the affluent groups covered by private arrangements might come to prefer tax cuts to higher replacement rates in the end. This is precisely the reason why during the postwar era the Social Democratic founding figures of the Swedish welfare state insisted on the universality of income replacement in the event of unemployment: Without the middle-class on board, social solidarity would have been hard to sustain. Seen in this way, it comes as no surprise that the center-right's agenda of linking tax cuts with welfare cuts appealed to a relatively large segment of working people (Lindvall and Rueda 2012). Proof of this electoral appeal came with the defeat of the SAP in the elections of 2006, which paved the way for a united center-right majority.

Dualization: the formation of a united center-right front

> We tried to discuss it. We didn't even get debates that we had organized with some prominent members of parliament from the Nya Moderaterna [Conservative Party]. The person didn't even show up! I was there, people were there listening, but he didn't come. And later on he stated: "This is because you are just going to criticize us."
>
> Interview with Sture Nordh, chairman of TCO (1999–2011), Sept. 30, 2015

> The difference was that we had worked really hard on these reforms in advance. This is what people forget: everything was already calculated!
>
> Interview with Eva Uddén Sonnegård, state secretary of Nya Moderaterna at the Ministry of Employment (2006–2010), Oct. 2, 2015

The 2006 elections reinforced the exclusion of organized labor from the policy-making process. It provided an unprecedented "Alliance for Sweden" (Allians för Sverige) between the conservative Moderate Party (26.2 percent), the Center Party (7.9 percent), the Liberals (7.5 percent), and the Christian Democrats (6.6 percent) with a majority of seats for the first time since 1932. As indicated by the quotations illustrated above, the election victory of this alliance gave rise to a meticulously planned "make work pay" agenda, which almost invariably ruled out significant political exchanges with the unions. Drawing on a united majority, the first Reinfeldt cabinet (2006–2010) pursued a unilateral strategy for the introduction of a series of profound tax and labor market reforms, which exacerbated the segmentation of the Swedish labor market. Most notably, the successful legislation of this reform path took place despite the presence of egalitarian welfare attitudes (Svallfors 2011) and opposition from the strongest union organization worldwide (Ebbinghaus et al. 2011). What adds to the puzzle is that the center-right bloc's agenda was not aided by any sort of economic crisis; on the contrary, the economy had grown in the second quarter of 2006 by a remarkable 5.1 percent, while public finances recorded an expected surplus of 3 percent that year (Aylott and Bolin 2007, 621).

So how did the Swedish Allians manage to pursue a powerful "make work pay" agenda, given the structural constraints of welfare state popularity and relative union strength? Existing partisanship or producer group explanations are of little explanatory service in this regard. A reference to center-right partisanship fails to explain why the Austrian ÖVP-FPÖ or the Danish V-K governments were much less successful than their Swedish counterparts in cutting back outsider protection. Partisanship theorists, therefore, miss the difference in government strength to overcome resistance from outsider-inclusive trade unions. Unlike the Austrian

ÖVP-FPÖ government, the Swedish alliance displayed a remarkable level of internal cohesiveness to formulate a common policy agenda, in part due to the absence of a right-wing populist party inside the coalition. Unlike the Danish V-K government, the Swedish alliance also had a majority of seats and was thus not reliant on exchanges with support parties from the opposition. Second, a reference to the erosion of Swedish macrocorporatism fails to explain why Swedish governments did not even pursue tripartite deals with the top-level associations in the first place. Producer group theorists, therefore, underestimate the autonomous reform capacity of strong governments. If anything, in fact, the central operator of the government—the Moderate Party—emphatically rejected significant influence from any other political actor in labor market policy, whereas the employers simply pushed for more radical policy changes. In the words of Eva Uddén Sonnegård, who was state secretary of the Moderate Party at the Ministry of Employment (2006–2010): "Everything that had to do with labor market policy came from us, because we had worked so much on this issue already before the Allians was formed."[8]

The autonomous reform capacity of the Reinfeldt cabinets essentially rested on two strategic properties: first, the unification process toward a common electoral platform allowed the government to formulate a cohesive policy agenda prior to the 2006 election, which reflected a clear transformation of the traditionally fragmented center-right bloc. The formation of the Allians started out with an invitation of the Center Party leader, Maud Olofsson, to the other three leaders of the center-right parties to her home in 2004 (Aylott and Bolin 2007, 625). Crucial to the formation of the subsequent electoral platform was the initiative of the Moderate Party leader, Fredrik Reinfeldt, to coordinate the different partisan platforms into a common program targeted against Social Democratic hegemony (Aylott and Bolin 2007, 625). In the words of Sven-Otto Littorin, minister of employment (2006–2010) in relation to the Moderate Party:

> We did something very fortunate: And that was forming the 'Alliance,' the four non-socialist parties into one group. We were lucky with that, because there were new leaders in the other three parties. There was a consensus that this has to be done. It was our only chance, we had to do it.[9]

Second, the extraordinary success in the 2006 election provided the "Alliance for Sweden" with an unprecedented majority of seats to pass their agenda in parliament—a peak-level "window of opportunity" in a Swedish context. This success may in large part be attributed to the Moderates' shift to the center ground on economic affairs in response to its massive defeat in the 2002 election. Following this centrist turn, the party successfully framed economic inactivity as a threat to the fiscal and moral sustainability of the Swedish welfare state. Unlike the neoliberal postures of the party's past, the Moderates thus claimed to safeguard the "Swedish model" by creating jobs for all through a "make work pay" agenda (Agius 2007). Despite robust economic growth and fiscal surpluses, the previous Social Democratic government indeed faced difficulties in responding to labor market exclusion: unemployment rates remained relatively high from a diachronic perspective, especially among immigrants and young people, as discussed earlier. In fact, the actual level of open unemployment became greatly contested, as a growing share of workers had become deemed "incapable to work" due to sickness or disability benefit receipt. Placing the labor market situation front and center, the Moderates managed to strike at the very heart of the SAP's core vocabulary of "full employment." In fact, as Lindbom (2008) pointed out, the party had at the ready a new problem for the mobilization of a traditionalist conservative reform program. Therefore, the major strategic change took place with respect to the rhetoric of the party, but not its genuine policy preference. On top of this centrist recast, Reinfeldt renamed his party the "New Moderates" (Nya Moderaterna) and the "New Worker's Party" (Nya Arbetarpartiet) to buttress the credibility of its agenda behind the classic SAP-like goal of full employment.

Thanks to a united parliamentary majority, the Allians was able to push through an impressive reform program within two months after its election victory in October 2006 (Davidsson 2011; Sjöberg 2011; Gordon 2012). At its most basic, the "make work pay" agenda implied reductions in the access to and generosity of social benefits to finance income tax cuts for low-income and middle income workers as well as payroll tax cuts for employers. By handling the agenda in this way, the official idea was to boost work incentives for people who were out of work by increasing the gap between wage income and transfer income, while actually pitting the interests of workers with stable jobs (insiders) against those with high unemployment risks (outsiders). First, the government legislated substantial cuts in unemployment benefit generosity: the replacement rate was cut from 80 to 70 percent for 200 days of unemployment and to 65 percent for unemployed with children after 300 days; the maximum benefit ceiling was reduced from 730 to 680 SEK to the level of 2002; the reference period for the calculation of benefit levels was extended from six to twelve months.

Second, the government tightened eligibility criteria in various ways. Firstly, and most notably, the possibility to qualify for unemployment benefits through periods at university was abolished for students—namely, 18 percent of the unemployed lost access to benefit receipt (Sjöberg 2011, 218). Additionally, the suitability criteria were substantially tightened by abolishing the right of unemployed workers to seek a job within their occupation and local residence within the first one hundred days of joblessness. Furthermore, the benefit duration for part-time unemployed was reduced from 300 to 75 days, thereby threatening the social rights of women in particular. Finally, the waiting period was extended from five to seven days; access to benefits for the long-term unemployed (more than three hundred days) were abolished unless they had children or participated in "job and development guarantee," which provided a replacement rate of 65 percent.

Third, and most controversially, the government increased and differentiated the level of fees for membership in the union-run and voluntary unemployment benefit funds (Clasen and Viebrock 2008, 444–445). This implied two changes in the funding mechanism. In the first place, the average monthly unemployment insurance contribution was raised more than threefold. Moreover, the level of contribution payments was differentiated according to the risk of unemployment, thereby making membership in the benefit funds less attractive for workers with high unemployment risks. In effect, the share of outlays covered by membership fees was raised from 9.5 percent in 2004 to 46 percent in 2007. As a result, the number of members covered by unemployment insurance fell from 3.8 million to 3.3 million, union density decreased from 75 percent to 68 percent, while the LO lost a full 15 percent of its membership within one year after reform had taken effect (Kjellberg 2011). Taken together, while the SAP achieved spending cuts primarily at the expense of active labor market policy and the benefit entitlements of middle-income and high-income workers, the 2006 reform of the center-right hit the unemployment protection of outsiders and the viability of encompassing union membership (Gordon 2012, 262).

The legislation of a reform of this profound scope within a period of two months suggests that the Allians was not in any way bothered by the opposition of the union confederations. In fact, the Ministry of Employment had to push this change through parliament without accepting the incorporations of any union demands that would lead to a deviation from the initial proposal of the government. Mats Wadman, senior official at the Ministry Employment from 1988 to 2007, described the formal hearing of union responses to the reform plans of the government in an interview with the author:

> They just took the society into a hearing and listened to them. And then they just said: "Okay, we heard what you said, but we will do this anyway." I have never seen the heads of the trade unions and others so angry, because it was a very strange meeting.[10]

Part of the explanation for this unilateral reform strategy comes from the central relevance of the 2006 reform to the overall "make work pay" agenda, which was the core of the government's election campaign. Another part of the explanation comes from the government's perception that the LO leadership would face difficulties in mobilizing their membership against its reform plan. In an interview with the author, the minister of employment (2006–2010), Sven-Otto Littorin, named the LO as the most forceful union confederation in opposition to the successful legislation of the reform, but also said:

> Even though the top of the LO would have liked to smash us, we felt we had a stronger support among the members than the leadership had because they had a long time trying to do something with the problems that we had seen before, but nothing happened. And that was what actually happened in the 2006 election: we got a much stronger support from the LO membership than never before I think.[11]

Perhaps not surprisingly, all three union confederations heavily opposed this policy package. In the month before the unemployment insurance reform had taken effect, in December 2006, the LO organized a nationwide protest of 39,000 participants and mobilized a petition against the reform signed by 280,000 people.[12] Despite these protest activities, the speed of the government in legislating this reform inhibited the mobilizing capacity of the LO. In the words of Thomas Carlén, labor market policy expert at the LO:

> I think they caught us off-guard and we started to protest quite late. We protested during the election in debates. We lost these debates, as you can see. And when the reform was decided in parliament, then we started to protest much more, but then it was too late, of course. So I think we woke up too late to realize that this is for real. Basically, we underestimated them.

The TCO also heavily opposed this reform in public debates, but did not dare to join the LO in mobilizing petitions or mass demonstrations. In the words of Sture Nordh:

> LO did some demonstrations here in Stockholm or other parts of the country. We were invited to join them but we said: No, thank you. That is due to the non-political status that we have. We have a trade union mission. We will criticize any government that does not do what we want, and we will try to influence any government. But we would not have the members to get out on the streets, because a lot of our members had voted for the Alliance. . . . It is also a risk for the union, given that we don't have the tradition of mobilizing people on the streets. What if we failed? Then we would lose the entire argument for the rest of the term as well.

At the same time, in 2006–2007, the Allians deregulated fixed-term contracts by doubling the maximum duration of temporary contracts to twenty-four months and abolishing the obligation on the part of the employer to justify the use of temporary work. To the great disappointment of the employers' association, the government, however, left the LAS framework for permanent workers untouched and kept the "last-in, first-out" principle. The Liberals and the Center Party would have preferred a liberalization of the LAS framework, but the Nya Moderaterna prevented any step in this direction. The official justification of this choice was that the LAS merely changes the composition, but not the level of unemployment.[13] Accordingly, the LAS would thus not contradict the government's ambition to achieve full employment. In response, the employers addressed the unions to find a new agreement—without success. The job security regulations for permanent workers remain strong, while the government expanded the subsidization of low-wage work through the gradual introduction of a series of in-work tax credits (Nystarjobben) and obligations in return for benefit entitlements (Spohr 2012, 244–251).

Judging from public opinion data, approval ratings of the center-right government's policies did not remain unaffected by the mobilization of union protests. In 2008, the center-left opposition was clearly in the lead in national representative surveys ("Opposition Opens Up Record Poll Lead" 2008). Yet the subsequent decline of unemployment rates boosted the efforts of the government to legitimize their reform agenda. In the 2010 election, the "Alliance for Sweden" lost its majority despite a modest increase in the vote, as the radical right-wing Sweden Democrats successfully entered parliament. The loss of a majority and the successful accomplishment of "make work pay" reforms in the first tenure of the center-right government restrained the reform frenzy of tax and welfare cuts in the subsequent period. If anything, however, the strength of the first Reinfeldt cabinet was sufficient to significantly reinforce a dualistic reform path.

Conclusion

The pronounced dualization path of Sweden cannot be understood without recognizing the power-distributional interaction between a weakened peak union confederation and a strengthened government. Membership losses and labor fragmentation definitely underpinned a decline in union strength during the neoliberal era. However, this in itself did not rule out political exchanges with the LO. In fact, governments in noncorporatist economies sought labor-inclusive "social pacts" with weakened union confederations precisely in the 1990s, when the SAP set in motion a relegation of the LO's influence in the interest of "sound public finances" (Hamann and Kelly 2007). Faced by the economic crisis of the early 1990s, the SAP came to follow the policy recommendations of liberal economists, and not the LO. The novel cross-class collaboration with the Center Party allowed the SAP to find the parliamentary majority necessary to eschew labor acquiescence. Ironically, the SAP's fiscal consolidation agenda against the opposition of the LO paved the way for a seemingly Social Democratic-like agenda for full employment; one, however, that came from the political right, and not the left. The subsequent "make work pay" agenda reinforced an ongoing trend by pushing the union movement out of the reform process. Sven-Otto Littorin made no secret of the Conservatives' unilateral reform strategy: "In the term I served, we were a majority government, so in that respect we felt fairly secure and confident in actually getting things through. And we were fairly confident that what we were doing was the right thing."

I argued that the strength of the SAP and Allians to formulate and pass policy change independent of union support put constraints on the capacity of organized labor to strike deals on behalf of outsiders. The active inclusion of trade unions in the deliberation of policy changes would have helped a minority coalition that lacks parliamentary support to establish a broad consensus around controversial issues. For example, if the Center Party had not provided the SAP with a majority through a cooperation agreement from 1995 to 1998, the SAP would not have been able to pursue its dualistic labor market policy changes. It is clear that the Left Party supported the LO in rejecting the ensuing cuts in benefit entitlements and job security for fixed-term contracts.

Perhaps the clearest demonstration of government strength came from the policy performance of the Allians. Equipped with a parliamentary majority, the center-right coalition did not even consider the idea of pursuing labor-inclusive exchanges. If the Reinfeldt government, however, had not had a united majority, it would have faced reform deadlocks similar to the previous center-right government in office from 1976 to 1982. The Danish case may provide a factual scenario to buttress this position. During the late 1980s, the Danish center-right minority government opted for a labor-inclusive reform strategy when the opposition refrained from supporting its policy proposals (see chapter 3). In consequence, the Danish prime minister, Poul Schlüter, considered a policy deal with the trade unions the most durable strategy to find parliamentary support for a structural reform of the labor market. The result of this labor-inclusive reform strategy was the expansion of active labor market policies, and not the government's initial plan of cutting benefit entitlements unilaterally.

While the *direction* of labor market reform was similar across different governments, this chapter also highlights significant partisan differences in the degree of *dualization*. In other words, it would be implausible to assume that a majoritarian center-left government would have introduced the same labor market reforms as the Allians in the late 2000s. The "modernization" of the SAP took place in response to the country's serious economic crisis at a time of weakened labor movements and enhanced capital mobility. Moderate dualization was thus a way of reconciling risk protection with the structural imperatives of fiscal consolidation and labor market flexibility. For the political right, by contrast, the crucial role of the Ghent system for union organization had always provided a strategic incentive to mobilize political support for radical cuts to unemployment insurance. The SAP's consent to an emergent dualism in connection with persistent unemployment created opportunities for the Allians to legitimize such an agenda.

The central driver of Swedish dualization was not the vote-seeking action of governments, as suggested by partisanship theorists. A view that puts voters front and center would have expected an outsider-oriented policy shift from the SAP to accommodate to the egalitarian preference structure of the Swedish electorate. At the same time, the political cause of Swedish dualization was not the action of cross-class coalitions, as suggested by producer group theorists. A producer group perspective would have assigned governments and employers an interest in maintaining cooperative relations with encompassing union movements. Both theoretical expectations are wrong, because they downplay the structural incentive for governments to prioritize business demands over the social protection of outsiders. With an (i) autonomous ideological outlook and (ii) a united majority, Swedish governments were strong enough to impose such a dualizing reform strategy without any reliance on union consent. These two assets of Swedish governments best explain why the LO was surprisingly unsuccessful in protecting outsiders.

STRONG GOVERNMENTS AND PRECARIOUS WORKERS IN THE ERA OF LIBERALIZATION

Governments and Unions in the Era of Liberalization

The defining political feature of the liberalization era has been a decline in union strength and an increase in business power. This shift in class power pushed governments in the preferred direction of employers and weakened the structural incentive to provide organized labor with a material compensation for public policy changes (Streeck 2009; Baccaro and Howell 2011; Culpepper and Regan 2014). But governments cannot impose any agreement on unions, when their autonomous reform capacity is constrained by intracoalitional divisions or a hung parliament. Under these conditions of weakness, governments faced a political incentive to trade policy concessions for union support in the mobilization of a durable consensus. This weakness has been instrumental in forcing governments to negotiate different forms of compensation for liberalizing reforms with unions.

This finding has significant implications for precisely those groups of workers who are most reliant on democratic state interventions in the operation of a capitalist economy: the "outsiders." They face the costs of liberalization in particular, as they are unemployed or have atypical jobs that often lack security. This is an increasingly numerous group of low-skilled, female, and young workers that is strongly exposed to the risks of being attached to the labor market in precarious ways (Häusermann and Schwander 2015). In popular democratic theory, we would expect the responsiveness of political parties to increase with the growing number of outsiders in the electorate. In reality, however, the governments in

Austria, Denmark, and Sweden only responded to the social needs of outsiders when their own weakness forced them to pursue exchanges with organized labor. Ironically, therefore, the protection of the weakest labor market segments relies on the presence of weak governments, since they lack the capacity to shield their economies from the political demands of organized labor.

My argument rests on a comparative investigation of one policy area that is of profound relevance to the social protection of outsiders: labor market policy. It provides social security and reintegration support in the event of unemployment, while regulating job security arrangements for those who are employed. The liberalization of labor market institutions has become the central tool available for job creation due to the structural constraints of monetarism and austerity in a globalizing capitalist economy. National political actors therefore pursued tighter obligations for the unemployed in return for benefit support, while deregulating temporary forms of employment to create entry points for those at the margins of the workforce. However, some countries compensated outsiders for this liberalization with changes that expand training-based active labor market policy (ALMP) and mitigate status divisions in employment and welfare standards, while others, in contrast, restricted the coverage of protection arrangements to workers with stable employment biographies and refused to provide enhanced training (or retraining) opportunities for the unemployed. These differences are fundamental to the distributive outcomes of economic liberalization in a given capitalist regime.

Yet, as of the 1990s, political parties of all orientations have shifted toward a market-conforming policy outlook and thus prioritized employer demands over the social protection of outsiders. In the absence of Keynesian policy instruments, governments instead aimed at job creation through the expansion of flexible low-wage employment and activation. While the political right was the main partisan force behind dualization, the Social Democratic parties supported at least moderate cuts in the employment and social rights of outsiders. As a result, partisanship influenced the *degree* of dualization. What made a difference with respect to the *direction* of reform, however, was the level of government strength. More specifically, weak center-right governments enhanced the protection of outsiders, because they were unable to exclude organized labor from the policy-making process. Strong center-left governments, by contrast, did the opposite by downgrading union influence.

Building on a strong electoral mandate, the policy performance of the Swedish SAP government (1994–2006) was perhaps the clearest example of a Social Democratic Party leadership that was willing (and able) to legislate moderate dualistic reforms in order to boost job creation without introducing rising public deficits.[1] To be sure, Sweden was hit particularly hard by the public debt crisis of the early 1990s. But the remarkably successful fiscal consolidation in following decades did not induce a significant compensation for growing unemployment and fixed-term employment (Palme et al. 2009; Haffert and Mehrtens 2015). The subsequent center-right majority government markedly reinforced this dualistic reform trend, suggesting that the SAP's previous reforms paved the way for a marked break with welfare universalism (Gordon 2017). In a similar vein, the Austrian SPÖ under Franz Vranitzky (1986–1997) and Viktor Klima (1997–2000) accepted social-spending cuts in response to the Maastricht criteria, whereas the ÖVP demanded more of the same market-conforming adjustment agenda. The Danish Socialdemokraterne (1993–2001) largely adhered to the Flexicurity deal reached by employers and unions under the previous center-right government, but the center-left cabinet under Thorning-Schmidt (2011–2015) refused to reverse previous cuts in unemployment protection and went even further than the political right by linking tax cuts for people in employment with welfare cuts for people out of work. In all these instances, the transformation of the center-left responded to shifts in class power that emerged from competitiveness demands in conjunction with austerity and monetarism.

An alternative way of explaining the partisan reform ambitions behind dualization is to claim that voters have a low level of political solidarity with unemployed wage earners relative to benefit recipients in sickness, disability, or old-age welfare plans (Alber 1982; Pierson 1994; Van Oorschot 2006; Giger and Nelson 2011). In that sense, as Rueda (2007) argues, the selective protection of "insiders" may be a vote-seeking device in hard times. That "outsiders" have indeed a lower probability to vote than "insiders" could have strengthened this electoral calculus all the more (Schäfer 2013). It could therefore be argued that parties have little to fear from an increasingly numerous group of outsiders, because their social needs are not significant in electoral terms.

But such a view is inconsistent with the fact that political parties imposed unilateral cutbacks on outsiders *despite* the presence of egalitarian welfare attitudes in Denmark and Sweden (see Larsen 2008; Goul Andersen 2011a; Svallfors 2011). Moreover, polling and survey data show that the electorate reacted negatively against cuts in the protection of outsiders in both countries. In Denmark, the Social Democratic Party lost support from its core voters due to tightened activation demands during the 1990s (Arndt 2013), while in 2000 and 2008, three quarters of nationwide representative surveys stated that access to unemployment benefits should be a universal social right (Goul Andersen 2011b, 16). The political right had thus faced wide criticism for retrenching the inclusiveness of unemployment protection in 2011, but the subsequent center-left government still broke its promise to reverse the reform. On the contrary, it lost a whole six percentage points when it presented the 2012 tax reform that linked cuts in taxes and welfare (Goul Andersen 2012a, 10). In a similar vein, voter demands played a minor role in Sweden. Survey evidence indicated ongoing high (albeit slightly declining) levels of support for unemployment benefits (Svallfors 2011), while the SAP paid a high price for stubbornly high levels of labor market exclusion at the 2006 election (Aylott and Bolin 2007). In addition, the subsequent center-right government lost its majority in approval ratings when it legislated comprehensive cuts in the generosity and inclusiveness of unemployment benefits in 2007 ("Opposition Opens Up Record Poll Lead" 2008).

Why, then, should even Social Democratic parties cut back the protection of outsiders? This leads me to the impact of class power on the policy preferences of governments. It is clear that governments not only have to respond to the electorate, but also the demands of job creation (Polanyi 1944). The gradual stages of liberalization—monetarism and capital account and trade liberalization (late 1970s), the prioritization of inflation control over unemployment (1980s), fiscal austerity and the creation of EMU (1990), and the socialization of bad loans (post-2008)—contributed to a macroeconomic context that favored the removal of constraints on employers' strategies of capital accumulation for successful employment performance (Baccaro and Howell 2011; Streeck 2011). This structural constraint on the governing capacities of political parties has clear class power implications by creating opportunities for employers to push for stronger discretion in setting the terms and conditions of employment (McCarthy 2017).

The partisan shift to dualization appears therefore to be more in line with a view that highlights the shift in class power from labor to capital during the era of liberalization. This explains why Social Democratic partisanship has become associated with (moderate) dualization (Emmenegger et al. 2012, 311), although such parties attract electoral support from outsiders (Häusermann et al. 2015). For example, Jens Christiansen, the campaign director of the Danish Social Democrats in the 2011 election, was quick to point out that the Thorning-Schmidt cabinet consented to employer demands as means to stimulate economic growth—and thus electoral success—in the face of capital mobility. In a similar vein, Dan Andersson, the chief economist from the Swedish Trade Union Confederation (LO), observed an "enormous influence of new liberal economists" inside the SAP when the Swedish postwar model broke down in the early 1990s, giving way to a fiscal policy, "which most Conservatives had advocated 100 years ago."[2]

An electoral claim along the lines of Rueda (2007) is also inconsistent with respect to the smoothening of status divisions in Austria, given that his account predicts a reinforcement of insider-outsider divides in countries with a Conservative institutional legacy. Contrary to these expectations, electoral dynamics had little effect, because the social partners remained the key political operators of labor market and welfare policies. Finally, his theoretical prediction that union movements do not push for the regulation (or reregulation) of temporary employment and an expansion of social security coverage and training-based ALMP spending—that is, outsider-supportive policies—was falsified in all three cases over the entire period of investigation.

Unlike political parties, *inclusive trade unions* with high levels of density and unity have an acute interest in the social protection of outsiders. High density rates integrate outsiders directly into the membership base of unions, while an administrative power position on social security and ALMP boards gives a strategic incentive to push for generous and inclusive labor market policy arrangements. It should thus come as no surprise that unions in the Ghent countries of Denmark and Sweden supported universal social rights for the unemployed. This finding is consistent with Thelen's (2014) claim that encompassing unionization is important for the incorporation of outsiders into union politics (see also Gordon 2015). Moreover, the case of Austria suggests that high levels of labor unity through concentration and centralization may compensate for rapidly falling membership rates in the representational scope of union politics. It broadens the inclusiveness of union confederations by providing affiliates from the low-value-added service sector with a relevant voice in the interest formation process. Their overwhelming problem is how to undermine the labor market competition from atypical employment contracts, which allow employers to circumvent the prevailing restrictions of employment and labor law. The successful extension of social rights to atypical workers was a way of undermining this competition in Austria, because it imposed the payment of social insurance contributions on employers. Following this line of action, the weaker member unions of the ÖGB could regain bargaining power vis-à-vis employers, shield their members from flexible low-wage competition, and reach out to atypically employed workers. Seen in this way, the Conservative welfare state architecture provided clear material incentives for centralized unions to oppose dualization and mobilize political support for outsiders instead.

Yet, regardless of organizational inclusiveness, trade unions in the advanced capitalist political economies lost a great deal of their political assertiveness in the reform process. Yet, conventional producer group approaches seem to have paid more attention to cross-national differences in class *preferences* than to the common shift in the balance of class *power*. Martin and Swank (2012, 171), for example, emphasize that encompassing peak-level associations of labor and business "allow for a wider range of interests to engage collectively in articulating and implementing updated policy intervention." Placing more emphasis on labor, Thelen (2014, 204) similarly concludes that high levels of inclusiveness on the part of unions are "indispensable for continued high levels of social solidarity." Their research was instructive in showing that the fragmentation of (postindustrial) interests on both sides of the class divide required the incorporation of broad segments into the peak-level associations to fulfill a "solidaristic" role in the politics of economic adjustment.

But the dominant focus on preferences implies that producer group approaches tend to underestimate the declining power of unions to impose constraints on the reform ambitions of governments. In spite of long-standing traditions of consensus democracy, the labor movements in Denmark and Sweden mobilized public protests in front of parliament against unilateral cuts in the inclusiveness (2011 in Copenhagen) and the general dismantling of unemployment protection (2007 in Stockholm). Moreover, the Austrian ÖGB organized unprecedented mass demonstrations and industrial action in response to the 2003 pension reform, which reduced the public pension entitlements of workers with discontinuous employment histories. But the impact of union protests on the final policy output remained largely absent because the governments proceeded unilaterally, without offering any form of compensation to organized labor. This shows that even inclusive unions are no longer powerful enough to stand in the way of unilateral government action, although they continue to be institutionally entrenched in the administration of unemployment protection arrangements.

Unlike trade unions, governments continue to be strong when they are equipped with a united majority in parliament. Ideological cohesiveness and a majority of seats makes them capable of overriding union organizations that refuse to consent to cutbacks for outsiders. Not surprisingly, therefore, the strongest government observed in my case selection—the Swedish center-right "Alliance"—had the most powerful impact on dualization by marginalizing the union movement in the policy-making process. Its political power stemmed from a common political program along the mantra of "make work pay." Notably, they achieved a united majority in the 2006 election without having to rely on the support from a right-wing populist party. Leaving aside other factors here, this was a notable difference to center-right governments in Austria and Denmark. Unlike the Swedish "Alliance," they had to incorporate the policy preferences of right-wing populist parties, which are often attached to the electoral demands of the (native) blue-collar working class (Afonso 2015; Röth et al. 2017). In Austria, the FPÖ, when in government, blocked significant parts of the ÖVP's labor market policy agenda, as this populist grassroots wing of the party aimed to represent the interests of the "common man." The Danish People's Party, by contrast, was merely a support party of the Liberal-Conservative minority government, but traded cuts in welfare universalism for restrictions in immigration and asylum policies.

Understanding how unions can still impose their claims on political parties requires detailed attention to the autonomous reform capacity of national governments. Governments are unable to suppress the claims of unions when they themselves are unable to formulate and pass reforms independent from organized interests. Under this condition, governments of *all* partisan orientation have a powerful political incentive to share policy-making authority with unions because they require an extraparliamentary channel of consensus mobilization. One way that governments become weak is through intracoalitional divisions between ideologically divided parties. The Austrian grand coalition instructively demonstrated this type of weakness, given that its recognition for the necessity of consensus went hand in hand with mutual reform blockages between similarly strong coalition partners. Another way that governments become weak is when they lack of parliamentary support in a polarized party system. The Danish center-right minority coalition of the late 1980s stood out in this regard, given its weak position in parliament due to low electoral support and the adversarial stance of the opposition. In both cases, national governments fell back on labor-inclusive negotiations to mobilize a durable consensus in the interest of successful economic adjustment.

In sum, I found the power-distributional interaction between an inclusive union movement and a politically weak government to be the dominant coalition behind the material compensation of outsiders for economic liberalization. An inclusive union organization incorporated the interests of outsiders into the producer group arena. But it was the presence of a politically weak government that created the necessary opportunities for unions to achieve policy influence on behalf of outsiders. Previous chapters therefore explored how variations in the strength of governments influenced the success of trade unions in enhancing the protection of outsiders. In the next section of this concluding chapter, I will discuss the potential limitations and extensions of this argument.

Limitations and Extensions

The argument of this book is a result of qualitative comparative research on labor market policy in Austria, Denmark, and Sweden. It is therefore rich in empirical depth and causal tests, but it could not be applied in detail to a broad range of cases within the confined space of a single book. To assess the generalizability of my argument, I first outline two potential limitations resulting from my selection of country cases. I then attempt to extend my argument to the cases of Italy and Spain to show how my argument may still provide us with a better understanding of the broader phenomenon of labor market reform in national contexts of liberalization that are diverse from the ones studied in this book.

The first potential limitation of my argument emerges from its empirical focus on three small Western European states with similar corporatist legacies (Katzenstein 1985). This similarity refers to the presence of institutionalized channels of tripartite macrobargaining and national peak-level associations that have strong microfoundations at the workplace level. It could therefore be argued that my argument has no explanatory merit for other states that are noncorporatist and large in size. Yet the fundamental fact that corporatist legacies were not sufficient for the policy-making influence of organized labor may point to mechanisms applicable to a broader set of countries. Tellingly, my argument on variations of government strength drew on the social pact literature, which primarily looked at countries *without* corporatist legacies. In fact, the claim that weak governments are more likely to strike policy deals with unions originated from studies on noncorporatist cases such as Ireland, Italy, and South Korea (Baccaro and Lim 2007; Baccaro and Simoni 2008). Tripartite policy-making forums today appear therefore less influential on the reform strategy pursued by national governments than in the Keynesian postwar era.

The second potential limitation, however, is more difficult to refute. As I have emphasized, my case selection covers only countries with relatively inclusive union movements. They may thus had stronger incentives to mobilize political support for outsiders than union movements in countries with lower levels of inclusiveness. Let us recall that the union movements of Denmark and Sweden pushed for the protection of outsiders, because they incorporated many workers at risk of unemployment into their membership base. High levels of density in connection with the Ghent systems gave unions a strategic incentive to strike policy deals for outsiders. The union movement of Austria, by contrast, had an acute interest in the protection of outsiders, because the strong authority of the confederate level in a highly concentrated labor movement empowered the voice of member unions hit hardest by precarious labor standards. By implication, where unions lack (i) members at risk of unemployment as well as (ii) the centralized structure to give voice to precarious workers, they should be less able to represent outsiders effectively.

The expectation that exclusive union movements are less able than their inclusive counterparts to protect outsiders requires a conceptual distinction between *preferences* and *priorities*. Preferences, on this reading, describe a number of first-best policy goals laid out in official statements and manifestos. For example, in Italy, all three union confederations established specific organizations for the interest representation of atypical workers during the late 1990s, which aimed to undermine the emergence of insider-outsider divides (Durazzi 2017). Yet trade unions face power relationships and institutional legacies that rule out the achievement of "ideal" policy outcomes vis-à-vis governments and business; that is to say, they have to pursue second-best policy choices. Priorities decide over the kind of preferences trade unions are willing to sacrifice to achieve concessions in areas to which they attach the highest strategic importance. Faced with organizational disunity and a declining (and aging) membership base in tandem with growing pressures for liberalization, such labor movements no longer had the political capacity to pursue maximalist solutions that satisfy the social needs of permanent workers ("insiders") and atypical or unemployed workers ("outsiders") at the same time. They thus prioritized the demands of their core membership over those of atypical workers, even though they *would* have preferred a redirection of labor market policy in the interest of *all* workers.[3] Or, in the words of Walter Korpi (2006), exclusive union movements should be seen as "consenters" to dualistic reforms (in case they were actually asked to consent), but the "protagonist" of this outcome remains capital.

The above reflections about the limitations of my case selection allow me to sharpen the theoretical propositions of my argument. First, I contend that variations in government strength have a *similar* impact on the level of union influence in a diverse set of European countries: the weaker the government, the stronger the influence of unions. This argument rests on the empirical observation that corporatist legacies were neither sufficient for union influence in Austria, Denmark, and Sweden, nor necessary for the conclusion of labor-inclusive social pacts in noncorporatist countries. Second, the involvement of unions has a *dissimilar* impact on the protection of outsiders in a diverse set of European countries: the higher the inclusiveness of union movements, the more they push for outsider-oriented policy choices when invited to reform negotiations. This claim rests on the empirical observation that differences in inclusiveness increased over time (Hassel 2015), and that these differences impact on the representational outlook of unions (Thelen 2014; Gordon 2015). It follows that I expect reform negotiations with unions characterized by low levels of inclusiveness—measured in terms of density and centralization rates—to be less effective in compensating outsiders for liberalizing government reforms.

The next section of this chapter briefly examines these two propositions in the Italian and Spanish cases based on an analysis of secondary literature. A brief consideration of these two countries has the methodological advantage that they are very different from the ones studied in this book. First, both cases are noncorporatist and large in size. Across these differences, I will show, variations in government strength had a remarkably similar impact on the capacity of trade unions to influence the policy output. Only when governments were weak—as in the case of Italy—did unions achieve formal policy influence. When governments were strong—as in the case of Spain—unions faced a gradual marginalization. Second, both cases feature relatively decentralized union movements that lack an encompassing membership base. Italian unions thus prioritized the protection of permanent workers, but their policy influence still moderated the *degree* of dualization relative to the unilateral government action that was dominant in Spain.

As a result, the process of dualization started later in time and was less pronounced in in Italy than in Spain (Bulfone 2016; Picot and Tassinari 2017). A crucial factor that helps understand this variation is the stronger autonomy of Spanish governments relative to their Italian counterparts (Molina and Rhodes 2007). A lower number of constitutional veto points and the dominance of single-party governments with relatively strong executive powers, formed either by the socialist PSOE (Partido Socialista Obrero Españo) or the right-wing PP (Partido Popular), allows political parties in Spain to pursue radical reforms against the interests of organized labor. This contrasts with the prevalence of either multiparty or technocratic governments in Italy, which were haunted by instable power relations and constitutional veto points.

Following the argument of this book, I claim that the variation in the strength of governments helps explain why Spanish unions were less successful in preventing growing insider-outsider divides than their Italian counterparts (see also Molina and Rhodes 2007, 2011; Hamann and Kelly 2011). During the Great Recession, however, the labor movements of both countries lost influence, which paved the way for a deregulation of dismissal protection at the expense of *permanent* workers in both countries. Notably, however, the Italian "Jobs Act" in 2014 linked reduced dismissal protection with expanded coverage of unemployment benefits (Picot and Tassinari 2017).

Evidence from the Mediterranean: Italy and Spain

Italy and Spain constitute the Mediterranean "mixed-market" type of capitalism (Molina and Rhodes 2007). Unlike the small and corporatist cases studied in this book, they display fragmented industrial relations with relatively weak coordination capacities and high levels of industrial conflict. The union movements of both countries developed a more conflict-oriented outlook than in Northwestern Europe, because their historical formation in the postwar era was met with state repression (Bonoli and Emmenegger 2010). This created ideological divisions between different wings of the labor movement, which were conducive to the formation of fragmented and particularistic interests. State interventions are therefore required to compensate for the lacking capacities of organized interests to coordinate the national political economy (Molina and Rhodes 2007).

In Spain, the PSOE's neoliberal turn to unilateral government action in the 1980s and 1990s seems to underline that government strength has become more influential than left-right differences in partisanship. After having signed a social pact on wage moderation and fixed-term contracts in return for increased public spending with one of the two dominant union confederations in 1984, the UGT (Unión General de Trabajadores), the socialist government ruled out any formal concessions and welcomed the rapid spread of temporary employment as a way of reducing labor costs to fight unemployment (Molina and Rhodes 2011, 180–181). Between 1984 and 1997, therefore, there was no formal policy agreement between the PSOE government and organized labor. In 1992, the single-party majority government of the PSOE effectively imposed a cut in the maximum benefit duration by one third on the unemployed, which led the entire union movement to call a general strike (Knotz and Lindvall 2015, 607–608). Public protests did not induce any form of compensation for this cutback. In a similar vein, the 1994 labor market reform was unilaterally legislated with the tacit support of the center-right Catalan CiU (Convergécia i Unió) because the union movement rejected the proposed expansion of part-time contracts, private employment agencies, and the decentralization of collective bargaining (Molina and Rhodes 2011, 184–185). Again, the 1994 general strike did not induce the government to renew talks with the unions. In sum, the PSOE successfully rejected the unions' demands for a reregulation of fixed-term contracts; although more than one third in total employment was in temporary contracts at that time, thereby displaying the highest figures in the OECD countries (Mato 2011).

With the 1996 election, the incoming center-right coalition between the PP and three right-wing regionalist parties was in a minority position and thus relatively weak by Spanish standards (Hamann and Kelly 2011, 118; Molina and Rhodes 2011, 185). Its weak position on the one hand, and the union's previous failure to threaten the PSOE with industrial action on the other, contributed to a favorable context for a political exchange. In the 1997 social pact, the unions successfully obtained measures to counter the spread of fixed-term contracts and recentralize collective bargaining. A change in government did not undermine union influence in Spain, as the PSOE was also in a minority position backed up by two small (leftist) parties. The unions could sign a bipartite pact that "included a general commitment to employment stability and quality" with the employers in 2001 (Molina and Rhodes 2011, 189) and another labor market reform aimed at limiting the incidence of temporary employment in 2006 (Molina and Rhodes 2011, 191). To sum up, in the words of Molina and Rhodes, "one of our more robust conclusions is that government weakness is the best predictor of successful pacting, alongside relations between and within the Spanish unions" (2011, 175). Responding to the rapid growth of temporary employment contracts, the union movement indeed used the conclusion of social pacts to enhance the protection of outsiders by countering the pronounced dualism in job security regulations. But the impact of their achievements remained limited, as the share of temporary contracts in the labor force fell only modestly from 33.5 percent in 1997 to 31.8 percent a decade later (Molina and Rhodes 2011, 175). At the same time, fiscal austerity undermined the expansion of unemployment support, while weak coordination capacities of the public employment service were detrimental to the activation of the unemployed (Mato 2011).

Building on a parliamentary majority, the PP government was able to respond to the Great Recession (and subsequent Eurozone crisis) with a unilateral reform strategy, which included a substantial dismantling of job security for permanent workers and another decentralization of collective bargaining (Picot and Tassinari 2017). Notably, the PP emphatically rejected increased spending on unemployment support to compensate organized labor for growing economic uncertainty on a volatile labor market with record high unemployment. Once again, a general strike had no effect on the final policy output. While principally remaining a Conservative regime in character, this state intervention was decisive in moving Spain in the direction of an Anglo-American type of deregulation (Picot and Tassinari 2017). The autonomous reform capacity of single-party majority governments appears to be a crucial factor behind the unions' inability to defend the job security of insiders (during the Great Recession) and strike concessions for outsiders (during the 1980s and 1990s). Importantly, the main union confederations were excluded from reform deliberations in most instances, so it would be questionable to attribute the distributive outcomes of the Spanish dualization path to union preferences. Rather, it was the lack of capacity to resist unilateral government action under the conditions of a strong government. If anything, in fact, the unions mobilized on various occasions public support for the growing number of fixed-term workers, albeit prioritizing the employment protection of permanent workers at the same time.

Italian governments were much weaker than their Spanish counterparts. During the early 1990s, the collapse of the party system in the wake of anti-corruption investigations led to a series of technocratic and instable party governments that relied on extraparliamentary support in the mobilization of political consensus and legitimacy (Baccaro and Lim 2007; Baccaro and Simoni 2008). Proof of this commitment to tripartite economic adjustment came with two important social pacts aimed at reforming the wage-setting regime in 1993 and 1994. Following the subsequent 1994 election, Silvio Berlusconi's center-right coalition received a substantial majority of 58 percent in the lower house of the parliament, albeit falling two seats short of a majority in the upper house (Hamann and Kelly 2011, 128). Still, the government had a relatively strong electoral mandate, which allowed Berlusconi to challenge the influence of organized labor in the areas of pension policy and fixed-term employment. Yet with the withdrawal of the Northern League (Lega Nord) from the coalition, Berlusconi had to give up his ambitions for unilateral reform and resign after a few months in office (Haman and Kelly 2011, 129). Unlike Berlusconi's short-lived center-right coalition, the subsequent government led by Lamberto Dini again consisted of technocrats with no affiliation to any political party in parliament. This had paved the way for another tripartite agreement on pension reform in 1995.

In the area of labor market policy, Italian governments negotiated two important reforms with the unions: the Treu law of 1997 on the one hand, and the Biagi reform of 2001 on the other. Although being legislated by governments of different partisan complexions, both reforms had a dualistic policy outlook in the interest of job creation. Named after the labor lawyer and minister of labor, Tiziano Treu, the first reform was driven by the center-left "Olive Tree" alliance led by Romano Prodi, which was a minority government supported by the Communist Refoundation Party (RC), a far-left opposition party. The government's reliance on a small far-left party posed constraints on its autonomy, especially in the area of workers' rights (OECD 2009, 254). Mindful of the unions' united opposition to changes in the statutory employment protection of permanent workers, the government aimed at easing restrictions of fixed-term employment instead. In other words, its principal objective was to facilitate the "hiring" of groups with weak labor market attachment through deregulations, while leaving untouched the legal constraints on the "firing" of established workers.

Faced by a relatively weak government, the unions successfully defended their past achievements for permanent workers, while consenting to the introduction of temporary agency work and a moderate liberalization of part-time employment in return for the introduction of labor grants in the area of ALMP for young people (OECD 2009, 254). While this outcome reflects the prioritization of the unions' core membership, the successful demand for ALMP measures also shows that the unions incorporated outsiders into their representational outlook. Still, the amount of social investment flowing to labor grants was quite limited (equivalent to 0.05 percent of GDP). By contrast, the employers accepted tax increases for state-funded job creation activities (Regini and Colombo 2011, 131).

Overall, during the 1980s and 1990s, Italian unions were more successful than their Spanish counterparts in taming the deregulatory agenda of partisan actors. The result was a late and moderate dualization of job security arrangements. The 2001 election paved the way for a center-right government led by Silvio Berlusconi, which had a majority both in the lower house (59 percent) and in the upper house (56 percent) (Hamann and Kelly 2011, 129). With a strong parliamentary position, the government threatened to eschew negotiations with unions and legislate another round of liberalization unilaterally. Eventually, this announcement split the union movement, since the two moderate union confederations, CISL

(Confederazione Italiana Sindacati Lavoratori) and UIL (Unione Italiana del Lavoro), proved willing to enter into negotiations on the basis of the government's reform proposals, while the main union confederation, the CIGL (Confederazione Generale Italiana del Lavoro), left the bargaining table. The final content of the "Biagi reform" removed restrictions on the usage of various temporary employment contracts, but the unions managed to block the government in its attempt to restrict the coverage of statutory employment protection for permanent workers in firms with more than fifteen employees (Article 18 of the Workers' Statute).

Unlike the "Treu law", the "Biagi reform" included no compensation for deregulations at the margins of the workforce, except for their successful veto on reforming Article 18 (EIRO 2002b). This absence of compensations reflects the strengthened position of the government vis-à-vis a weakened and divided union movement (Regini and Colombo 2011, 133). Due to these changes, between the mid-1990s and 2007, the share of atypical employment in total employment almost doubled to about 20 percent, consisting of 8.0 percent part-time workers and 11.9 percent fixed-term workers (Jessoula and Vesan 2011, 146). As described above, these figures are much lower compared to the ones in Spain.

In 2012, at the height of the Eurozone crisis, the appointment of a technocratic government led by Mario Monti put an end to the era of social pacts in Italy (Culpepper and Regan 2014). Its political mandate came with external pressure from the European Central Bank and the public's concerns that Berlusconi's center-right government lacked the capacity to tackle the Italian sovereign debt problem. Unlike previous technocratic governments of the early 1990s, the Monti cabinet pursued a unilateral approach when it faced opposition from both sides of the class divide for different reasons. Named after the labor and welfare minister, the labor market proposal of the "Fornero reform" followed EU Council recommendations within the constraints of the tightened EMU governance framework. First, it was presented as an attempt to smoothen divisions in the level of job security between permanent and temporary employment contracts. The unions opposed changes to Article 18 that required employers with more than fifteen employees to reinstate workers who are found to be unfairly dismissed, whereas the employers protested against additional restrictions on the usage of temporary contracts (Tiraboschi 2012, 81).

In contrast to the parliamentary majority of the PP government in Spain, the Monti cabinet faced internal divisions because a composite parliamentary majority that included both left- and right-wing components had to support it. As a result, it was reliant on the consent of the union-friendly wing inside the center-left Democratic Party (PD). In response to sustained lobbying efforts by the PD, the Monti cabinet indeed watered down the liberalization of Article 18 in favor of the unions (Culpepper and Regan 2014). Moreover, the "Fornero reform" was an attempt to extend the coverage of unemployment protection to workers with fixed-term contracts by replacing the ordinary benefit scheme with the so-called ASP and the Mini-ASPI. Notably, the new system reduced the number of workers not covered by unemployment insurance by two thirds (Sacchi 2013). At the same time, however, the benefit system remains insurance-based in character, tying the level and duration of benefit entitlements to the individual contribution record.

The so-called Jobs Act in 2014 under the PD-leadership of Matteo Renzi combined a deregulation of dismissal protection with an extension in the coverage of unemployment benefits. Even though the unions welcomed enhanced unemployment support, they fiercely opposed the package as it included the dismantling of Article 18 (EIRO 2015). This seems to confirm the expectation that exclusive unions prioritize the established rights of permanent workers when faced with a policy trade-off along the lines of the Jobs Act, even though they clearly increased their bargaining efforts for precarious workers at the same time (Durazzi 2017). Emmenegger (2014, chap. 5) points out that the unions' defense of Article 18 was not only driven by the aim to protect their core membership, but also a way of retaining their institutionalized role at the workplace. With respect to the government, Picot and Tassinari (2017) observe that Renzi himself had initially planned to leave Article 18 untouched, but changed his mind in response to growing pressures from EU institutions. Accordingly, the serious confrontation with the unions might be seen as a way of enhancing business confidence to generate more leeway with respect to the Eurozone's fiscal deficit targets. This seems necessary to secure long-term funding for the expansion of unemployment support (Picot and Tassinari 2017, 136).

This very cursory evidence from Italy and Spain supports the view that variations in government strength and union inclusiveness help us understand differences in the protection of outsiders outside the three Northwestern European countries studied in the previous chapters. In short, from the 1980s until 2008, the unions of both countries opposed the governments' ambitions to deregulate temporary forms of employment. However, only in Italy were the unions able to mitigate such deregulation at the margins, because technocratic and multiparty governments mobilized their consent in return for maintaining Article 18 and expanding labor grants. This contrasts with the marginalization of Spanish unions under single-party governments, which led to an earlier and more pronounced pattern of dualization relative to Italy.

The PP's high level of government strength also explains why it was able to respond to the Eurozone crisis with a unilateral dismantling of dismissal protection without offering any form of compensation to organized labor. This unilateral intervention moved Spain toward an Anglo-American type of across-the-board deregulation at the expense of both insiders and outsiders (Bulfone 2016; Picot and Tassinari 2017). In Italy, by contrast, the government not only cut back dismissal protection against union protests as in Spain; it also contributed to enhanced unemployment support (Bulfone 2016; Picot and Tassinari 2017). The latter part of the deal reflects a notable deviation from the previous path of dualization in the interest of outsider protection. Yet the implementation of the Jobs Act and its effects on risk protection remain uncertain, given that weak aggregate demand in tandem with public debt levels at a record high threaten the employment-enhancing effects and thus the fiscal sustainability of the Jobs Act.

In response to the dismantling of Article 18, the CGIL has strengthened its efforts to mobilize political support for precarious workers. In 2016, it collected 1.5 million signatures to present a new legislative proposal entitled "Charter of Universal Labor Rights" aimed at the universalization of labor rights across different employment contracts in 2016. Moreover, at the time of writing, it has collected signatures for the reintroduction of mandatory contribution payments for social security entitlements in the event of outsourcing and the abolition of 10-euro vouchers to remunerate "occasional work." It seems that the unions' primary goal to defend the established rights of their core membership gives way to an agenda of universal rights once there are hardly any past achievements left to defend. What is sure is that these recent mobilization efforts—as well as the unions' collective bargaining agenda for temporary agency work—suggest a gradual shift in policy priorities toward a greater representation of precarious workers (Benassi and Vlandas 2015; Durazzi 2017), which can be observed in Spain (Pulignano et al. 2016) and elsewhere in Europe too (Doellgast et al. 2017).

While the evidence from the Mediterranean cases draws our attention to the strategic challenges faced by decentralized and shrinking union movements, it also highlights the impact of EMU accession on domestic class power relations. The Austrian experience gave some insight into how the fiscal requirements of the Eurozone created opportunities for employers to push governments toward social-spending cuts during the 1990s (which did not affect Denmark and Sweden, because they did not sign up for EMU). Yet in the former soft-currency regimes of Italy and Spain, the economic adjustment pressure was undeniably higher as they used to restore competitiveness through currency devaluations; an option that was no longer available (Johnston and Regan 2016). They thus had the hardest work to remake their labor market regimes in the interest of EMU entry, involving a mix of wage restraint, job security deregulation, and fiscal consolidation (Hancké and Rhodes 2005). This exogenous pressure helped governments to legitimize liberalizing moves and thus shield them from domestic opposition, which put unions in a defensive position (see, e.g., Durazzi 2017, 271). I will conclude by discussing the theoretical and political implications of my findings for current debates in comparative political economy and the study of comparative capitalism.

Government Strength and Varieties of Liberalization

A growing literature of comparative political economy makes the case for liberalization as the dominant trend of institutional change in the advanced capitalist countries (e.g., Streeck and Thelen 2005; Streeck 2009; Emmenegger 2014; Thelen 2014; Baccaro and Howell 2017). This shift in the empirical perspective of recent scholarship also implied a shift in theoretical attention. Whereas previous research has been dominated by arguments highlighting the organization of employers (Swenson 2002) and the path-dependent nature of institutions (Steinmo et al. 1992), the study of power and conflict was central to explaining the *"varieties of liberalization"* (Thelen 2014) that followed the building of *"varieties of capitalism"* (Hall and Soskice 2001). The argument of this book on the relationship between strong governments and precarious workers fundamentally confirms the relevance accorded to power in recent empirical studies of liberalization.

One way of how my findings contribute to this debate is the conceptual distinction between *preferences* and *power* on the part of organized labor, and the implications this has for national paths of liberalization. To be sure, producer group theories widely recognized the relevance of representational inclusiveness for the preference formation of trade unions: the more inclusive they are organized, the more they incorporate precarious workers (Becher and Pontusson 2011; Thelen 2014; Gordon 2015). This assumption relates to the observation of growing intralabor heterogeneity, which may confront trade unions with representational trade-offs in the interest formation process (Rueda 2007; Häusermann 2010). Yet as the findings of this book suggest, shifts in class power were more influential than changes in union preferences per se. For example, the labor movements of Denmark and Sweden had clear stakes in the protection of outsiders, but their egalitarian preferences did not prevent strong governments from legislating unilateral cuts in the union-administered unemployment insurances. While the employers' associations welcomed such interventions, the union confederations organized public protests—without success. The shadow case studies pointed in the same direction. Although the labor movement of Italy prioritized the defense of dismissal protection, the Renzi government put an end to the so-called Article 18. The labor movement of Spain found itself largely excluded from the policy-making process and thus unable to resist the gradual across-the-board deregulation of the labor market. In all these instances, union protests against unilateral government action did not include any form of material compensation. It would thus be difficult to contend that the policy outputs described previously can be attributed to changes in union preferences rather than shifts in class power.

That governments prioritized business demands over the social protection of outsiders has theoretical implications for the role of *partisanship*. It is clear that the policy choices of political parties are influenced by new electoral cleavages that result from changing work- and family patterns: the "old" working class wants income and dismissal protection; the "new" middle class wants social investment (Beramendi et al. 2015). Yet the findings of this book make obvious that we must not only look at the interaction between parties and voters, but also the fact that governments are obliged to facilitate capital accumulation for *job creation*. Otherwise, the economy goes down the drain, followed by the electoral fortunes of governments. Understanding how governments deal with this structural constraint requires taking the balance of class forces seriously (McCarthy 2017). The gradual stages of liberalization since the collapse of the Keynesian class compromise have created an environment that favored employer demands for wage differentiation and labor market flexibility over policy tools governments once used to tighten labor supply or adapt social protection for workers (Silver 2003; Glyn 2007; Streeck 2009; Culpepper and Regan 2014; Emmenegger 2014; Baccaro and Howell 2017). In this way, the capitalist context of labor market reform created opportunities for employers to push governments in their preferred direction.

The third theoretical contribution of this book relates to the "delivery mechanism" that links declining union power to the legislation of insider-outsider divides in employment and welfare: *government strength*. One popular way of looking at the neoliberal transformation of capitalism is to say that the strengthening of market mechanisms required the weakening of governments. This notion refers to the gradual decline in the relevance of the nation state in managing the social outcomes of capitalist market expansion. The return of unemployment and precarious jobs that lack security across all national sovereign democratic states of the Western world seems to justify this idea of a weak government vis-à-vis capitalism. But the politics of liberalization required a government strong enough to insulate the expansion of markets mechanisms from popular demands of voters and unions. It is in this sense that the past four decades of liberalization were characterized by a dialectic between a government weak in relation to the capitalist economy but strong in relegating calls for market correction at the same time (Gamble 1988; see also Streeck 2015).

This dialectic might resolve the theoretical paradox of why precisely the weakest governments were most responsive to the social needs of workers hit hardest by the liberalization of national models of capitalism. Regardless of partisanship, when governments are not sufficiently united or encompassing to act unilaterally in the policy-making process, they will be unable to fend off political demands from organized labor. In response they will reach out to trade unions, because labor-inclusive negotiations provide them with an extraparliamentary channel of consensus mobilization. The price for this consensual adjustment is a material compensation to workers for the costs of liberalization. When unions are sufficiently inclusive to the margins of the workforce, this compensation predicts outsiders. But strong governments dismiss the policy demands from others to prevent a distortion of their political agenda. This is especially the case when these demands come from trade unions whose structural power and electoral significance have faded over time.

A Long Goodbye to Trade Unions—and Social Solidarity?

This book has political implications for economic reform in contemporary capitalism. The first one seems most obvious in light of my findings: precarious workers need inclusive trade unions. Otherwise, they lack political representation. High levels of inclusiveness often result from an encompassing membership (as in Denmark and Sweden) or labor unity through concentration and centralization (as in Austria). However, does this mean that outsiders are "doomed" in countries *without* inclusive trade unions? To be sure, the evidence from Italy suggests that fragmented union movements with shrinking membership bases might well prioritize the defense of established rights for their remaining core membership when faced with the liberalizing reform ambitions of governments. However, this does not mean that they do no longer care about precarious workers (see Pulignano et al. 2016). On the contrary, recent scholarship observes a broader shift in union priorities toward social solidarity in studies on collective bargaining and industrial relations (Doellgast et al. 2017), pension policy (Naczyk and Seeleib-Kaiser 2015), temporary agency work (Benassi and Vlandas 2016), and union revitalization (Baccaro et al. 2003; Heery and Adler 2004; Jódar et al. 2011). European trade unions across the continent have thus become increasingly aware of the fact that the representation of precarious workers is nothing less than a question of their own survival. Flexible low-wage competition from outsiders gradually eats into the core workforce and broader commitments to social solidarity are necessary to attract popular support (Doellgast et al. 2017). Still, unions obviously need unity and members among precarious workers to mobilize effectively against dualizing reform ambitions. In this sense, the fate of outsiders lies in their own hands.

Second, from the perspective of trade unions, institutionalized channels of corporatist bargaining are no longer sufficient to influence government reforms. That governments can exclude labor movements from policy-making has become clear in the countries hit hardest by the Eurozone crisis in the past decade: Greece, Ireland, Italy, Portugal, and Spain (Armingeon and Baccaro 2012; Culpepper and Regan 2014). While in the 1990s these labor movements had entered deals with "least worst outcomes" (Gumbrell-McCormick and Hyman 2013, 103), this time they were not even offered a deal. Yet, union exclusion is by no means confined to noncorporatist countries, given the evidence from Austria, Denmark, and Sweden. Across diverse European political economies, governments no longer seem to attribute union leaders the legitimacy to speak on behalf of the workforce in economic policy-making. The reasons for this are not hard to discern. It is commonplace to observe that unions lost members, unity, and thus influence over time. Yet, the fragmentation of the working class—in union members and non-members or "insiders" and "outsiders"—is by no means a "natural" phenomenon beyond the reach of agency; it resulted from political interventions that expanded market forces and thus put workers in competition to each other.[4] Such a policy would have been impossible to achieve without downgrading union influence in the first place.

While the decline of continuous macro-corporatist bargaining seems to be of lasting nature, the ability of governments to impose austerity is not. In an acute stage of crisis, the Great Recession certainly strengthened the executive powers of governments vis-à-vis trade unions, but it also caused long-term political costs. As Hernández and Kriesi (2016) show, the economic strain of the Great Recession led to a further fragmentation of Western European party systems, meaning a decrease in support for the political mainstream to the benefit of challengers from both sides of the partisan divide. Growing divisions within the parliamentary arena are hard to reconcile with unilateral government action and may thus require a more consensual approach to the political demands of trade unions in order to mobilize a durable consensus around controversial areas of economic reform. The ongoing demands of austerity *beyond* the immediate period of economic crisis may thus reach a point whereby the internal unity and external size of governments crumble away, and new forums of consensus mobilization are needed. This would create (or re-create) opportunities for union influence.

Third, and finally, the increased importance of government strength in tandem with the declining relevance of corporatist legacies bears political insights for the future strategies of organized labor. When faced with a weak government, trade unions must be willing and able to develop a consensus-oriented outlook to secure themselves an influential role in the reform process. Internally divided governments are often unable to formulate a common reform proposal and thus in need of union support in the preparation of economic policies. In this situation, the main asset unions can lay before governments is active collaboration with employers in trilateral negotiations to overcome reform deadlocks. Minority governments in adversarial party systems, on the other hand, often require union consent to convince the parliamentary opposition of its reform plans. Here trade unions can play an instrumental role in mobilizing political support for government reforms among working people. Taken together, when trade unions attempt to influence the policies of weak governments, they can promote their inclusion in the reform process by supporting economic problem solving and political consensus building. While such a reform-friendly strategy will be difficult to follow for decentralized union movements that lack internal unity, it is the most likely source of union influence under weak governments.

Trade unions must be prepared to shift toward a more confrontational strategy when faced with the formation of a strong government. Single-party minority governments (with multiple options to build a majority) or ideologically united majority governments are able to develop liberalizing policies autonomously, which often leads them to reject lengthy and costly union consultations. In this situation, unions have no other option than to mobilize their members and public opinion against the government. Such a confrontational strategy requires the anticipation of unilateral reform plans and a subsequent mandate from union membership for industrial action and mass demonstrations. A shift towards a conflict-oriented outlook poses challenges for union confederations that used to be involved in corporatist policy concertation, but the findings of this book suggest that trade unions can no longer rely on previous traditions of consensus democracy when confronted with a strong government.

The future of social solidarity continues to depend on the historically specific balance of class forces in the capitalist economy. Weak governments may be unable to dualize labor markets unilaterally, but this in itself does not undermine the power relationships on which the motives behind their policy choices rest. An impetus against the imperatives of competitiveness and liberalization, it seems, may come from two different directions, with fundamentally different implications for social solidarity however. The first one stems from the nativist agenda of the populist radical right. Although its position on economic reform appears "blurred," it is outspoken on the rejection of free trade and, above all, immigration (Rovny 2013). Growing support for such parties reflects, at least in part, the convergence of the political mainstream toward neoliberal economic positions

(Kitschelt 1995; see also Spies and Franzmann 2011), which opened up a new playing field over cultural matters around which the radical right could gain issue ownership (Meguid 2008). But the boundaries between economic and cultural conflicts have become increasingly unclear along the dimension of "distributive deservingness" (Häusermann and Kriesi 2015; see also Van Oorschot 2006). Here the populist radical right advocates "welfare chauvinism," which implies the restriction of employment and social rights to natives at the expense of immigrants, thereby creating new divisions within the workforce.

The other impetus on behalf of the working class comes from organized labor in cooperation with progressive civil society organizations and (new) parties on the left. Trade unions may be tempted to side with the populist radical right against immigration to control labor supply. However, the nativist agenda of the populist radical right cannot be reconciled with a trade union agenda, because welfare chauvinism facilitates precarious employment and thus wage dumping in the long run. Organized labor may instead aim to incorporate migrants as much as other labor market outsiders to strengthen its membership base and undermine labor market competition. In the end, these political forces and understandings of social solidarity—populist nativism versus working-class universalism—are likely to shape the distributive outcomes of the postliberalization era.

Notes

2. LABOR MARKET POLICY IN AUSTRIA, DENMARK, AND SWEDEN

1. In comparison with Belgium, Germany, France, and the Netherlands, Austria displayed the lowest shares of involuntary fixed-term contracts in total fixed-term employment (12.4 percent) and involuntary part-time contracts in total part-time employment (11.2 percent) (Eichhorst and Marx 2012).

2. I restricted the time period of figure 2.1 to the year of 1997 because the OECD does not provide data on temporary employment from before this date for Austria and Sweden.

3. RELYING ON THE WEAK: AUSTRIAN UNIONS AND SMOOTHED DUALIZATION

1. Means testing in this second tier of the unemployment protection system derives from the condition that the unemployed, whose partners receive a certain wage level, are not eligible for unemployment assistance. The benefit level of unemployment assistance is slightly less generous than the first-tier unemployment insurance (92–95 percent of the previous benefit level).

2. For a description of the types of "atypical" employment contracts, see Bock-Schappelwein and Mühlberger (2008).

3. The package included the reduction of the net replacement rate for the unemployed from 57.9 percent to 56.0 percent, an increased in the requalification period from twenty to twenty-six weeks, and the abolition of the family surcharge for partners of unemployed people (Tálos and Wörister 1998, 272).

4. Interview with Andreas Khol, party whip of the ÖVP (1994–1999, 2000–2002), Dec. 9, 2014.

5. According to his memoirs, Wolfgang Schüssel ruled out the formation of a coalition with the FPÖ at that time, but he openly announced this option as part of his calculations to exert pressure on the SPÖ during the election campaign (Schüssel 2009, 22–25). It took him another four years to break with the grand coalition.

6. Interview with Alexander Prischl, ÖGB, head of the Labor Market and Education Division, Mar. 5, 2015.

7. Interview with Eleonora Hostasch, minister of the Labor Market, Health Care, and Social Affairs Division of the SPÖ, Jan. 27, 2015.

8. Hostasch interview.

9. Drawing on interview evidence from Tobias Hinterseer (2014, 127–128), representatives of the FPÖ even contacted experts from the Chamber of Labor to get a more informed view of upcoming reform projects.

10. Khol interview.

11. The level of severance pay amounted to 2 months of the gross wage after 3 years of service; 3 months of the gross wage after 5 years of service; 4 months after 10 years; 6 months after 15 years; 9 months after 20 years; and 12 months after 25 years. The severance pay was subject to a flat-rate income tax of 6 percent.

12. Interview with Walter Neubauer, senior official in the Ministry of Labor Market and Social Affairs, May 29, 2015.

13. Khol interview.

14. Interview with Stefan Potmesil, head of the Labor Market Department in the Ministry of Social Affairs (2000–2010), Aug. 27, 2015.

15. Interview with Erwin Buchinger, minister of the Labor Market, Social Affairs, and Consumer Protection Division of the SPÖ (2007–2008), Dec. 18, 2015.

16. Interview with a senior official of the Labor Market Policy Division of the BAK, Dec. 11, 2014.

17. Interview with René Schindler, confederal secretary of PRO-GE (Union of Production Workers), Dec. 17, 2014.

18. Schindler interview.

19. Prischl interview.

4. STRENGTHENED GOVERNMENTS AND THE EROSION OF DANISH FLEXICURITY

1. The savings package in the pension system reduced the benefit duration of the early retirement scheme from five to three years, increased the minimum age for the entitlement to early retirement to sixty-four years, and increased the retirement age from sixty-five to sixty-seven years. In a similar vein, spending cuts in the employment subsidy scheme for people with disabilities (Flexjob) and restricted access to disability pensions for people below the age of forty point in the direction of less inclusive social security.

2. Belgium, Denmark, Finland and Sweden are the four countries with Ghent systems, which in large part explains their high levels of union organization. Unlike the Nordic countries, however, Belgian unemployment insurance is not voluntary, as membership contributions are mandatory for every wage earner (Clegg 2012).

3. Similar to the Austrian Freedom Party, however, the Danish People's Party was attached to the blue-collar working class and thus followed the strategy of the Liberals to refrain from radical welfare cuts, at least until the onset of the Great Recession.

4. Interview with Jørgen Rosted, leader of the state secretariat of the Zeuthen Commission, Aug. 11, 2014.

5. As Anthonsen et al. (2011) argue, the resurgence of corporatism in wage bargaining (1987) and occupational pensions (early 1990s) may be attributed to the emerging willingness of the unions to cooperate with a center-right coalition whose policies they had fiercely opposed for five years in a polarized political environment. This argument may account for the emergence of negotiated wage restraint in 1987 but misses the weakened parliamentary power base of the government in the policy-making processes (see Green-Pedersen et al. 2001).

6. Rosted interview.

7. The reform extended the minimum contribution period in an unemployment benefit fund to twenty-five years, introduced a separate early retirement contribution, and included reduced benefit levels for people retiring at the age of sixty.

8. For example, Commission of Administrative Structures (2002–2004), Welfare Commission (2004–2007), Labor Market Commission (2007–2009), and Tax Commission (2007–2009).

9. Interview with a consultant of LO, Dec. 13, 2013; former consultant in the Ministry of Employment.

10. Interview with Jan Kaeraa Rasmussen, chief economist of LO, Dec. 12, 2013.

11. Interview with Thomas Qvortrup Christensen, senior adviser of Danish Industries (DI), Dec. 9, 2013.

12. Three major cutbacks were imposed on people on social assistance under the Liberal-Conservative government during the 2000s. First, the so-called start-assistance—a reduced level of social assistance for immigrants who had been in Denmark for fewer than

seven of the last eight years—was introduced in order to undermine the perceived danger of increasing welfare abuse. However, Danish citizens returning from abroad were also included under its umbrella. Second, after having tightened employment requirements for spouses on social assistance in 2004 and 2008, the Liberal-Conservative government introduced a work requirement of 225 hours a year for all married recipients in order to be eligible for social assistance in 2010. Third, a benefit ceiling was imposed on families with "extraordinary" expenses, namely, the maximum level of social assistance benefits that uninsured unemployed people could receive.

13. Interview with Karsten Lorentsen, press spokesperson of the Danish People's Party, Dec. 11, 2013.

14. Interview with Jan Birkemose, chief editor of *Ugebrevet A4* (magazine published by the LO between 2002 and 2013; since then published by the media company Avisen.dk Aps), Dec. 10, 2013.

15. Interview with Kristian Madsen, journalist at *Politiken* (a Danish newspaper), former PR consultant (Informationschef) at the trade union 3F (2008–2010), and consultant at LO (2004–2008), Dec. 18, 2013.

16. Interview with Claus Hjort Frederiksen, Liberal Party (Venstre), minister of employment (2001–2009) and minister of finance (2009–2011), Dec. 10, 2013.

17. Lorentsen interview.

18. Frederiksen interview.

19. Rasmussen interview.

20. Thomas Qvortrup Christensen interview.

21. Frederiksen interview.

22. The new severance pay scheme entitles dismissed employees after three, six, or eight years' seniority in a firm to receive a lump sum that is calculated as the difference between the monthly unemployment benefit payment and the monthly wage deducted by 15 percent. Depending on job tenure, the employer has to pay one, two, or three times the base-level severance pay. Therefore, this measure rewards "insiders" with continuous employment relationships more than people with temporary contracts.

23. Interview with Anita Vium Jørgensen, chief economist of 3F (Danish workers' union), Dec. 16, 2013.

24. "The point of departure for the government is the economic policy of the VK-government in the widest sense, including the consolidation agreement and the pension reform of spring" (Regeringen 2011, 9).

25. Interview with Jens Christiansen, Managing Director of Advice *A/S*, Campaign Director for the Social Democratic Party (Socialdemokraterne) in the election of 2011, Aug. 12, 2014.

26. Rasmussen interview.

27. Interview with a political consultant, Social Democratic Party (Socialdemokraterne), Dec. 16, 2013.

5. GOODBYE TO SWEDISH SOCIAL DEMOCRACY AND UNIVERSAL WELFARE

1. This paragraph is based on evidence from Emmenegger (2010).

2. Interview with Patrik Karlsson, labor market policy official at the peak employers' association, Swedish Business (Svenskt Näringsliv; SAF until 2001), Sept. 29, 2015.

3. Interview with Mats Wadman, senior official at the Ministry of Employment (1988–2007), Oct. 2, 2015.

4. Interview with Dan Andersson, chief economist of the LO (2000–2008), May 5, 2015.

5. Interview with Sture Nordh, chairman of TCO (1999–2011), Sept. 30, 2015.

6. Interview with Dan Andersson, chief economist of the LO (2000–2008), May 5, 2015.

7. Interview with Mats Wadman, director at the Ministry of Employment (1988–2007), Oct. 2, 2015.

8. Interview with Eva Uddén Sonnegård, Conservative Party (Nya Moderaterna), state secretary at the Ministry of Employment (2006–2010), Oct. 2, 2015.

9. Interview with Sven-Otto Littorin, Conservative Party (Nya Moderaterna), minister of employment (2006–2010), Dec. 4, 2015.

10. Interview with Mats Wadman, director at the Ministry of Employment (1988–2007), Oct. 2, 2015.

11. Interview with Sven-Otto Littorin, Nya Moderaterna, minister of employment (2006–2010), Dec. 4, 2015.

12. Interview with Thomas Carlén, labor market policy expert of the LO, Oct. 1, 2015.

13. Interview with Sven-Otto Littorin, Nya Moderaterna, minister of employment, Dec. 4, 2015.

6. STRONG GOVERNMENTS AND PRECARIOUS WORKERS IN THE ERA OF LIBERALIZATION

1. Walter Korpi was probably among the first to anticipate the dualistic policies of the SAP. For him, it was the emerging crisis tendencies in the Rehn-Meidner model that posed threats to the practical viability of redistributive state action. Writing in 1978, he illustrated this claim by referring to the 1976 election in Sweden, where the center-right bloc took office for the first time since 1932: "The interpretation suggested here is thus that electoral difficulties of the Social Democrats have arisen largely from the continued superiority of the capitalist class, which has constrained Social Democratic policies, necessitating compromises with dualistic consequences for potential supporters" (Korpi 1978, 322).

2. Interview with Dan Andersson.

3. Durazzi (2017) documents a number of union proposals (and actions) toward the extension of prevailing employment and social rights to all types of workers. Most recently, the largest union confederation (CGIL, Confederazione Generale Italiana del Lavoro) has launched a Charter of Universal Labor Rights, which ranges from fair pay and freedom of expression to health and safety as well as equal opportunities and lifelong learning (see below).

4. However, the socially corrosive effects of the Great Recession seem to have reenhanced public trust in trade unions as a "sword of justice," especially among socially vulnerable groups with weak attachments to the labor market (Frangi et al. 2017).

Bibliography

"Abfertigung neu: Koalition weiter uneins." 2001. *Der Standard*, June 25. https://derstandard.at/625722/Abfertigung-neu-Koalition-weiter-uneins

Afonso, Alexandre. 2013. *Social Concertation in Times of Austerity. European Integration and the Politics of Labour Market Reforms in Austria and Switzerland.* Amsterdam: Amsterdam University Press.

Afonso, Alexandre. 2015. Choosing whom to betray: Populist right-wing parties, welfare state reforms and the trade-off between office and votes. *European Political Science Review* 7 (2): 271–292.

Agius, Christine. 2007. "Sweden's Parliamentary Election 2006 and After: Contesting or Consolidating the Swedish Model?" *Parliamentary Affairs* 60 (4): 585–600.

Alber, Jens. 1982. *Vom Armenhaus zum Wohlfahrtsstaat. Analysen zur Entwicklung der Sozialversicherung in Westeuropa.* Frankfurt and New York: Campus Verlag.

Alber, Jens. 2002. "Modernisierung als Peripetie des Sozialstaats?" *Berliner Journal für Soziologie* 12 (1): 5–35.

Alexiadou, Despina. 2013. "In Search of Successful Reform: The Politics of Opposition and Consensus in OECD Parliamentary Democracies." *West European Politics* 36 (4): 704–725.

Allern, Elin Haugsgjerd, Nicholas Aylott, and Flemming J. Christiansen. 2007. "Social Democrats and Trade Unions in Scandinavia: The Decline and Persistence of Institutional Relationships." *European Journal of Political Research* 46 (5): 607–635.

Anderson, Karen M. 2001. "The Politics of Retrenchment in a Social Democratic Welfare State: Reform of Swedish Pensions and Unemployment Insurance." *Comparative Political Studies* 34 (9): 1063–1091.

Andersson, Dan. 2005. *Vem ansvarar för arbetslösheten?* Sweden: Landsorganisationen i Sverige.

Andersson, Dan. 2008. "Vilken arbetslinje väljer socialdemokratin?" *Tiden* 101 (3): 6–11.

Anker, Jørgen, Jonas Lindén, Marie H. Wegner, and Jacob A. Holch. 2009. *Overview and Analysis of Minimum Income Schemes in Denmark.* A Study of National Policies on Behalf of the European Commission, DG Employment, Social Affairs and Equal Opportunities.

Anthonsen, Mette, and Johannes Lindvall. 2009. "Party Competition and the Resilience of Corporatism." *Government and Opposition* 44 (2): 167–187.

Anthonsen, Mette, Johannes Lindvall, and Ulrich Schmidt-Hansen. 2011. "Social Democrats, Unions and Corporatism: Denmark and Sweden Compared." *Party Politics* 17 (1): 118–134.

Armingeon Klaus, and Lucio Baccaro. 2012. "Political Economy of the Sovereign Debt Crisis." *Industrial Law Journal* 41 (3): 254–275.

Arndt, Christoph. 2013. "The Electoral Consequences of Welfare State Reforms for the Danish Social Democrats." *World Political Science Review* 9 (1): 319–335.

Arndt, Christoph. 2014. "Beating Social Democracy on Its Own Turf: Issue Convergence as Winning Formula for the Centre-Right in Universal Welfare States." *Scandinavian Political Studies* 37 (2): 149–170.

Atzmüller, Roland. 2009. "Die Entwicklung der Arbeitsmarktpolitik in Österreich. Dimensionen von Workfare in der österreichischen Sozialpolitik." *Kurswechel* 4: 24–34.

Atzmüller, Roland, Manfred Krenn, and Ulrike Papouschek. 2012. "Innere Aushöhlung und Fragmentierung des österreichischen Modells: Zur Entwicklung von Erwerbslosigkeit, prekärer Beschäftigung und Arbeitsmarktpolitik." In *Neue Prekarität. Die Folgen aktivierender Arbeitsmarktpolitik—europäische Länder im Vergleich*, ed. Karin Scherschel, Peter Streckeisen, and Manfred Krenn, 75–110. Frankfurt and New York: Campus Verlag.

Avdagic, Sabina. 2010. "When Are Concerted Reforms Feasible? Explaining the Emergence of Social Pacts in Western Europe." *Comparative Political Studies* 43 (5): 628–657.

Aylott, Nicholas. 2003. "After the Divorce: Social Democrats and Trade Unions in Sweden." *Party Politics* 9 (3): 369–390.

Aylott, Nicholas, and Niklas Bolin. 2007. "Towards a Two-Party System? The Swedish Parliamentary Election of September 2006." *West European Politics* 30 (3): 621–633.

Baccaro, Lucio, Kerstin Hamann, and Lowell Turner. 2003. "The Politics of Labour Movement Revitalisation: The Need for a Revitalised Perspective." *European Journal of Industrial Relations* 9 (1): 119–133.

Baccaro, Lucio, and Chris Howell. 2011. "A Common Neoliberal Trajectory: The Transformation of Industrial Relations in Advanced Capitalism." *Politics & Society* 39 (4): 1–43.

Baccaro, Lucio, and Chris Howell. 2017. *Trajectories of Neoliberal Transformation: European Industrial Relations since the 1970s.* Cambridge: Cambridge University Press.

Baccaro, Lucio, and Sang-Hoon Lim. 2007. "Social Pacts as Coalitions of the Weak and the Moderate." *European Journal of Industrial Relations* 13 (1): 27–46.

Baccaro, Lucio, and Richard M. Locke. 1998. "The Politics of Labour Movement Revitalization: The Need for a Revitalized Perspective." *European Journal of Industrial Relations* 9 (1): 119–133.

Baccaro, Lucio, and Marco Simoni. 2008. "Policy Concertation in Europe: Explaining Government's Choice." *Comparative Political Studies* 41 (10): 1323–1348.

Bale, Tim, and Torbjörn Bergman. 2006. "Captives No Longer, but Servants Still? Contract Parliamentarism and the New Minority Governance in Sweden and New Zealand." *Government and Opposition* 41 (3): 422–449.

Barbier, Jean-Claude. 2005. "Citizenship and the Activation of Social Protection: A Comparative Approach" In *The Changing Face of Welfare. Consequences and Outcomes from a Citizenship Perspective*, ed. Jørgen G. Andersen, Anne-Marie Guillemand, Per H. Jensen, and Birgit Pfau-Effinger, 113–134. Bristol, UK: Policy Press.

Bartolini, Stefano. 2000. *The Political Mobilization of the European Left, 1860–1980: The Class Cleavage.* Cambridge: Cambridge University Press.

Becher, Michael, and Jonas Pontusson. 2011. "Whose Interests Do Unions Represent? Unionization by Income in Western Europe." *Research in the Sociology of Work* (22) 2: 181–211.

Benassi, Chiara, and Tim Vlandas. 2016. "Union Inclusiveness and Temporary Agency Workers: The Role of Power Resources and Ideology." *European Journal of Industrial Relations* 22 (1): 5–22.

Beramendi, Pablo, Silja Häusermann, Herbert Kitschelt, and Hanspeter Kriesi. 2015. "Introduction: The Politics of Advanced Capitalism." In *The Politics of Advanced Capitalism*, ed. Pablo Beramendi, Silja Häusermann, Herbert Kitschelt, and Hanspeter Kriesi, 1–64. Cambridge: Cambridge University Press.

Bergh, Andreas, and Gissur Ò. Erlingsson. 2008. "Liberalization without Retrenchment: Understanding the Consensus on Swedish Welfare State Reforms." *Scandinavian Political Studies* 32 (1): 71–93.

Bergmark, Åke, and Joakim Palme. 2003. "Welfare and the Unemployment Crisis: Sweden in the 1990s." *International Journal of Social Welfare* 12 (2): 108–122.

Blair, Tony, and Gerhard Schröder. 1998. Der Weg nach vorne für Europas Sozialdemokraten. Ein Vorschlaf von Gerhard Schröder und Tony Blair. http://www.glas nost.de/pol/schroederblair.html.

Blatter, Joachim, and Markus Haverland. 2012. *Designing Case Studies: Explanatory Approaches in Small-N Research*. Basingstoke, UK: Palgrave Macmillan.

Blom-Hansen, Jens. 2001. "Organized Interests and the State: A Disintegrating Relationship? Evidence from Denmark." *European Journal of Political Research* 39 (3): 391–416.

Blyth, Mark. 2001. "The Transformation of the Swedish Model: Economic Ideas, Distributional Conflicts and Institutional Change." *World Politics* 54 (1): 1–26.

Bock-Schappelwein, Julia, and Ulrike Mühlberger. 2008. *Beschäftigungsformen in Österreich: Rechtliche und quantitative Aspekte*, WIFO Monatsbericht. Vienna: Austrian Economic Research Institute.

Bonoli, Giuliano. 2003. "Social Policy through Labor Markets: Understanding National Differences in the Provision of Economic Security to Wage Earners." *Comparative Political Studies* 36 (9): 1007–1030.

Bonoli, Guiliano. 2007. "Time Matters: Postindustrialzation, New Social Risk, and Welfare State Adaptations." *Comparative Political Studies* 40 (5): 495–520.

Bonoli, Giuliano. 2010. "The Political Economy of Active Labor-Market Policy." *Politics and Society* 38 (4): 435–457.

Bonoli, Guiliano, and Patrick Emmenegger. 2010. "Why Not Flexicurity? State-Society Relationships, Social Trust and the Development of Labour Market Policies in Italy and Sweden." *West European Politics* 33 (4): 830–850.

Bredgaard, Thomas. 2013. "Flexibility and Security in Employment Regulation: Learning from Denmark." In *Rethinking Workplace Regulation: Beyond the Standard Contract of Employment*, ed. Katherine V. W. Stone, and Harry Arthurs, 213–233. New York: Russell Sage Foundation.

Bulfone, Fabio. 2016. "Still South European Capitalism? The Divergence of Corporate and Labour Relations in Italy and Spain." Paper presented at the 23rd International Conference of Europeanists, Philadelphia, April 14–16.

Bundesministerium für Arbeit, Soziales, Gesundheit und Konsumentenschutz (BMASK). 2010. *Überblick über Arbeitsbedingungen in Österreich. Studie der Forschungs- und Beratungsstelle Arbeitswelt (FORBA) im Auftrag des BMASK*. Vienna: Sozialpolitische Studienreihe Band 4.

Bundesministerium für Arbeit, Soziales, Gesundheit und Konsumentenschutz (BMASK). 2012. "Aktive Arbeitsmarktpolitik in Österreich." http://www.ams.at/_docs/001 _Aktive_Arbeitsmarktpolitik.pdf.

Bundesministerium für Arbeit, Soziales, Gesundheit und Konsumentenschutz (BMASK). 2013. "Aktive Arbeitsmarktpolitik in Österreich." http://www.sozialministerium .at/cms/site/attachments/2/7/9/CH2124/CMS1249975678352/doku_aamp_1994 -2013_webversion.pdf.

Bundesministerium für Arbeit, Soziales, Gesundheit und Konsumentenschutz (BMASK). 2014. *Überblick über Arbeitsbedingungen in Österreich. Follow-up Studie. Studie der Forschungs- und Beratungsstelle Arbeitswelt (FORBA) im Auftrag des BMASK*. Vienna: Sozialpolitische Studienreihe Band 15.

Burroni, Luigi, and Maarten Keune. 2011. "Flexicurity: A Conceptual Critique." *European Journal of Industrial Relations* 17 (1): 75–91.

Calmfors, Lars. 2012. "Sweden—From Macroeconomic Failure to Macroeconomic Success." Center for Economic Studies, University of Munich, *CESIFO Working Paper*, no. 3790.

Castles, Francis G. 1978. *The Social Democratic Image of Society. A Study of the Achievements and Origins of Scandinavian Social Democracy in Comparative Perspective.* London: Routledge & Kegan Paul.

Christensen, Johan. 2013. "Economists and Neoliberal Reform. Profession and Power in Tax Policy-Making, 1980–2010." PhD diss., EUI Florence.

Christiansen, Peter Munk, and Michael Baggesen Klitgaard. 2010. "Behind the Veil of Vagueness: Success and Failure in Institutional Reforms." *Journal of Public Policy* 30 (2): 183–200.

Clasen, Jochen, and Daniel Clegg. 2006. "Beyond Activation: Reforming European Unemployment Protection Systems in Post-Industrial Labour Markets." *European Societies* 8 (4): 527–553.

Clasen, Jochen, and Daniel Clegg. 2011. "Unemployment Protection and Labour Market Change in Europe: Towards 'Triple Integration'?" In *Regulating the Risk of Unemployment. National Adaptions to Post-Industrial Labour Markets in Europe*, ed. Jochen Clasen, and Daniel Clegg, 1–12. Oxford: Oxford University Press.

Clasen, Jochen, and Elke Viebrock. 2008. "Voluntary Unemployment Insurance and Trade Union Membership: Investigating the Connections in Denmark and Sweden." *Journal of Social Policy* 37 (3): 433–451.

Clasen, Jochen, and Elke Viebrock. 2009. "Flexicurity and Welfare Reform: A Review." *Socio-Economic Review* 7 (2): 305–331.

Clegg, Daniel. 2012. "Solidarity or Dualization? Social Governance, Union Preferences and Unemployment Benefit Adjustment in Belgium and France." In *The Age of Dualization. The Changing Face of Inequality*, ed. Patrick Emmenegger, Silja Häusermann, Bruno Palier, and Martin Seeleib-Kaiser, 253–276. Oxford: Oxford University Press.

Crombez, Christophe. 1996. "Minority Governments, Minimal Winning Coalitions and Surplus Majorities in Parliamentary Systems." *European Journal of Political Research* 29 (1): 1–29.

Crouch, Colin. 2009. "Privatised Keynesianism: An Unacknowledged Policy Regime." *British Journal of Politics and International Relations* 11 (3): 382–399.

Crouch, Colin, and Maarten Keune. 2012. "The Governance of Economic Uncertainty. Beyond the 'New Social Risks' Analysis." In *The Politics of the New Welfare State*, ed. Giuliano Bonoli, and David Natali, 22–45. Oxford: Oxford University Publications.

Culpepper, Pepper D. 2002. "Puzzling, Powering and 'Pacting': The Informational Logic of Negotiated Reform." *Journal of European Public Policy* 9 (5): 774–790.

Culpepper, Pepper D., and Aidan Regan. 2014. "Why Don't Governments Need Trade Unions Anymore? The Death of Social Pacts in Ireland and Italy." *Socio-Economic Review* 12 (4): 723–745.

Davidsson, Johan Bo. 2011. "Unions in Hard Times. Labour Market Politics in Western Europe: Two Patterns of Reform." PhD diss., European University Institute.

Davidsson, Johan Bo, and Patrick Emmenegger. 2012. "Defending the Organisation, Not the Members. Unions and the Reform of Job Security Legislation in Western Europe." *European Journal of Political Research* 53 (3): 339–363.

Denmark Government. 2016. *Denmark's National Reform Programme*. Copenhagen: Ministry of Finance.

Dingeldey, Irene. 2007. "Wohlfahrtsstaatlicher Wandel zwischen 'Arbeitszwang' und 'Befähigung.' Eine vergleichende Analyse aktivierender Arbeitsmarktpolitik in Deutschland, Dänemark und Großbritannien." *Berliner Journal für Soziologie* 17 (2): 189–209.

Doellgast, Virginia, Nathan Lilie, and Valeria Pulignano. "From Dualization to Solidarity." In *Reconstructing Solidarity: Labour Unions, Precarious Work, and the Politics of Institutional Change in Europe*, ed. Virginia Doellgast, Nathan Lilie, and Valeria Pulignano 1–41. Oxford: Oxford University Press.

Due, Jesper, Jørgen Madsen, and Christian L. Ibsen. 2012. "A-kassernes medlemstal er stagneret trods krisen, FAOS Analyse." http://www.faos.ku.dk/pdf/artikler/ovrige _artikler/2012/a- kassernes_medlemstal_er_stagneret150312.pdf.

Durazzi, Niccolo. 2017. "Inclusive Unions in a Dualized Labour Market? The Challenge of Organizing Labour Market Policy and Social Protection for Labour Market Outsiders." *Social Policy and Administration* 51 (2): 265–285.

Ebbinghaus, Bernhard. 2006. *Reforming Early Retirement in Europe, Japan and the USA*. Oxford: Oxford University Press.

Ebbinghaus, Bernhard, Claudia Göbel, and Sebastian Koos. 2011. "Social Capital, 'Ghent' and Workplace Contexts: Comparing Union Membership in Europe." *European Journal of Industrial Relations* 17 (2): 107–124.

Ebbinghaus, Bernhard, and Anke Hassel. 2000. "Striking Deals: Concertation in the Reform of Continental European Welfare States." *Journal of European Public Policy* 7 (1): 44–62.

Eichhorst, Werner, and Regina Konle-Seidl. 2008. "Contingent Convergence: A Comparative Analysis of Activation Policies." Institute of Labor Economics, *IZA Discussion Paper*, no. 3905.

Eichhorst, Werner, and Paul Marx. 2012. "Whatever Works: Dualization and the Service Economy in Bismarckian Welfare States." In *The Age of Dualization. The Changing Face of Inequality*, edited by Patrick Emmenegger, Silja Häusermann, Bruno Palier, and Martin Seeleib-Kaiser, 73–99. Oxford: Oxford University Press.

Eichhorst, Werner, and Ole Wintermann. 2005. "Generating Legitimacy for Labor Market and Welfare State Reforms: The Role of Policy Advice in Germany, the Netherlands and Sweden." Institute of Labor Economics, *IZA Discussion Paper*, no. 1845.

Emmenegger, Patrick. 2010. "The Long Road to Flexicurity: The Development of Job Security Regulations in Denmark and Sweden." *Scandinavian Political Studies* 33 (3): 271–294.

Emmenegger, Patrick. 2014. *The Power to Dismiss: Trade Unions and the Regulation of Job Security in Western Europe*. Oxford: Oxford University Press.

Emmenegger, Patrick, Silja Häusermann, Bruno Palier, and Martin Seeleib-Kaiser. 2012. *The Age of Dualization. The Changing Face of Inequality*. Oxford: Oxford University Press.

Esping-Andersen, Gøsta. 1985. *Politics against Markets: The Social Democratic Road to Power*. Princeton, NJ: Princeton University Press.

Esping-Andersen, Gøsta. 1990. *The Three Worlds of Welfare Capitalism*. Cambridge: Polity Press.

Etherington, David, and Martin Jones. 2004. "Welfare-through-Work and the Reregulation of Labour Markets in Denmark." *Capital and Class* 28 (2): 19–45.

European Commission. 2010. "Council Recommendation with a View to Bringing an End to the Situation of an Excessive Government Deficit in Denmark." *European Commission*, June 15, 2010.

European Industrial Relations Observatory (EIRO). 1997. "Controversial Changes in Employment Protection Act Provide for More Bargaining at Company Level."

European Industrial Relations Observatory (EIRO). 2001. "Reform of Severance Pay under Discussion." http://eurofound.europa.eu/observatories/eurwork/articles /reform-of-severance-pay-under-discussion.

European Industrial Relations Observatory (EIRO). 2002a. "Government and Social Partners Sign Pact for Italy." http://www.eurofound.europa.eu/observatories /eurwork/articles/government-and-social-partners-sign-pact-for-italy.

European Industrial Relations Observatory (EIRO). 2002b. "Social Partners Agree Far-Reaching Reform of Severance Pay." http://www.eurofound.europa.eu/eiro/2001/12/feature/at0112231f.htm.

European Industrial Relations Observatory (EIRO). 2007. "Social Partners Tackle Unemployment and Skills Deficit." http://www.eurofound.europa.eu/eiro/2007/11/articles/at0711039i.htm.

European Industrial Relations Observatory (EIRO). 2010. "Decline in Union Density Threatens Collective Bargaining." http://www.eurofound.europa.eu/eiro/2010/12/articles/dk1012019i.htm.

European Industrial Relations Observatory (EIRO). 2013. "New Training to Plug Skills Gap." http://www.eurofound.europa.eu/eiro/2013/04/articles/at1304011i.htm.

European Industrial Relations Observatory (EIRO). 2015. "Italy: Reforms to System of Unemployment Benefits." http://www.eurofound.europa.eu/observatories/eurwork/articles/industrial-relations-law-and-regulation/italy-reforms-to-system-of-unemployment-benefits.

European Monitoring Centre on Change (EMCC). 2013. "Sweden: Young People and Temporary Employment in Europe." http://www.eurofound.europa.eu/observatories/emcc/comparative-information/national-contributions/sweden-young-people-and-temporary-employment-in-europe.

Fallend, Franz. 2006. "Die ÖVP." In Schwarz-Blau. Eine Bilanz des "Neu-Regierens," ed. Tálos Emmerich, and Marcel Fink, 3–18. Vienna: LIT Verlag.

Fichtelius, E. 2007. Aldrig ensam, alltid ensam. Samtalen med Göran Persson 1996–2006. Stockholm: Norstedts.

Fervers, Lukas, and Hanna Schwander. 2015. "Are Outsiders Equally Out Everywhere? The Economic Disadvantage of Outsiders in Cross-national Perspective." European Journal of Industrial Relations 21 (4): 369–387.

Fink, Marcel. 2006. "'Zwischen "Beschäftigungsrekord' und 'Rekordarbeitslosigkeit': Arbeitsmarkt und Arbeitsmarktpolitik unter Schwarz-Blau/Orange." In Schwarz-Blau. Eine Bilanz des "Neu-Regierens," ed. Tálos Emmerich, and Marcel Fink, 170–187. Vienna: LIT Verlag.

Fink, Marcel, and Manfred Krenn. 2014. "Prekariat und Working Poor: Zum Verhältnis von Erwerbsarbeit und sozialer Inklusion in Österreich." In Handbuch Armut in Österreich. 2nd edition, ed. Nikolaus Dimmel, Martin Schenk, and Christine Stelzer-Orthofer, 289–308. Vienna: Studienverlag.

Frangi, Lorenzo, Sebastian Koos, and Sinisa Hadziabdic. 2017. "In Unions We Trust! Analysing Confidence in Unions across Europe." British Journal of Industrial Relations 55 (4): 831–58.

Gamble, Andrew. 1988. The Free Economy and the Strong State: The Politics of Thatcherism. London: Macmillan.

Garrett, Geoffrey. 1995. "Capital Mobility, Trade and the Domestic Politics of Economic Policy." International Organizations 49 (4): 657–678.

George, Alexander L., and Andrew Bennett. 2005. Case Studies and Theory Development. Cambridge, MA: MIT Press.

Giger, Nathalie, and Moira Nelson. 2011. "The Electoral Consequences of Welfare State Retrenchment: Blame Avoidance or Credit Claiming in the Era of Permanent Austerity?" European Journal of Political Research 50 (1): 1–23.

Gingrich, Jane, and Silja Häusermann. 2015. "The Decline of the Working-class Vote, the Reconfiguration of the Welfare Support Coalition and Consequences for the Welfare State." Journal of European Social Policy 25 (1): 50–75.

Glyn, Andrew. 2007. *Capitalism Unleashed: Finance Globalisation and Welfare.* Oxford: Oxford University Press.

Goldthorpe, John H. 1984. *Order and Conflict in Contemporary Capitalism.* New York: Oxford University Press.

Gordon, Joshua. 2012. "Bringing Labor Back In: Varieties of Unionism and the Evolution of Employment Protection and Unemployment Benefits in the Rich Democracies." PhD diss., University of Toronto.

Gordon, Joshua. 2015. "Protecting the Unemployed: Varieties of Unionism and the Evolution of Unemployment Benefits and Active Labour Market Policy in the Rich Democracies." *Socio-Economic Review* 13 (1): 79–99.

Gordon, Joshua. 2017. "The Perils of Vanguardism: Explaining Radical Cuts to Unemployment Insurance in Sweden." *Socio-Economic Review* (preview).

Goul Andersen, Jørgen. 2003. "The General Election in Denmark, November 2001." *Electoral Studies* 22 (22): 186–193.

Goul Andersen, Jørgen. 2011a. "Ambivalent values: Universalism or targeting? Welfare State Attitudes in Denmark." *CCWS Working Paper no. 2011–73.* Aalborg, Denmark: University of Aalborg

Goul Andersen, Jørgen. 2011b. "Denmark: Ambiguous Modernization of an Inclusive Unemployment Protection." In *Regulating the Risk of Unemployment. National Adaptions to Post-Industrial Labour Markets in Europe,* ed. Jochen Clasen, and Daniel Clegg, 187–207. Oxford: Oxford University Press.

Goul Andersen, Jørgen. 2011c. *From the Edge of the Abyss to Bonanza—and Beyond. Danish Economy and Economic Policies 1980–2011.* Aalborg, Denmark: University of Aalborg, Department of Political Science.

Goul Andersen, Jørgen. 2012a. "Crisis Narratives and Welfare Reform in Denmark. A Critical Juncture?" Paper prepared for Conference on Labour Markets and Welfare State Research, CARMA and CCWS, first draft, October.

Goul Andersen, Jørgen. 2012b. "Universalization and De-universalization of Unemployment Protection in Denmark and Sweden." In *Welfare State, Universalism and Diversity,* ed. Anneli Anttonen, Liisa Häikiö, and Kolbeinn Stefánsson, 162–186. Cheltenham and Northhamptom, UK: Edward Elgar.

Goul Andersen, Jørgen, and Kasper Møller Hansen. 2013. "Vælgernes krisebevidsthed." In *Krisevalg. Økonomien og Folketingsvalget 2011,* ed. Rune Stubager, Kasper Møller Hansen, and Jørgen Goul Andersen, 137–162. Copenhagen: Jurist-og Økonomforbundets Forlag.

Goul Andersen, Jørgen, and Jacob J. Pedersen. 2007. "Continuity and Change in Danish Active Labour Market Policy: 1990–2007. The Battlefield between Activation and Workfare." Center for Comparative Welfare Studies, Aalborg University, Denmark, *CCWS Working Paper,* no. 54.

Government of Austria. 1994. *Das Arbeitsübereinkommen zwischen der Sozialdemokratischen Partei Österreichs und der Österreichischen Volkspartei.*

Green-Pedersen, Christoffer. 2001. "Minority Governments and Party Politics: The Political and Institutional Background to the 'Danish Miracle.'" *Journal of Public Policy* 21 (1): 53–70.

Green-Pedersen, Christoffer, Flemming J. Christiansen, Eva-Maria Euchner, Carsten Jensen, and John Turnpenny. 2012. "Dismantling by Default? The Indexation of Social Benefits in Four Countries." In *Dismantling Public Policy. Preferences, Strategies and Effects,* ed. Michael W. Bauer, Andrew Jordan, Christoffer Green-Pedersen, and Adrienne Héritier, 129–155. Oxford: Oxford University Press.

Green-Pedersen, Christoffer, Kees Van Keesbergen, and Anton Hemerijck. 2001. "Neo-liberalism, the 'Third Way' or What? Recent Social Democratic Welfare Policies in Denmark and the Netherlands." *Journal of European Social Policy* 8 (2): 307–325.

Gumbrell-McCormick, Rebecca, and Richard Hyman. 2013. *Trade Unions in Western Europe: Hard Times, Hard Choices*. Oxford: Oxford University Press.

Hacker, Jacob. 2004. "Privatizing Risk without Privatizing the Welfare State: The Hidden Politics of Social Policy Retrenchment in the United States." *American Political Science Review* 98 (2): 243–260.

Hacker, Jacob, and Paul Pierson. 2002. "Business Power and Social Policy: Employers and the Formation of the American Welfare State." *Politics and Society* 30 (2): 277–326.

Hacker, Jacob, and Paul Pierson. 2010. *Winner-Take-All Politics: How Washington Made the Rich Richer and Turned Its Back on the Middle Class*. New York: Simon & Schuster.

Haffert, Lukas, and Philip Mehrtens. 2015. "From Austerity to Expansion? Consolidation, Budget Surpluses, and the Decline of Fiscal Capacity." *Politics and Society* 43 (1): 119–148.

Hall, Peter A. 1997. "The Role of Interests, Institutions, and Ideas in the Comparative Political Economy of the Industrialized Nations." In *Comparative Politics: Rationality, Culture and Structure*, ed. Mark I. Libach, and Alan S. Zuckerman, 174–207. Cambridge: Cambridge University Press.

Hall, Peter A. 2003. "Aligning Ontology and Methodology in Comparative Politics." In *Comparative Historical Analysis in the Social Sciences*, ed. James Mahoney, and Dietrich Rueschemeyer, 373–404. New York: Cambridge University Press.

Hall, Peter A. 2006. "Systematic Process Analysis: When and How to Use It." *European Management Review* 3 (1): 24–31.

Hall, Peter A. 2008. "Systematic Process Analysis: When and How to Use It." *European Political Science* 7 (3): 304–317.

Hall, Peter A., and David Soskice. 2001. "An Introduction to Varieties of Capitalism." In *Varieties of Capitalism. The Institutional Foundations of Comparative Advantage*, ed. Peter A. Hall, and David Soskice, 1–68. Oxford: Oxford University Press.

Hancké, Bob, and Martin Rhodes. 2005. "EMU and Labor Market Institutions in Europe. The Rise and Fall of National Social Pacts." *Work and Occupations* 32 (2): 196–228.

Hamann, Kerstin, and John Kelly. 2007. "Party Politics and the Reemergence of Social Pacts in Western Europe." *Comparative Political Studies* 40 (8): 971–994.

Hamann, Kerstin, and John Kelly. 2011. *Parties, Elections, and Policy Reforms in Western Europe. Voting for Social Pacts*. London and New York: Routledge.

Harvey, David. 2010. *The Enigma of Capital and the Crisis of Capitalism*. London: Profile Books.

Hassel, Anke. 2009. "Policies and Politics in Social Pacts in Europe." *European Journal of Industrial Relations* 15 (1): 7–26.

Hassel, Anke. 2015. "Trade Unions and the Future of Democratic Capitalism." In *The Politics of Advanced Capitalism*, ed. Pablo Beramendi, Silja Häusermann, Herbert Kitschelt, and Hanspeter Kriesi, 231–256. Cambridge: Cambridge University Press.

Häusermann, Silja. 2010. *The Politics of Welfare State Reform in Continental Europe. Modernization in Hard Times*. Cambridge: Cambridge University Press.

Häusermann, Silja and Hanspeter Kriesi. 2015. "What Do Voters Want? Dimensions and Configurations in Individual-Level Preferences and Party Choice." In *The Politics of Advanced Capitalism*, ed. Pablo Beramendi, Silja Häusermann, Herbert Kitschelt, and Hanspeter Kriesi, 202–230. Cambridge: Cambridge University Press.

Häusermann, Silja, Thomas Kurer, et al. 2015. "High-Skilled Outsiders" https://academic.oup.com/ser/article/13/2/235/2885309.

Häusermann, Silja, Thomas Kurer, and Hanna Schwander. 2015. "High-Skilled Outsiders? Labor Market Vulnerability, Education and Welfare State Preferences." *Socio-Economic Review* 13 (2): 235–258.

Häusermann, Silja, and Hanna Schwander. 2015. "Who Is In and Who Is Out? A Risk-Based Conceptualisation of Insiders and Outsiders." *Journal of European Social Policy* 23 (3): 248–269.

Hayek, Friedrich August von. 1979. *Law, Legislation and Liberty, Volume 3: The Political Order of a Free People*, chap. 3. Chicago: University of Chicago Press.

Heery, Edmund, and Lee Adler. 2004. "Organizing the Unorganized." In *Varieties of Unionism: Strategies for Union Revitalization in a Globalizing Economy*, ed. Carola Frege, and John Kelly, 45–69. Oxford: Oxford University Press.

Heinisch, Reinhard. 1999. "Modernization Brokers: Explaining the Resurgence of Austrian Corporatism in the Mid-1990s." *Current Politics and Economics of Europe* 9 (1): 65–94.

Heinisch, Reinhard. 2000. "Coping with Economic Integration: Corporatist Strategies in Germany and Austria in the 1990s." *West European Politics* 23 (3): 67–96.

Heinisch, Reinhard. 2001. "Defying Neoliberal Convergence: Austria's Successful Supply-Side Corporatism in the 1990s." *Environment and Planning C: Government and Policy* 19 (1): 29–44.

Hemerijck, Anton, Brigitte Unger, and Jelle Visser. 2000. "How Small Countries Negotiate Change. Twenty-Five Years of Policy Adjustment in Austria, the Netherlands, and Belgium." In *Welfare and Work in an Open Economy: Volume 2I, Diverse Responses to Common Challenges*, ed. Fritz Scharpf, and Vivianne Schmidt, 176–263. New York: Oxford University Press.

Henkes, Christian. 2006. "Schweden." In *Die Reformfähigkeit der Sozialdemokratie. Herausforderungen und Bilanz der Regierungspolitik in Westeuropa*, ed. Wolfgang Merkel, Christoph Egle, Christian Henkes, Tobias Ostheim, and Alexander Petring, 272–314. Wiesbaden, Germany: VS Verlag für Sozialwissenschaften.

Hernández, Enrique, and Hanspeter Kriesi. 2016. "The Electoral Consequences of the Financial and Economic Crisis in Europe" *European Journal of Political Research* 55 (2): 203–224.

Hofer, Helmut, Andrea Weber, and Rudolf Winter-Ebmer. 2014. "Labor Market Policy during the Crises." *Working Paper n. 1326*. Linz: Department of Economics, Johannes Kepler University of Linz.

Horaczek, Nina. 2007. *Das Streikjahr 2003. Von der sozialpartnerschaftlichen Konsens- zur Konfliktdemokratie? Die politischen Auswirkungen der Streiks 2003 unter besonderer Berücksichtigung des ÖGB*. Vienna: ÖGB-Verlag.

Huber, Evelyne, and John D. Stephens. 2001. *Development and Crisis of the Welfare State. Parties and Policies in Global Markets*. Chicago: University of Chicago Press.

Huo, Jingjing. 2009. *Third Way Reforms: Social Democracy after the Golden Age*. Cambridge: Cambridge University Press.

Huo, Jingjing, Moira Nelson, and John D. Stephens. 2008. "Decommodification and Activation in Social Democratic Policy: Resolving the Paradox." *Journal of European Social Policy* 18 (1): 5–20.

Ibsen, C. Lyhne. 2013. "Consensus or Coercion? Collective Bargaining Coordination and Third Party Intervention." PhD diss., Department of Sociology, University of Copenhagen.

Ibsen, C. Lyhne, Jesper Due, and Jørgen S. Madsen. 2014. *Fald i organisationsgraden igen*. FAOS Analyse. Copenhagen University.

Ibsen, Flemming, Laust Høgedahl, and Steen Scheuer. 2013. "Free Riders: The Rise of Alternative Unionism in Denmark." *Industrial Relations Journal* 44 (5): 444–461.

Iversen, Torben. 1996. "Power, Flexibility, and the Breakdown of Centralized Wage Bargaining: Denmark and Sweden in Comparative Perspective." *Comparative Politics* 28 (4): 399–436.

Iversen, Torben. 1998. "The Choices for Scandinavian Social Democracy in Comparative Perspective." *Oxford Review of Economic Policy* 14 (1): 59–75.

Jensen, Carsten. 2014. *The Right and the Welfare State.* Oxford: Oxford University Press.

Jessoula, Matteo, and Patrik Vesan. "Italy: Limited Adaption of an Atypical System." In *Regulating the Risk of Unemployment: National Adaptions to Post-Industrial Labour Markets in Europe,* ed. Jochen Clasen and Daniel Clegg, 142–163. Oxford: Oxford University Press.

Jodár Pere, Sergi Vidal, and Ramon Alós. 2011. "Union Activism in an Inclusive System of Industrial Relations: Evidence from a Spanish Case Study." *British Journal of Industrial Relations* 49 (s1): 158–180.

Jørgensen, Henning. 2009. "From a Beautiful Swan to an Ugly Duckling: The Renewal of Danish Activation Policy." *European Journal of Social Security* 11 (4): 337–367.

Jørgensen, Henning, and Michaela Schulze. 2011. "Leaving the Nordic Path? The Changing Role of Trade Unions in the Welfare Reform Process." *Social Policy and Administration* 45 (2): 206–219.

Jupskås, Anders R. 2015. "Institutionalised Right-Wing Populism in Times of Economic Crisis: A Comparative Study of the Norwegian Progress Party and the Danish People's Party." *In European Populism in the Shadow of the Great Recession,* ed. Hanspeter Kriesi and Takis S. Pappas, 23–40. Colchester: ECPR Press.

Kalina, Josef. 2007. "'Mission Impossible'—am Ende siegen die Guten." In *Wahl 2006—Kanzler, Kampagnen, Kapriolen. Analysen zur Nationalratswahl 2006,* ed. Thomas Hofer and Barbara Tóth, 33–46. Vienna: LIT.

Karlhofer, Ferdinand. 2006. "Arbeitnehmerorganisationen." In *Politik in Österreich. Das Handbuch,* ed. Herbert Dachs et al., 425–442. Vienna: LIT.

Katzenstein, Peter J. 1976. *Disjoined Partners: Austria and Germany since 1815.* Berkeley: University of California Press.

Katzenstein, Peter J. 1984. *Corporatism and Change. Austria, Switzerland and the Politics of Industry.* Ithaca, NY, and New York: Cornell University Press.

Katzenstein, Peter J. 1985. *Small States in World Markets: Industrial Policy in Europe.* Ithaca, NY, and New York: Cornell University Press.

Kaufmann, Franz-Xaver. 1997. *Herausforderungen des Sozialstaates.* Frankfurt am Main: Suhrkamp.

Khol, Andreas. 2001. *Die Wende ist geglückt. Der schwarze-blaue Marsch durch die Wüste Gobi.* Vienna: Molden.

Kitschelt, Herbert. 1995. *The Radical Right in Western Europe: A Comparative Analysis.* Ann Arbor: University of Michigan Press.

Kjellberg, Anders. 2011. "The Decline in Swedish Union Density since 2007." *Nordic Journal Of Working Life Studies* 1 (1): 67–93.

Kjellberg, Anders. 2015. "Kollektivavtalens täckningsgrad samt organisationsgraden hos arbetsgivarförbund och fackförbund." *Lund University Studies in Social Policy, Industrial Relations, Working Life and Mobility,* Research Reports 2013:1, updated version.

Klenner, Fritz. 1967. *Die österreichischen Gewerkschaften. Eine Monographie.* Vienna: Verlag des Österreichischen Gewerkschaftsbundes.

Klitgaard, Michael B., and Christian Elmelund-Præstekær. 2013. "The Partisanship of Systemic Retrenchment: Tax Policy and Welfare Reform in Denmark 1975–2008." *European Political Science Review* 6 (1): 1–19.

Klitgaard, Michael B., and Asbjørn S. Nørgaard. 2010. "Afmagtens mekanismer: Den danske fagbevægelse og arbejdsmarkedspolitikken siden 1960'erne." *Politica* 42 (1): 5–26.

Klitgaard, Michael B., and Asbjørn S. Nørgaard. 2014. "Structural Stress or Deliberate Decision? Government Partisanship and the Disempowerment of Unions in Denmark." *European Journal of Political Research* 52 (2): 1–18.

Klos, M. 2014. *33.900 har mistet deres dagpengeret i 2013, Status for hele 2013.* Copenhagen: AK-Samvirke.

Knotz, Carlo, and Johannes Lindvall. 2015. "Coalitions and Compensation: The Case of Unemployment Benefit Duration." *Comparative Political Studies* 48 (5): 586–615.

Konle-Seidl, Regina. 2008. *Hilfereformen und Aktivierungsstrategien im internationalen Vergleich, IAB-Forschungsbericht 7.* Nuremberg, Germany: IAB.

Korpi, Walter. 1978. *The Working Class in Welfare Capitalism. Work, Unions and Politics in Sweden.* London: Routledge.

Korpi, Walter. 1983. *The Democratic Class Struggle.* London: Routledge.

Korpi, Walter. 2006. "Power Resources and Employer-Centered Approaches in Explanations of Welfare State and Varieties of Capitalism: Protagonists, Consenters and Antagonists." *World Politics* 58 (2): 167–206.

Korpi, Walter, and Joakim Palme. 2003. "New Politics and Class Politics in the Context of Austerity and Globalization: Welfare State Regress in 18 Countries, 1975–95." *American Political Science Review* 97 (3): 425–446.

Kriesi, Hanspeter, Edgar Grande, Romain Lachat, Martin Dolezal, and Simon Bornschier. 2008. *West European Politics in the Age of Globalization.* Cambridge: Cambridge University Press.

Lafer, Gordon. 2017. *The One Percent Solution: How Corporations Are Remaking America One State at a Time.* Ithaca, NY: ILR Press.

Larsen, Christian A. 2008. "The Institutional Logic of Welfare Attitudes: How Welfare Regimes Influence Public Support." *Comparative Political Studies* 41 (2): 145–168.

Larsen, Christian A., and Jørgen Goul Andersen. 2009. "How New Economic Ideas Changed the Danish Welfare State: The Case of Neoliberal Ideas and Highly Organized Social Democratic Interests." *Governance* 22 (2): 239–261.

Lavalle, Ashley. 2008. *The Death of Social Democracy: Political Consequences in the 21st Century.* Aldershot, UK: Ashgate.

Laver, Michael, and Kenneth A. Shepsle. 1996. *Making and Breaking Governments: Cabinets and Legislatures in Parliamentary Democracies.* Cambridge: Cambridge University Press.

Lehmbruch, Gerhard, and C. Philippe Schmitter. 1982. *Patterns of Corporatist Policy Making.* London: Sage Publications.

Levy, Jonah. 1999. "Vice into Virtue: Progressive Politics and Welfare Reform in Continental Europe." *Politics and Society* 27 (2): 239–273.

Lind, Jens. 2009. "The End of the Ghent System as a Trade Union Recruitment Machinery?" *Industrial Relations Journal* 40 (6): 510–523.

Lindbom, Anders. 2008. "The Swedish Conservative Party and the Welfare State: Institutional Change and Adapting Preference." *Government and Opposition* 43 (4): 539–560.

Lindgren, Karl-Oskar. 2011. "The Variety of Capitalism in Sweden and Finland: Continuity Through Change." In *The Changing Political Economies of Small West European Countries,* ed. Uwe Becker, 45–72. Amsterdam: Amsterdam University Press.

Lindvall, Johannes. 2004. "The Politics of Purpose. Macroeconomic Policy in Sweden after the Golden Age." PhD diss., Göteborg University.

Lindvall, Johannes. 2010. *Mass Unemployment and the State*. Oxford: Oxford University Press.

Lindvall, Johannes, and Bo Rothstein. 2006. "Sweden: The Fall of the Strong State." *Scandinavian Political Studies* 29 (1): 47–63.

Lindvall, Johannes, and David Rueda. 2012. "Insider-Outsider Politics: Party Strategies and Political Behavior in Sweden." In *The Age of Dualization*, ed. Patrick Emmenegger, Silja Häusermann, Bruno Palier, and Martin Seeleib-Kaiser, 277–303. Oxford: Oxford University Press.

Lindvall, Johannes, and Joakim Sebring. 2005. "Policy Reform and the Decline of Corporatism in Sweden." *West European Politics* 28 (5): 1057–1074.

Lipset, Seymour M., and Stein Rokkan. 1990. "Cleavage Structures, Party Systems, and Voter Alignments." In *The West European Party System*, ed. Peter Mair, 91–111. Oxford: Oxford University Press.

Landsorganisationen i Sverige. 2015. *Vägen till full sysselsättning och rättvisare loner*. Final Report to the Statutory Congress of LO Sweden in 2016, Swedish Trade Union Confederation.

Locke, Richard, and Kathleen Thelen. 1995. "Apples and Oranges Revisited: Contextualised Comparisons and the Study of Comparative Labor Politics." *Politics and Society* 23 (3): 337–367.

Luther, Kurt. 2003. "The Self-Destruction of a Right-Wing Populist Party? The Austrian Parliamentary Election of 2002." *West European Politics* 26 (2): 136–152.

MacLean, Nancy. 2017. *Democracy in Chains: The Deep History of the Radical Right's Stealth Plan for America*. New York: Viking.

Madsen, Kongshøj Per. 1999. "Denmark: Flexibility, Security, and Labour Market Success." *Employment and Training Papers no. 53*, ILO Geneva.

Mailand, Mikkel. 2006. "Dynamic Neo-Corporatism–Regulating Work and Welfare in Denmark." *Tranfer: European Review of Labour and Research* 12 (3): 371–387.

Mahoney, James, and Gary Goertz. 2004. "The Possibility Principle: Choosing Negative Cases in Comparative Research." *American Political Science Review* 98 (4): 653–669.

Mair, Peter. 2013. *Ruling the Void: The Hollowing of Western Democracy*. London and New York: Verso Book.

Mares, Isabella. 2003. *The Politics of Social Risk: Business and Welfare State Development*. Cambridge: Cambridge University Press.

Mares, Isabella. 2006. *Taxation, Wage Bargaining, and Unemployment*. Cambridge: Cambridge University Press.

Martin, Cathie J., and Duane Swank. 2012. *The Political Construction of Business Interests: Coordination, Growth, and Equality*. Cambridge: Cambridge University Press.

Martin, Cathie J., and Kathleen Thelen. 2007. "The State and Coordinated Capitalism. Contributions of the Public Sector to Social Solidarity in Postindustrial Societies." *World Politics* 60 (1): 1–36.

Mato, Javier F. 2011. "Spain: Fragmented Unemployment Protection in a Segmented Labour Market." In *Regulating the Risk of Unemployment. National Adaptions to Post-Industrial Labour Markets in Europe*, ed. Jochen Clasen, and Daniel Clegg, 164–186. Oxford: Oxford University Press.

McCarthy, Michael A. 2017. *Dismantling Solidarity: Capitalist Politics and American Pensions since the New Deal*. London and Ithaca, NY: ILR Press, an imprint of Cornell University Press.

Meguid, Bonnie. 2008. *Party Competition between Unequals: Strategies and Electoral Fortunes in Western Europe*. Cambridge and New York: Cambridge University Press.

Mehrtens, Philip. 2014. *Staatsschulden und Staatstätigkeit. Zur Transformation der politischen Ökonomie Schweden*. Frankfurt, Germany, and New York: Campus Verlag.

Meidner, Rudolf, and Anna Hedborg. 1984. *Modell Schweden. Erfahrungen einer Wohl-fahrtsgesellschaft.* Frankfurt am Main: Campus.

Milanovic, Branko. 2016. *Global Inequality. A New Approach for the Age of Globalization.* Harvard, MA: Harvard University Press.

"Mindestsicherung: Fleckerlteppich statt engmaschiges Netz." 2015. *Der Standard*, January 2. http://derstandard.at/2000009956876/Mindestsicherung-Fleckerlteppich-statt-dichtmaschiges-Netz.

Molina, Oscar, and Martin Rhodes. 2007. "The Political Economy of Adjustment in Mixed Market Economies: A Study of Spain and Italy." In *Beyond Varieties of Capitalism Conflict, Contradictions and Complementarities in the European Economy*, ed. Bob Hancké, Martin Rhodes, and Mark Thatcher, 223–252. Oxford: Oxford University Press.

Molina, Oscar, and Martin Rhodes. 2011. "Spain: From Tripartite Pacts to Bipartite Pacts." In *Social Pacts in Europe. Emergence, Evolution, and Institutionalization*, ed. Sabrina Avdagic, Martin Rhodes, and Jelle Visser, 174–202. Oxford: Oxford University Press.

Müller, Wolfgang C. 1988. "Die neue Große Koalition in Österreich." *Österreichische Zeitschrift für Politikwissenschaft* 17 (4): 321–347.

Müller, Wolfgang C., and Franz Fallend. 2004. "Changing Patterns of Party Competition in Austria: From Multipolar to Bipolar System." *West European Politics* 27 (5): 801–835.

Naczyk, Marek, and Martin Seeleib-Kaiser. 2015. "Solidarity against All Odds: Trade Unions and the Privatization of Pensions in the Age of Dualization." *Politics & Society* 43 (3): 361–384.

"Neue Sozialhilfeobergrenze: 33.000 Dänen ab 1. Oktober betroffen." Der Nordschleswiger, September 23.

"Neue Sozialpartnerschaft." 2008. *Der Standard*, May 21. http://derstandard.at/3319100.

Nickell, Stephen, and Richard Layard. 1999. "Labour Market Institutions and Economics Performance." In *Handbook of Labour Economics, Vol. 3, Part C*, ed. Orley Ashenfelter and David Card, 3029–3084. Amsterdam: North-Holland.

Nordt, Carlos, Ingeborg Warnke, Erich Seifritz, and Wolfram Kawohl. 2015. "Modelling Suicide and Unemployment: A Longitudinal Analysis Covering 63 Countries, 2000–11." *The Lancet Psychiatry* 2 (3): 239–245.

Obinger, Herbert. 2002. "Veto Players, Political Parties and Welfare State Retrenchment." *International Journal of Political Economy* 32 (2): 44–66.

Obinger, Herbert. 2009. "Sozialpolitische Bilanz der Großen Koalition in Österreich." In *Wohlfahrtsstaatlichkeit in entwickelten Demokratien. Herausforderungen, Reformen und Perspektiven, Schriften des Zentrums für Sozialpolitik*, ed. Herbert Obinger, and Elmar Rieger, 347–374. Frankfurt and New York: Campus Verlag.

Obinger, Herbert, Peter Starke, and Alexandra Kaasch. 2012. "Responses to Labor Market Divides in Small States since the 1990s." In *The Age of Dualization. The Changing Face of Inequality in Deindustrializing Countries*, ed. Patrick Emmenegger, Silja Häusermann, Bruno Palier, and Martin Seeleib-Kaiser, 176–200. New York: Oxford University Press.

Obinger, Herbert, Peter Starke, Julia Moser, Claudia Bogedan, Edith Gindulis, and Stephan Leibfried. 2010. *Transformations of the Welfare State. Small States, Big Lessons.* Oxford/New York: Oxford University Press.

Obinger, Herbert, and Emmerich Tálos. 2006. *Sozialstaat Österreich zwischen Kontinuität und Umbau. Eine Bilanz der ÖVP/FPÖ/BZÖ-Regierung.* Wiesbaden, Germany: Verlag für Sozialwissenschaften.

OECD. 1994. *The OECD Jobs Study. Facts, Analysis, Strategies.* Paris.

OECD. 2008. *Growing Unequal? Income Distribution and Poverty in OECD Countries.* Paris.

OECD. 2009. *The Political Economy of Reform Lessons from Pensions, Product Markets and Labour Markets in Ten OECD Countries.* Paris.

OECD. 2011. *Divided We Stand? Why Inequality Keeps Rising.* Paris.

OECD. 2013. *Crisis Squeezes Income and Puts Pressure on Inequality and Poverty, Results from the OECD Income Distribution Database.* Paris.

OECD. 2015. *In It Together: Why Less Inequality Benefits All.* Paris.

Öberg, PerOla., Torsten Svensson, Peter M. Christiansen, Asbjørn S. Nørgaard, Hilmar Rommetvedt, and Gunnar Thesen. 2011. "Disrupted Exchange and Declining Corporatism: Government Authority and Interest Group Capability in Scandinavia." *Government and Opposition* 46 (3): 365–391.

Oesch, Daniel. 2006. "Coming to Grips with a Changing Class Structure. An Analysis of Employment Stratification in Britain, Germany, Sweden and Switzerland." *International Sociology* 21 (2): 263–288.

ÖKSA (Österreichisches Komitee für Soziale Arbeit). 2012. *Evaluierung zur Umsetzung der Bedarfsorientierten Mindestsicherung.* Dokumentation der Jahreskonferenz 2012.

"Opposition Opens Up Record Poll Lead." 2008. *The Local,* January 25. http://www.thelocal.se/20080125/9767.

Palier, Bruno. 2006. "The Politics of Reforms in Bismarckian Welfare Systems." *Revue Francaise des Affaires Sociales* (1) 5: 47–72.

Palier, Bruno, and Silja Häusermann. 2008. "The State of the Art: The Politics of Employment-Friendly Welfare Reforms in Post-Industrial Economies." *Socio-Economic Review* 6 (3): 559–586.

Palier, Bruno, and Kathleen Thelen. 2010. "Institutionalizing Dualism: Complementarities and Change in France and Germany." *Politics and Society* 38 (1): 119–148.

Palme, Joakim, Johann Fritzell, and Åke Bergmark. 2009. "Das Ende der Gleichheit? Der schwedische Wohlfahrtsstaat nach der Krise." *WSI-Mitteilungen* 1, 2009: 46–51.

Paster, Thomas. 2012. *The Role of Business in the Development of the Welfare State and Labor Markets in Germany. Containing Social Reforms.* London: Routledge.

Paster, Thomas. 2013. "Why Did Austrian Business Oppose Welfare Cuts? How the Organization of Interests Shapes Business Attitudes Toward Social Partnership." *Comparative Political Studies* 47 (7): 966–992.

Pernicka, Susanne. 2003. "Arbeitsbeziehungen nach der rechtskonservativen Wende. Sozialpartnerschaft in der Krise?" *Kurswechsel* 3, 2006: 84–87.

Pernicka, Susanne. 2005. "The Evolution of Union Politics for Atypical Employees: A Comparison between German and Austrian Trade Unions in the Private Service Sector." *Economic and Industrial Democracy* 26 (2): 205–228.

Picot, Georg, and Arianna Tassinari. 2014. "Liberalization, Dualization, or Recalibration? Labor Market Reforms under Austerity, Italy and Spain 2010–2012." *Nuffield College Working Paper in Politics* 2014-01.

Pierson, Paul. 1994. *Dismantling the Welfare State? Reagan, Thatcher and the Politics of Retrenchment.* Cambridge: Cambridge University Press.

Pierson, Paul. 1996. "The New Politics of the Welfare State." *World Politics* 48 (2): 143–179.

Pierson, Paul. 1998. "Irresistible Forces, Immovable Objects, Post-Industrial Welfare States Confront Permanent Austerity." *Journal of European Public Policy* 5 (4): 539–560.

Polanyi, Karl. 1944. *The Great Transformation.* Reprint 1957. Boston: Beacon Press.

Pontusson, Jonas. 1992. "At the End of the Third Road: Swedish Social Democracy in Crisis." *Politics and Society* 20 (3): 305–332.

Pontusson, Jonas. 1993. "The Comparative Politics of Labor-Initiated Reforms. Swedish Success and Failure." *Comparative Political Studies* 25 (4): 548–578.

Pontusson, Jonas. 2011. "Once again a Model: Nordic Social Democracy in a Globalized World." In *What's Left of the Left? Futures of the Left*, ed. James Cronin, George Ross, and James Shoch, 89–115. Durham, NC: Duke University Press.

Pontusson, Jonas, and Peter Swenson. 1996. "Labor Markets, Production Strategies, and Wage Bargaining Institutions. The Swedish Employer Offensive in Comparative Perspective." *Comparative Political Studies* 29 (2): 223–250.

Pulignano, Valeria, Luis Ortíz Gervasi and Fabio de Franceschi. 2016. "Union Responses to Precarious Workers: Italy and Spain Compared." *European Journal of Industrial Relations* 22 (1): 39–55.

Rasmussen, Peter. 2014. "Privatizing Unemployment Protection—The rise of Private Unemployment Insurance in Denmark and Sweden." *CCWS Working Paper no. 2014-83*.

Rathgeb, Philip. 2017. "No Flexicurity without Trade Unions: The Danish Experience." *Comparative European Politics*: 1–21.

Regeringen. 2011. *ET DANMARK, DER STÅR SAMMEN*. Regeringsgrundlaget.

Regini, Marino. 2000. "The Dilemmas of Labour Market Regulation." In *Why Deregulate Labour Markets?*, ed. by Gøsta Esping-Andersen, 11–29. Oxford: Oxford University Press.

Regini, Marino, and Sabrina Colombo. 2011. "Italy: The Rise and Decline of Social Pacts." In *Social Pacts in Europe. Emergence, Evolution, and Institutionalization*, ed. Sabrina Avdagic, Martin Rhodes, and Jelle Visser, 118–146. Oxford: Oxford University Press.

Rhodes, Martin. 1996. "Globalization and West European Welfare States: A Critical Review of Recent Debates." *Journal of European Social Policy* 6 (4): 305–327.

Riesenfelder, Andreas, Susi Schelepa, and Petra Wetzel. 2011. *Geringfügige Beschäftigung in Österreich*. Vienna: Sozialpolitische Studienreihe Band 9.

Rommetvedt, Hilmar, Gunnar Thesen, Peer M. Christiansen, and Asbjørn S. Nørgaard. 2013. "Coping with Corporatism in Decline and the Revival of Parliament: Interest Group Lobbyism in Denmark and Norway, 1980–2005." *Comparative Political Studies* 46 (4): 457–485.

Röth, Leonce, Alexandre Afonso, and Dennis Spies. 2017. "The Impact of Radical Right Parties on Socio-Economic Policies." *European Political Science Review* (preview).

Rothstein, Bo. 1992. "Labor Market Institutions and Working Class Strength." In *Structuring Politics. Historical Institutionalism in a Comparative Perspective*, ed. Sven Steinmo, Kathleen Thelen, and Frank Longstreth, 33–56. Cambridge: Cambridge University Press.

Rovny, Jan. 2013. "Where Do Radical Right Parties Stand? Position Blurring in Multidimensional Competition." *European Political Science Review* 5 (1): 1–26.

Rovny, Allison. 2014. "The Capacity of Social Policies to Combat Poverty among New Social Risk Groups." *Journal of European Social Policy* 24 (5): 405–423.

Rueda, David. 2006. "Social Democracy and Active Labour-Market Policies: Insiders, Outsiders and the Politics of Employment Promotion." *British Journal of Political Science* 36 (3): 385–406.

Rueda, David. 2007. *Social Democracy Inside Out: Government Partisanship, Insiders, and Outsiders in Industrialized Democracies*. Oxford: Oxford University Press.

Rueda, David. 2008. "Left Government, Policy, and Corporatism: Explaining the Influence of Partisanship on Inequality." *World Politics* 60 (3): 349–389.

Rueda, David. 2015. "The State of the Welfare State: Unemployment, Labor Market Policy and Inequality in the Age of Workfare." *Comparative Politics* 47 (3): 296–314.

Rydgren, Jens. 2014. "Explaining the Emergence of Radical Right-Wing Populist Parties: The Case of Denmark." *West European Politics* 27 (3): 474–502.

Ryner, Magnus. 2004. "Neoliberalization of Social Democracy: The Swedish Case." *Comparative European Politics* 2 (1): 97–119.

Sacchi, Stefano. 2013. "Social Policy Reform in the Italian Debt Crisis: Pensions, Labor, Unemployment Benefits." *Italian Politics* 28 (1): 207–226.

Schäfer, Armin. 2013. "Liberalization, Inequality and Democracy's Discontents." In *Politics in the Age of Austerity*, ed. Armin Schäfer, and Wolfgang Streeck, 169–195. Cambridge: Polity Press.

Scharpf, Fritz. 1987. *Sozialdemokratische Krisenpolitik in Europa.* Frankfurt am Main, Germany: Campus.

Scharpf, Fritz. 1997. *Games Real Actors Play. Actor-Centred Institutionalism in Policy Research.* Boulder, CO: Westview.

Scharpf, Fritz. 2000. "The Viability of Advanced Welfare States in the International Economy: Vulnerabilities and Options." *Journal of European Public Policy* 7 (2): 190–228.

Scharpf, Fritz. 2002. "The European Social Model: Coping with the Challenges of Diversity." *Journal of Common Market Studies* 40 (4): 645–670.

Scheuer, Steen. 1992. "Denmark: Return to Decentralisatin." In *Industrial Relations in the New Europe*, ed. Anthony Ferner, and Richard Hyman, 168–198. Oxford: Blackwell.

Schmitt, Carl. 1932. *Gesunde Wirtschaft im starken Staat. Mitteilungen des Vereins zur Wahrung der gemeinsamen wirtschaftichen Interessen in Rheinland und Westfalen ("Langnamverein").* English translation cited in Cristi (1998).

Schmitter, Philippe, and Wolfgang Streeck. 1999. "The Organization of Business Interests: Studying the Associative Action of Business in Advanced Industrial Societies." *MPIfG Discussion Paper* 99 (1).

Schnyder, Gerhard. 2012. "Like a Phoenix from the Ashes? Reassessing the Transformation of the Swedish Political Economy since the 1970s." *Journal of European Public Policy* 19 (8): 1126–1145.

Schulze, Michaela. 2011. *Gewerkschaften im Umbau des Sozialstaates. Der Einfluss der Dachverbände im Welfare-to-Work-Reformprozess in Dänemark, Deutschland und den USA.* Wiesbaden, Germany: VS Verlag für Sozialwissenschaften.

Schüssel, Wolfgang. 2009. *Offen gelegt.*Vienna: Ecowin.

"Schüssel verweist auf Regierungsabkommen." 2001. *Wiener Zeitung*, May 23, 2001. http://www.wienerzeitung.at/nachrichten/oesterreich/politik/208420_Schuessel-verweist-auf-Regierungsabkommen.html.

Schwander, Hanna. 2012. "The Politicisation of the Insider-Outsider Divide in Western Europe: Labour Market Vulnerability and its Political Consequences." PhD diss., University of Zurich.

Scruggs, Lyle. 2002. "The Ghent System and Union Membership in Europe, 1970–1996." *Political Research Quarterly* 55 (2): 275–297.

Scruggs, Lyle. 2007. "Welfare State Generosity across Time and Space." In *Investigating Welfare State Change. The 'Dependent Variable Problem' in Comparative Analysis*, ed. Jochen Clasen, and Nico Siegel, 133–166. Cheltenham, UK: Edward Elgar.

Scruggs, Lyle, Detlef Jahn, and Kati Kuitto. 2014. *Comparative Welfare Entitlements Dataset 2. Version 2014–03.* University of Connecticut and University of Greifswald.

Sebald, Marisa. 1998. *Sozialpartnerschaft und Sozialpolitik.* Diploma Thesis, Department of Government, University of Vienna.

Seeleib-Kaiser, Martin, Silke Van Dyk, and Martin Roggenkamp. 2008. *Party Politics and Social Welfare. Comparing Christian and Social Democracy in Austria, Germany and the Netherlands.* Cheltenham and Northampton, UK: Edward Elgar.

Silver, Beverly J. 2003. *Forces of Labor: Workers' Movements and Globalization since 1870.* Cambridge: Cambridge University Press.

Sjöberg, Ola. 2011. "Sweden: Ambivalent Adjustment." In *Regulating the Risk of Unemployment. National Adaptions to Post-Industrial Labour Markets in Europe*, ed. Jochen Clasen, and Daniel Clegg, 208–231. Oxford: Oxford University Press.

"Sozialpartnerschaft ist Eliteherrschaft." 2009. *Der Standard*, January 16. http://derstandard.at/1231151776063/Interview-mit-Emmerich-Talos-Sozialpartnerschaft-ist-Eliteherrschaft.

Spies, Daniel, and Simon Franzmann. 2011. "A Two-Dimensional Approach to the Political Opportunity Structure of Extreme Right Parties in Western Europe." *West European Politics* 34 (5): 1044–1069.

Spohr, Florian. 2015. *Pfadwechsel in der Arbeitsmarktpolitik. Eine Analyse aktivierender Reformen in Großbritannien, Deutschland und Schweden anhand des Multiple Stream Ansatzes.* Baden-Baden, Germany: Nomos.

Steinmo, Sven. 1988. "Social Democracy vs. Socialism: Goal Adaptation in Social Democratic Sweden." *Politics and Society* 16 (4): 403–446.

Steinmo, Sven. 2010. *The Evolution of Modern States: Sweden, Japan and the United States.* Cambridge: Cambridge University Press.

Steinmo, Sven. 2013. "Governing as an Engineering Problem: The Political Economy of Swedish Success." In *The Politics of Austerity*, ed. Wolfgang Streeck, and Armin Schäfer, 84–107. Cambridge: Polity Press.

Steinmo, Sven, Kathleen Thelen and Frank Longstreth. 1992. *Structuring Politics: Historical Institutionalism in Comparative Analysis.* Cambridge: Cambridge University Press.

Stelzer-Orthofer, Christine. 2011. "Mindestsicherung und Aktivierung—Strategien der österreichischen Arbeitsmarktpolitik." In *Aktivierung und Mindestsicherung: Nationale und europäische Strategien gegen Armut und Arbeitslosigkeit*, ed. Christine Stelzer-Orthofer and Josef Weidenholzer, 141–156. Vienna: Mandelbaum.

Stenographisches Protokoll des Nationalrates, XXIII. GP, 27. Sitzung, 4.7.2007, 116.

Stockhammer, Engelbert. 2004. "Financialisation and the Slowdown of Accumulation." *Cambridge Journal of Economics* 28 (5): 719–741.

Streeck, Wolfgang. 1997. "Beneficial Constraints: On the Economic Limits of Rational Voluntarism." In *Contemporary Capitalism: The Embeddedness of Institutions*, ed. J. Rogers Hollingsworth and Robert Boyer, 197–239. Cambridge: Cambridge University Press.

Streeck, Wolfgang. 2009. *Re-Forming Capitalism: Institutional Change in the German Political Economy.* Oxford and New York: Oxford University Press.

Streeck, Wolfgang. 2011. "The Crises of Democratic Capitalism." *New Left Review* 71 (Sept.-Oct.: 5–29.

Streeck, Wolfgang. 2013. *Gekaufte Zeit. Die vertagte Krise des demokratischen Kapitalisus.* Frankfurt am Main, Germany: Suhrkamp.

Streeck, Wolfgang. 2015. "Heller, Schmitt and the Euro." *European Law Journal* 21 (3): 361–370.

Streeck, Wolfgang, and Daniel Mertens. 2011. "Fiscal Austerity and Public Investment. Is the Possible the Enemy of the Necessary?" Max Plank Institute for the Study of Societies, *MPIfG Discussion Paper* 11/12.

Streeck, Wolfgang, and Kathleen Thelen. 2005. "Introduction: Institutional Change in Advanced Political Economies." In *Beyond Continuity: Institutional Change in Advanced Political Economies*, ed. Wolfgang Streeck, and Kathleen Thelen, 1–39. Oxford: Oxford University Press.

Stubager, Rune, Jakob Holm, Maja Smidstrup, and Katrine Kramb. 2013. *Danske vælgere 1971–2011. En oversigt over udviklingen i vælgernes holdninger mv. Det danske valgprojekt, 2. Udgave.*

Svallfors, Stefan. 2011. "A Bedrock of Support? Trends in Welfare Attitudes in Sweden, 1981–2010." *Social Policy and Administration* 45 (7): 806–825.

Svallfors, Stefan. 2015. "Politics as Organized Combat: New Players and New Rules of the Game in Sweden." Max Plank Institute for the Study of Societies, *MPIfG Discussion Paper* 15/2.

Svensson, Torsten, and PerOla Öberg. 2002. "Labour Market Organisations' Participation in Swedish Public Policy-Making." *Scandinavian Political Studies* 25 (4): 295–315.

Swedish Public Employment Service (*Arbetsförmedlingen*). 2014. *Arbetsmarknadsrapport 2014.* Stockholm: Arbetsförmedlingen.

Swedish Unemployment Insurance Board (IAF). 2009. *Arbetssökande med och utan arbetslöshetsersättning: En redovisning till regeringen i samverkan mellan Inspektionen för arbetslöshetsförsäkringen och Arbetsförmedlingen, 2009:7.* Katrineholm/Stockholm: IAF.

Swenson, Peter. 2002. *Capitalists against Markets: The Making of Labor Markets and Welfare States in the United States and Sweden.* Oxford: Oxford University Press.

Tálos, Emmerich. 1999. "Atypische Beschäftigung in Österreich." In *Atypische Beschäftigung. Internationale Trends und sozialstaatliche Regelungen,* edited by Emmerich Tálos, 36–81. Vienna: LIT.

Tálos, Emmerich. 2008a. "Armutspolitik am Beispiel Österreichs: Bedarfsorientierte Mindestsicherung." *WSI-Mitteilungen* 3/2008: 159–163.

Tálos, Emmerich. 2008b. *Sozialpartnerschaft. Ein zentraler politischer Gestaltungsfaktor in der Zweiten Republik.* Innsbruck, Austria: Studienverlag.

Tálos, Emmerich, and Bernhard Kittel. 2001. *Gesetzgebung in Österreich. Akteure, Netzwerke und Interaktionen in politischen Entscheidungsprozessen,* Vienna: Wiener Universitätsverlag.

Tálos, Emmerich, and Bruno Rossmann. 1992. "Materielle Sicherung im Wohlfahrtsstaat. Am Beispiel der Pensions- und Arbeitslosenversicherung." In *Der geforderte Wohlfahrtsstaat. Traditionen—Herausforderungen—Perspektiven,* ed. Emmerich Tálos, 17–59. Vienna: Löcker.

Tálos, Emmerich, and Karl Wörister. 1998. "Soziale Sicherung in Österreich." In *Soziale Sicherung im Wandel,* ed. Emmerich Tálos, 209–288. Vienna: Böhlau.

Taylor-Gooby, Peter. 2004. *New Risks, New Welfare: The Transformation of the European Welfare State.* Oxford and New York: Oxford University Press.

Thelen, Kathleen. 2012. "Varieties of Capitalism: Trajectories of Liberalization and the New Politics of Social Solidarity." *Annual Review of Political Science* (15): 137–159.

Thelen, Kathleen. 2014. *Varieties of Liberalization: The New Politics of Social Solidarity.* New York: Cambridge University Press.

Thörnqvist, Christer. 2007. "From Blue-Collar Wildcats in the 1970s to public Sector Resistance at the Turn of a New Millennium. Strikes in Sweden 1970–2005." In *Strikes around the World, 1968–2005. Case-Studies of 15 Countries,* ed. Sjaak van der Velden, Heiner Dribbusch, Dave Lyddon, and Kurt Vandaele, 321–338. Amsterdam: Aksant.

Tiraboschi, Michele. 2012. "Italian Labour Law after the so-called Monti-Fornero Reform (Law No. 92/2012)." *E-Journal of International and Comparative Labour Studies* (1), (Oct.-Dec.): 3–4.

Tomlinson, Mark, and Robert Walker. 2012. "Labour Market Disadvantage and the Experience of Recurrent Poverty." In *The Age of Dualization. The Changing Face of Inequality in Deindustrializing Countries,* ed. Patrick Emmenegger, Silja Häusermann,

Bruno Palier, and Martin Seeleib-Kaiser, 52–70. New York: Oxford University Press.

Torfing, Jacob. 1999. "Workfare with Welfare: Recent Reforms of the Danish Welfare State." *Journal of European Social Policy* 9 (1): 5–28.

Traxler, Franz. 1998. "Austria: Still the Country of Corporatism." In *Changing Industrial Relations in Europe*, ed. Anthony Ferner, and Richard Hyman, 239–261. Oxford: Blackwell.

Traxler, Franz. 2010. "The Long-Term Development of Organised Business and Its Implications for Corporatism." *European Journal of Political Research* 49 (2): 151–173.

Treib, Oliver. 2012. "Party Patronage in Austria: From Reward to Control." In *Party Patronage and Party Government in European Democracies*, ed. Petr Kopecky, Peter Mair, and Maria Spirova, 31–51. Oxford: Oxford University Press.

Traxler, Franz, and Susanne Pernicka. 2007. "The State of Unions: Austria." *Journal of Labor Research* 28 (2): 207–232.

Unger, Brigitte. 2001. *Österreichs Beschäftigungspolitik 1970–2001*. Vienna: Forum für politische Bildung.

Unger, Brigitte. 2003. "Austrian Social Partnership. Just a Midlife Crisis?" In *Renegotiating the Welfare State: Flexible Adjustment through Corporatist Concertation*, ed. Frans Van Waarden, and Gerhard Lehmbruch. 97–114. New York: Routledge.

Van Oorschot, Wim. 2006. "Making the Difference in Social Europe: Deservingness Perceptions among Citizens of European Welfare States." *Journal of European Social Policy* 16 (1): 23–42.

Van Peijpe, Taco. 1998. *Employment Protection under Strain. Sweden, Denmark and the Netherlands*. The Hague: Kluwer Law International.

Van Vliet, Olaf, and Koen Caminada. 2012. "Unemployment Replacement Rates. Dataset among 34 Welfare States, 1971–2009. An Update, Modification and Extension of the Scruggs' Welfare State Entitlements Data Set." *Neujobs Special Report* 2, January 2012.

Vis, Barbara. 2009. "Governments and Unpopular Social Policy Reform: Biting the Bullet or Steering Clear?" *European Journal of Political Research* 48 (1): 31–57.

Visser, Jelle, and Anton Hemerijck. 1997. *A Dutch Miracle*. Amsterdam: Amsterdam University Press.

Vlandas, Tim. 2013. "The Politics of Temporary Work Deregulation in Europe: Solving the French Puzzle." *Politics and Society* 41 (3): 425–460.

Vranitzky, Franz. 2004. *Politische Erinnerungen*. Wien: Paul Zsolnay Verlag.

Wagschal, Uwe, and Georg Wenzelburger. 2008. *Haushaltskonsolidierung*. Wiesbaden, Germany: VS Verlag für Sozialwissenschaften.

Western, Bruce. 1997. *Between Class and Market. Postwar Unionization in the Capitalist Democracies*. Princeton, NJ: Princeton University Press.

Wilensky, Harold L. 2012. *American Political Economy in Global Perspective*. New York: Cambridge University Press.

Index

CPSIA information can be obtained
at www.ICGtesting.com
Printed in the USA
BVHW030115071118
531826BV00002B/30/P